ANTIDIPLOMACY

SPIES, TERROR, SPEED, AND WAR

For Arthur Rebel, Betty Ann, Debra Ann,
Christine Ivy, and Elisabeth Lee —
my father, mother, and sisters

ANTIDIPLOMACY

SPIES, TERROR, SPEED, AND WAR

JAMES DER DERIAN

BLACKWELL
Cambridge MA & Oxford UK

First published 1992

Blackwell Publishers
238 Main Street, Suite 501
Cambridge MA 02142 USA

108 Cowley Road
Oxford OX4 1JF
UK

Library of Congress Cataloging-in-Publication Data

Der Derian, James.
    Antidiplomacy: spies, terror, speed, and war/James Der Derian.
        p.   cm.
    Includes bibliographical references and index.
    ISBN 1−55786−151−X.−ISBN 1−55786−344−X (pbk.)
    1. Intelligence service. 2. Terrorism. 3. International relations.
    4. World politics−1945− I. Title.
    JF1525.I6D47   1992
    327.1′17′09048−dc20   91−40169
                                                                                CIP

British Library Cataloguing in Publication Data

A CIP catalogue record for this book is available from the British Library.

Typeset in 10/12 pt Sabon
by Setrite Typesetters Ltd.
Printed in Great Britain by
T.J. Press, Padstow.

This book is printed on acid-free paper

CONTENTS

———

PREFACE

—

All books suffer from convenient beginnings and arbitrary endings. This one begins the year that I was born, 1955, when B-52 Stratofortresses began to fly continuous 24-hour circuits over the United States and Ronald Reagan opened the Magic Kingdom on television. It ends with a fax from an editor several thousand miles and a few minutes away, saying to end it now before now ends.

This book does not pretend to cover all of the events in between. It is a series of freeze-frames of the historical confrontation between the US (the all-inclusive "us") and its enemies (the excluded "them") that has preoccupied international politics from the beginning to the end of the Cold War. Since 1955 much has changed and, recently, much for the better: reform in the Soviet Union, withdrawal from Afghanistan, freedom and democracy movements in East and Central Europe, removal of intermediate nuclear forces from Europe, reunification of Germany, new coalitions of force against pariah states – and all B-52s stand down. These transformative events have been justly celebrated. Berliners have danced on the Wall and General Schwarzkopf was feted by Mickey Mouse in Disneyworld. But with increasing celerity in international relations, historical endings collapse into ambiguous beginnings: the long war of fifty years between East and West into the Serbo-Croatian war; the short war of Six Weeks and One Hundred Hours between Iraq and the Western coalition into the massacre of the Kurds; the instant coup of 72 hours into the disintegration of the Soviet Union.

What preoccupies in the international order are the great spectacles and instant banalization of security and terror, surveillance and speed, simulation and war. Textually represented and globally conveyed by the media, they have come to pervade everyday life. Yet they never seem to make it into the protected realm of international theory. This is a first attempt to do so, by applying a poststructuralist approach to a late modern condition of international relations which I call *antidiplomacy*. "Antidiplomacy" represents a challenge to traditional diplomatic practices, a new discursive formation of statehood based on a techno-strategic triad of surveillance, terror, and speed, and paradoxically, the possibility for a radical transformation of the states-system. Through a critical reading of antidiplomacy, this book seeks to identify new global dangers and opportunities that have emerged from the rise and fall of a bipolar empire of estrangement. It signals the loss of one mimetic other, and asks whether antidiplomacy will continue as war by an admixture of new otherness in a unipolar order — or as peace by the mediation of difference in an international society.

The much-heralded "death of the author" can be both boon and bane when it comes to the acknowledgment of intellectual debts. In spite of the best of authorial intentions, they often read as rituals of initiation, exchange, ingratiation. I find myself over-compensating, remembering the dissident and forgetting the central (to the discipline) figures who made important contributions to this book. But it was in the dialogues, and sometime polemics, invoked by public presentations of various parts of this book that I found the reason (in a very literal sense) to assess and reassert the significance of rhetoric in International Relations. So my first appreciation goes to responsive audiences at the University of Southern California, Rand Corporation, University of Hawaii, US Institute of Peace, Johns Hopkins University, Vanderbilt University, Columbia University, Northwestern University, Princeton University, University of California at Santa Cruz, MIT, and University of Toronto.

There are as well individual debts to be recognized. Hayward Alker, Thomas Biersteker, Richard Ashley, Michael Shapiro, and Rob Walker helped to open up a critical discursive space in the field of International Relations that made this book possible. Jean Bethke Elshtain, William Connolly, and Nicholas Xenos supplied the theoretical acuity, professional advice, and unstoppable humor that have made them the best of friends. On panels, with reviews, or in correspondence of one form or another, David Campbell, Daniel Deudney, Paul Gootenberg, Peter Hayes, Mark Hoffman, Alex Hybel, Robert Keohane, Michael Klare, Bradley Klein, Timothy Luke, Dwain Mefford, Nicholas Rengger, Jim Rosenau, John Ruggie, Anders Stephanson, Gerard Toal, and the late John Vincent offered insightful criticisms. The support and sound suggestions of my colleagues Eric Einhorn, Peter Haas, and M. J. Peterson kept me in a closer orbit to planet Earth. Bret Brown,

Timothy Cloyd, Jeneen Hobby, Adam Lerner, and the students from my seminars on Classical and Poststructural Theories of International Relations provided the close readings and gloves-off commentary that made a difference in the final product. Ruth Abbey stands out as a cosmopolitan critic, Naomi Mobed as an inspired researcher. And a special thanks to Paul Shoul for the use of the darkroom.

This book might be short on lessons for the reader. But in the writing of it I learned an important one: on the high and low roads of theory and life there could be found no better fellow traveler than John Santos, no better companion than Kiaran Honderich.

Earlier versions and shorter sections of some of the chapters were published in *International Studies Quarterly; Millennium Journal of International Affairs; USA: Economics, Politics, Ideology; Social Text; Radical America; Alphabet City; Cultural Politics in Contemporary America* (edited by Ian Angus and Sut Jhally, Routledge, 1988); *International/Intertextual Relations: Postmodern Readings of World Politics* (edited by James Der Derian and Michael Shapiro, Lexington, 1989); and *World Security: Trends and Challenges at Century's End* (edited by Michael Klare and Dan Thomas, St Martin's, 1991). I wish to thank the editors for permission to reprint. I would also like to thank three editors from Blackwell Publishers (at one time or another): Sean Magee, who taught me as much about the track as the trade; Simon Prosser, who adroitly mixed carrots, sticks, and fine dinners to get the book done; and Stephen Ball, whose editorial marginalia kept me honest and constantly amused.

1

INTRODUCTION: A CASE FOR A POSTSTRUCTURALIST APPROACH

—

Diplomacy is the art of saying "Nice doggie" until you can find a rock.

Will Rogers

THE DOG, THE CAVE, AND THE BEEF

I approach the front of the cave. The guard dog barks: "Where's the beef?" I don't have any. I try humor: there's more on the menu of life than beef; why not tofu? The dog growls. I stall, ask, what kind of beef? Did the dog know that the French prefer beef cut with the grain, Americans against? The dog snarls: "beef is beef." I agree, but say that in some cultures beef is used as a ritual sacrifice to the gods, and in others as a metaphor, believe it or not, for something of substance like, say, a research program. Suddenly a little old lady, Walter Mondale, and Ronald Reagan are in the dream. She's hitting Mondale over the head with an umbrella for taking her beef patty. Reagan, having no beef, is grinning widely. The dog goes for my leg. I grab the meat from Mondale and give it to the dog. The dog lets go of my leg and disappears into the cave. I'm left alone in front of the cave, until a strange creature approaches me. I ask it: "Where's the beef?"

At the most difficult moments of my struggle with the central claim and dilemma of this book — that the late modern condition of diplomacy requires a poststructuralist approach that is barely tolerated and poorly

INTRODUCTION

understood in the discipline of International Relations – this dream would dog me. This book aspired after a cure, but at some point, after a fair amount of rocks had been thrown and not a few bones offered, I came to realize that I was only treating the symptoms of a permanent condition that was much larger than the dog, the cave, the dream itself.

This book, then, should be read first as a symptomology, or, as it once was known in medicine and now is in literary theory, as a *semiology* of International Relations: of how it makes order out of disorder by the establishment of signifying boundaries (geographical, conceptual, epistemological) between the inside and outside of the cave, the constitution of essentialist identities (the state, democracy, research programs) like beef, and the construction of binary differences (war/peace, realism/idealism, us/them) between dog and non-dog. I argue in this book that in world politics it is increasingly not what is inside or outside the cave that really matters: it is the map of the borders – the *textualization* of reality – that has come to matter most. Drawn to keep at bay what Nietzsche called the "breath of empty space," these textual borders have taken on more substance as the immateriality of late modernity spreads.[1] Not substantial enough, I am afraid: for the dog, this book brings no thing; worse, it brings news of the nothingness that lurks outside its sovereign cave.

Some, understandably anxious about "empty space" left by the end of the cold war, might feel that textualism, relativism, or worse, nihilism is now more than ever a biteable offense. However, when the mandarin response is to ply an Hegelian dream of a liberal "end to history," and to reassert a unipolar order through a martial simulation of might against minor powers, then relativism takes on a certain appeal. The literary critic Maurice Blanchot makes a good case for relativism in a nihilist age:

> Here, then, is a first approach to Nihilism: it is not an individual experience or a philosophical doctrine, nor is it a fatal light cast over human nature, eternally vowed to nothingness. Rather, Nihilism is an event achieved in history, and yet it is like a shedding off of history, a moulting period, when history changes its direction and is indicated by a negative trait: that values no longer have value by themselves. There is also a positive trait: for the first time the horizon is infinitely opened to knowledge – "All is permitted."[2]

ANTIDIPLOMACY AND LATE MODERNITY

If this book attempts to open up a field known for its closure, it is so that we might better understand late modern challenges to traditional diplomatic practices, to which I have given the name *antidiplomacy*. A prior work of mine, *On Diplomacy: A Genealogy of Western Estrangement*, included a genealogy of the conflict between particularist states and universalist forces which gave rise to an earlier ideological form of antidiplomacy.[3] With Hegel as my guide, I attempted to show how a universal alienation, when mediated through particular interests, produces new and often violently antithetical forms of diplomatic relations. In this book I argue that new technological practices and universal dangers, mediated by the particular interests of the national security state, have generated a new antidiplomacy. In short, what distinguishes late modern antidiplomacy from earlier forms is how it constitutes and mediates estrangement by new techniques of power and representations of danger.

These new techniques of power are transparent and pervasive, more "real" in time than in space, and produced and sustained through the exchange of signs rather than goods. They have proven to be resistant if not invisible to traditional methods of analysis. They do not "fit" and therefore they elude the traditional and the re-formed delimitations of the International Relations field: the geopolitics of realism, the structural political economy of neorealism, the possessive institutionalism of neoliberalism. In contrast, I believe that poststructuralism can grasp – but never fully capture – the significance of these new forces for international relations.

In this book I will examine three forces that stand out for their discursive power and shared problematic. Their discursive power is *chronopolitical* and *technostrategic*, and they have generated a *late modern* problematic for a system of states which increasingly seems resistant to comprehension by traditional styles and systems of thought. To clarify: they are "chronopolitical" in the sense that they elevate chronology over geography, pace over space in their political effects;[4] they are "technostrategic" in that they use and are used by technology for the purpose of war;[5] they have a discursive power in that they produce and are sustained by historically transient discourses which mediate our relations with empirical events;[6] and the problematic is late (or post-) modern because it defies the grand theories or definitive structures which impose rationalist identities or binary oppositions to explain international relations.[7] Hence, a poststructuralist analysis is called for, to show us how these new technological and discursive practices mediate and often dominate relations with other states, but also to tell us about their relationship to ourselves; that is, how their power is manifested in the boundaries they establish for what can be said and who can say it with authority in international theory.

The three forces challenging traditional diplomacy that I will examine are *spies* (intelligence and surveillance), *terror* (global terrorism and the national security culture), and *speed* (the acceleration of pace in war and diplomacy). The problematic they have generated can be simply put: the closer technology and scientific discourse brings us to the "other" — that is, the more that the model is congruent with the reality, the image resembles the object, the medium becomes the real-time message — the less we see of ourselves in the other. Theoretical reflection loses out to techno-scientific reification.

This can be simply expressed but not fully explained. Why is this so? A full answer would surely lead us into an ontological bog that I prefer to avoid, so instead I offer in this introduction a partial explanation — and a provocation that might prompt others to lead the way on the onto-theological question that I have begged. I imagine that many of our leaders and scholars, like earlier estranged tribes who sought in heaven what they could not find on earth, have given up on peace on earth and now seek peace of mind through the worship of new techno-deities. They look up to the surveillance satellite, deep into the entrails of electronic micro-circuitry, and from behind Stealth protection to find the omniscient machines and incontrovertible signs that can help us see and, if state reason necessitates, *evade* or *destroy* the other. And should anyone pause too long to reflect skeptically on this reification of technical reason, they too are consigned to the ranks of the dissident other, as infidels who refuse to believe that there can be a single power or sovereign truth that can dispel or control the insecurities, indeterminacies, and ambiguities that make up international relations. In *The Twilight of the Idols* Nietzsche exposes the origins of this tyranny of reason which first appears as — but soon fences out — dissident knowledge:

> If one needs to make a tyrant of *reason*, as Socrates did, then there must exist no little danger of something else playing the tyrant. Rationality was at that time divined as a *saviour*; neither Socrates nor his "invalids" were free to be rational or not, as they wished — it was *de rigueur*, it was their *last* expedient. The fanaticism with which the whole of Greek thought throws itself at rationality betrays a state of emergency: one was in peril, one had only *one* choice: either to perish or — be *absurdly rational* ...[8]

A CASE FOR A POSTSTRUCTURALIST APPROACH   5

International Relations theory has not been immune to this eschatology of rationalism. In a very short period the field has oscillated: from *realist* theory, in which world-historical figures mean what they say and say what they mean, and diplomatic historians record it as such in Rankean fashion ("wie es eigentlich gewesen ist"); to *neorealist*, in which politico-economic structures do what they do, and we do what they make us do, at least up until 1989; to *hyperrealist*, in which the model of the real becomes more real than the reality it models, and we become confused.

Now, more than ever, the either/or tyranny of the Cold War that privileged absurdly rational theories of international relations is susceptible to new intellectual challenges. In this book, I take up this opportunity, to offer theoretical approaches which may help us to identify a neglected set of dangers that have emerged from the Cold War and survived its end. In each of the three parts that follow I intend to investigate the impact of surveillance, terrorism, and speed on international relations by providing an introductory theoretical chapter on the relevant work of poststructuralist and other critical thinkers, followed by an intertextual analysis of antidiplomatic discourses which have emerged with these new technostrategic practices. The final part on war is a recombinant effort, to show how the three antidiplomatic forces reached their highest expression in the Persian Gulf War.

The sources of this analysis are diverse, and exceed the range of materials that make up a conventional "research program" in International Relations. I have drawn from interviews with specialists in terrorism and modeling at the Rand Corporation, the late Hedley Bull's papers on diplomatic culture, and discussions with lieutenant colonels from the War Colleges. But I have also undertaken an intertextual analysis of over 520 issues (two years' worth) of the US Defense Department's *Current News*; the absorption of over fifty espionage novels; and the deciphering of formerly classified CIA documents and the National Security Council's computer PROF notes on the Iran hostage crisis and the Iran—Contra affair that had been shredded or erased, rewoven like rugs or recovered from computer disks, and collected by the National Security Archive in Washington, DC.

This book seeks to establish that these new forces, in their theorization and practical application, respond better to *interpretation* than *verification*. Examples will follow, of how the radar operator on the USS *Vincennes* based his interpretation of data about an approaching Iranian aircraft on training simulations; a former head of Air Force Intelligence found in surveillance photographs and computerized data evidence of systematic violations of arms control agreements while the head of the CIA saw an occasional misdemeanor; and how speed as the essence of modern warfare has radically changed the image of battle.[9]

POSTSTRUCTURALISM AND INTERNATIONAL RELATIONS

This book relies on intellectual approaches adapted by a new generation of IR scholars inspired by the works of Nietzsche, Bakhtin, Barthes, Foucault, Deleuze, Derrida, Rorty, Kristeva, Said, Lacan, Spivak, Baudrillard, Virilio and others. They go by different names: "post-modernism," "poststructuralism," "post-positivism" and "radical inter-pretivism" are some examples; none alone captures the diversity of the practitioners. I do not intend here to rehearse the so-called "Third Debate": this I have already done; and it has been done better by others.[10] Besides, this book is not *about* poststructuralism: it is the product of an inquiry using a set of intellectual instruments that make up one form among many poststructuralisms. However, since I believe that critical comments about the approach have arisen as much from confusion and willful ignorance as from disagreement, I will make a few prefatory points about the protocols of this poststructuralism that inform this work and distinguish it from the traditional approaches of IR.

First, poststructuralism is not, as many critics have claimed, inherently anti-empirical. This book does in fact contain a "research program," but not one which assumes that the object of research is immaculately reproduced by the program. Poststructuralism differs from rationalist approaches in that it does not hold that international theorists mirror the reality of world politics through their intellectual analysis. Both use and are used by language: meaning endlessly differs and is deferred through the linguistic interaction of theorist and text. Rationalists cling to the faith that there is an object, a truth, a reality out there, that is waiting for the right method to come along and in the name of scientific progress make use of, make sense of, give order to it. Moreover, the realities of world politics increasingly are generated, mediated, simulated by technical means of production, further distancing and alienating them from some original, unproblematic meaning. It is this very hetero-logical nature of discourse that the traditional theories of IR, in a demonstrative, hegemonic act, always dream of fixing, reducing, subject-ing to a single, monological meaning.

This is not to reduce IR to a linguistic practice, nor to claim there is *no* truth, *no* values, *no* reality. Rather, it is to refute the claim that there is an external being, supreme epistemology, ultimate theory that can prove, adjudicate, confirm an existence independent of its representation. A poststructuralist approach proceeds by recognizing and investigating the interrelationship of power and representational practices that elevate one truth over another, that subject one identity to another, that make, in short, one discourse matter more than the next. Such an investigation requires a *semio-critical* approach, one that might problematize and dismantle empirico-positivist categories by revealing their interdiscursive origins, logical inconsistencies and interpretive inadequacies.

Many thinkers have been associated with this approach, but two in particular guide this inquiry: Roland Barthes and Michel Foucault. First, Barthes on "semio-criticism":

> Hence, there exists today a new perspective of reflection − common, I insist, to literature and to linguistics, to the creator and the critic, whose tasks, hitherto absolutely self-contained, are beginning to communicate, perhaps even to converge, at least on the level of the writer, whose action can increasingly be defined as a critique of language ... This new conjunction of literature and linguistics, which I have just mentioned, might provisionally be called, for lack of a better name, *semio-criticism*, since it implies that writing is a system of signs.[11]

And second, Foucault on the genealogy of "problematiques":

> I am not looking for an alternative; you can't find the solution of a problem in the solution of another problem raised at another moment by other people. You see, what I want to do is not a history of solutions, and that's the reason why I don't accept the word *alternative*. I would like to do the genealogy of problems, of *problematiques*.[12]

These thinkers and other poststructuralists provide the intellectual means to reverse the acts of theoretical enclosure that have been instituted in North American IR theory, that assume rational choice, game theoretic, or formal modeling are sufficient representations of world politics. It is my belief that the accelerating, transparent, hyper-mediated diplomacy of late modernity *exceeds* the representational capabilities of traditional IR theory.

But more is needed. Poststructuralism is not simply a negative critique − although it has, by its more modish uses, been confused as such. In most cases − and certainly in the case of Foucault − it clears but does not destroy or deny the existence of the ground for a constructive theory. Even in the more radical applications of deconstruction it takes aim at totalist, transcendentalist, closed theory — not *all* theory. Lending critical support to an essay by Richard Ashley, the political theorist William Connolly outlines the features of a constructive theory in poststructuralism:

> One might seek, not to impose one reading on the field of discourse, but to elaborate a general reading that can contend with others by broadening the established terms of debates; not to create a transformation of international life grounded in a universal project, but to contribute to a general perspective that might support reconstitution of aspects of international life; not to root a theory in a transcendental ground, but to problematize the grounding any theory presupposes while it works out the implications of a particular set of themes; not merely to invert hierarchies in other theories (a useful task), but to construct alternative hierarchies that support modifications in relations between identity and difference.[13]

THE DOGGED REACTION TO POSTSTRUCTURALISM

Rationalists might well carry on, simply ignoring the problematic of discourse, in the vain hope that it will ignore them. But poststructuralists are always aware of — and always irritating others by demonstrating — the stickiness of the web of meaning. Inevitably, there is a reaction. A leading North American IR scholar, Robert Keohane, deserves credit for making it more difficult for the rationalists to ignore the discourse problematic. In his 1988 presidential address to the International Studies Association Robert Keohane gave notice of a new approach to the study of international relations. "Reflective", is how he labeled it, in the sense of reflecting, for the most part critically, on how one and others think and write about institutions in international relations. In an edited version of the address that appeared in the *International Studies Quarterly*, Keohane went on to criticize the reflective approach for failing to research the empirical reality of institutions. Within the criticism lies an implicit imprecation: if one is to find a "genuine research program" it is better to take the enlightened road of rationalist reflection than the benighted wood of poststructuralist reflexivity.[14]

There is, moreover, a metaphoric power operating in Keohane's choice of terms which insinuates a kind of (onto) generic passivity in the reflectivist camp. It would seem that the reflectivist, by definition, prefers (or has little choice but) to reflect others' thoughts and actions rather than to engage in the more productive work of empirically testing hypotheses. Then, after dazzling the reflective creature on this familiar road (the enlightenment tradition) with an impressive pair of twin high-beams (rationalist theory and empirical research), Keohane concludes that "eventually, we may hope for a synthesis between the rationalistic and reflective approaches."[15]

If we take time to reflect on Keohane's well-traveled road, to weigh his quite reasonable rules and to consider his ultimate destination of the higher "normative grounds" of "international cooperation," we can find much that is laudable, and indeed, much that is shared by those wandering in the dark wood. But his conclusion only makes the unbeaten track seem more appealing if not necessary: it is not in synthesis, but by learning to live with irreconcilable differences and multiple identities — in high theory and in everyday practices — that we might find our best hope for international relations. Unless we are willing now and then to head the big American car of international relations theory off in untried, untestable, even *unreasonable* directions, the only perpetual peace — to update Kant — will be that of the roadside kill. For critical enlightenment, as well as for casualty insurance for this book, it is worth repeating Kant's opening remarks to his essay *Perpetual Peace*.[16]

To Perpetual Peace

Whether this satirical inscription on a certain Dutch shopkeeper's sign, on which a graveyard was painted, holds for *men* in general, or especially for heads of state who can never get enough of war, or perhaps only for philosophers who dream that sweet dream, is not for us to decide. However, the author of this essay does set out one condition: the practical politician tends to look down with great smugness on the political theorist, regarding him as an academic whose empty ideas cannot endanger the nation, since the nation must proceed on principles derived from experience; consequently, the theorist is allowed to fire his entire volley, without the *worldly-wise* statesman becoming the least bit concerned. Now if he is to be consistent — and this is the condition I set out — the practical politician must not claim, in the event of a dispute with a theorist, to detect some danger to the nation in those views that the political theorist expresses openly and without ulterior motive. By this *clausula salvatoria*, the author of this essay will regard himself to be expressly protected in the best way possible from all malicious interpretation.

This book is not a polemic against Keohane's rationalist institutionalism or, in general, the new traditionalism in IR theory. Nor does it, admittedly, amount to a theoretical defense of poststructuralism. That double need, I think, has passed, for it seems that both sides have begun to recognize the legitimacy of the dialogue if not the epistemological claims of the other. In one of his last interviews Foucault presents a good case for this position when he defends a dialogical approach over against a polemical one:

> Questions and answers depend on a game — a game that is at once pleasant and difficult — in which each of the two partners takes pains to use only the rights given him by the other and by the accepted form of the dialogue. The polemicist, on the other hand, proceeds encased in privileges that he possesses in advance and will never agree to question. On principle, he possesses rights authorizing him to wage war and making that struggle a just undertaking; the person he confronts is not a partner in the search for the truth, but an adversary, an enemy who is wrong, who is harmful and whose very existence constitutes a threat. For him, then, the game does not consist of recognizing this person as a subject having the right to speak, but of abolishing him, as the interlocutor, from any possible dialogue; and his final objective will be, not to come as close as possible to a difficult truth, but to bring about the triumph of the just cause he has been manifestly upholding from the beginning.[17]

Perhaps I am overly sanguine in my assessment of the disposition of the field toward poststructuralism. There has been and probably will continue to be hostility towards the approach. Indeed, attacks have been directed against another latecomer to the field: feminism. In the British journal *Millennium*, Keohane issued an early warning to those feminists who might be attracted to the postmodernist Sirens, declaiming "that this postmodern project is a dead-end in the study of international relations — and that it would be disastrous for feminist international relations theory to pursue this path."[18] In his essay none of the views or arguments of postmodernist feminists within IR, nor any of the rich and diverse debates going on outside the field, are noted.[19] Instead he rests

his case for a "neoliberal institutionalist" feminism solely on the secondary opinions of a few feminists opposed to postmodernism.

Another example of recent hostility surfaced in a newly instituted
series in the *International Studies Quarterly*, in which an assortment of
individuals are invited to give status reports on the various sub-fields of
International Relations (note: IR in general, not just North American).
If the inaugural piece on the state of strategic studies is anything to
go by, the series does not intend to open up the discipline but to close
it down to new, dissident, or simply different approaches and view-
points.[20] After acknowledging that "the boundaries of intellectual disci-
plines are permeable," The author proceeds not only to raise the
drawbridge but to close every chink.[21] Recent attempts to broaden the
concept of "security" to include issues like global environmental dangers,
disease, and economic and natural disasters endanger the field, by
threatening "to destroy its intellectual coherence and make it more
difficult to devise solutions to any of these important problems."[22] The
field is surveyed in the most narrow and parochial way: out of 200+
works cited, esteemed Third World scholars of strategic studies receive
no mention, British and French scholars receive short shrift, and Soviet
writers do not make it into the pantheon at all. In short, the big
American car of IR theory takes another spin.

The author of the essay, Stephen Walt, has written one of the better
books on alliance systems;[23] here he seems intent on constructing a
new alliance within the discipline against "foreign" others, with the
"postmodernist" as arch-alien. The tactic is familiar: like many of the
neoconservatives who have launched the recent attacks on "political
correctness", the "neoliberals" of IR make it a habit to base their
criticisms on secondary accounts of a category of thinking rather than
on a primary engagement with the specific (and often differing) views of
the thinkers themselves.[24] In this case, Walt cites Keohane on the
hazards of "reflectivism," to warn off anyone who by inclination or
error might wander into the foreign camp: "As Robert Keohane has
noted, until these writers 'have delineated . . . a research program and
shown . . . that it can illuminate important issues in world politics, they
will remain on the margins of the field.'"[25] By the end of the essay, one
is left with the suspicion that the rapid changes in world politics have
triggered an "insecurity crisis" in security studies that requires extensive
theoretical damage control.

But these are lesser concerns. Hopefully a law of combined and
uneven development is operating in the social sciences that will spare
the field of IR from the "infantile liberalism" that demonstrates its
inclusionary principles by excluding theoretical practices closest to it on

the epistemological spectrum. In the end, I believe that the proponents
of the reformed schools of realism, who have already added layers of
structuralist, structurationist, institutionalist, and historicist interpretations upon its shaky empirico-positivist foundations, shall see that
they have more in common with poststructuralism than the formal
modelers and game theoreticians who hover on neorealism's other,
hyper-rationalist, flank.

Yet probably no argument can dispel the irrationalist fear that poststructuralism is some kind of insidious virus that needs to be quarantined,
or worse, a hegemonic conspiracy intent on taking over the field. Inevitably, poststructuralism will come to be accepted as one of many critical,
pluralist approaches needed to understand the multiple challenges to
traditional forms of power and statecraft in late modernity. I believe
this will happen because of influence and pressure from below and
outside the discipline, because of the good poststructuralist scholarship
going on within it, and, as in the land of dreams that opens this book,
because every dog has its day.[26]

Notes

1   Two terms receive preferential treatment in this book. First, "international
theory," defined as a set of representational practices which constitutes our
thinking about "international relations," is preferred over "International
Relations theory." Reflecting its British classical roots, international
theory connotes a more speculative, philosophical and historical approach
than its North American variant, IR theory. Second, I prefer to use the
term "late modernity" rather than "postmodernity," not out of some
semantic purism, but to better distinguish a historical condition ("late
modernity," "postmodernity") from a variety of theoretical responses
("postmodernism," "poststructuralism"), and because "postmodernism" in
general has begun to take on more meanings than it can sensibly carry.
These terms will be elucidated throughout the book, but at the outset a
common understanding of what I mean by late modernity/postmodernity
in international relations might be useful:
   [I]ncreasingly postmodern world politics is very much in need of poststructural readings. The basis for the claim, and our written response
   to its implications, can be traced to an overdetermined (yet under-
   documented) "crisis" of modernity, where foundational unities (the
   autonomous subject, the sovereign state, grand theory) and synthetic
   oppositions (subject–object, self–other, inside–outside) are undergoing serious and sustained challenges. We are witnessing changes in
   our international, intertextual, inter*human* relations, in which objective
   reality is displaced by textuality (Dan Quayle cites Tom Clancy to
   defend anti-satellite weapons), modes of production are supplanted by
   modes of information (the assemblyline workplace shrinks, a computer

and media-generated cyberspace expands), representation blurs into simulation (Hollywood, and Mr Smith, goes to Washington), imperialism gives way to the Empire of Signs (the spectacle of Grenada, the fantasy of Star Wars serve to deny imperial decline). With these tectonic shifts, new epistemological fault lines develop: the legitimacy of tradition is undermined, the unifying belief in progress fragments, and conventional wisdom is reduced to one of many competing rituals of power used to shore up a shaky (international) society.
See J. Der Derian, Preface to *International/Intertextual Relations: Postmodern Readings of World Politics*, edited by J. Der Derian and M. Shapiro (Lexington, MA: Lexington Books, 1989), pp. ix−x, 10.

2 Maurice Blanchot, "The Limits of Nihilism," in *The New Nietzsche*, ed. D. Allison (Boston: MIT Press, 1985), p. 122. Less historically inclined and more politically incisive is William Connolly's appraisal of relativism:
Nor is relativism the consummate danger in the late-modern world, where every culture intersects with most others in economies of interdependence, exchange, and competition. Relativism is an invention of academics who yearn for a type of unity that probably never existed, who worry about an alienation from established culture that seldom finds sufficient opportunity to get off the ground, and who insist that ethical discourse cannot proceed unless it locates its authority in a transcendental command.
See *Identity\Difference: Democratic Negotiations of Political Paradox* (Ithaca: Cornell University Press, 1991), p. 174.

3 See J. Der Derian, *On Diplomacy: A Genealogy of Western Estrangement* (Oxford: Blackwell, 1987), pp. 134−67.

4 On the displacement of "geopolitics" by "chronopolitics" see P. Virilio, *Pure War* (New York: Semiotext(e), 1983) and *Speed and Politics* (New York: Semiotext(e), 1986), and below.

5 See C. von Clausewitz, *On War*, trans. and edited by M. Howard and P. Paret (Princeton: Princeton University Press, 1976), pp. 128 and 177; J. Der Derian, "Techno-diplomacy," chapter 9 of *On Diplomacy: A Genealogy of Western Estrangement* (Basil Blackwell, 1987), pp. 199−209; and B. Klein, "The Textual Strategies of the Military: Or Have You Read Any Good Defense Manuals Lately?" in *International/Intertextual Relations: Post-modern Readings of World Politics*, ed. by J. Der Derian and M. Shapiro (Lexington, MA: Lexington Books, 1989), pp. 100−2.

6 See M. Foucault, *The Archaeology of Knowledge* (London: Tavistock, 1972), pp. 21−39, 46−7, and 181−4.

7 See J. Der Derian, "Philosophical Traditions in International Relations," *Millennium Journal of International Affairs* (Summer, 1988), XVII, 2, p. 189.

8 F. Nietzsche, *The Twilight of the Idols* (New York: Penguin Books, 1968), p. 33.

9 And for those rationalists of IR who might concede that what follows constitutes a sufficient body of empirical evidence but not *proof* unless it is scientifically tested, there is a *model*, constructed from a kit for a Stealth fighter-bomber three years before it officially existed, which sits on my desk, demonstrating that credible proof in national security matters is as much a function of hegemonic discursive power as it is the product of visible knowledge.

10 See Der Derian, "Philosophical Traditions in International Relations," *Millennium*, pp. 189–93; Yosef Lapid, "The Third Debate: On the Prospects of International Relations in a Post-Positivist Era," *International Studies Quarterly* (1989), 33, pp. 235–54; and Richard Ashley and R. B. J. Walker (eds), Special Issue on "Speaking the Language of Exile: Dissident Thought in International Studies," *International Studies Quarterly* (1990), 34, especially the essays by Ashley, and by Walker, Campbell and George.

11 R. Barthes, "To Write: An Intransitive Verb?", in *The Rustle of Language*, trans. by R. Howard (New York: Hill and Wang, 1986), pp. 11–12.

12 M. Foucault, "On the Genealogy of Ethics: An Overview of Work in Progress," *The Foucault Reader*, ed. P. Rabinow (New York: Pantheon, 1984), p. 343.

13 W. Connolly, *Identity\Difference: Democratic Negotiations of Political Paradox*, pp. 56–7.

14 See R. Keohane, "International Institutions: Two Approaches," *International Studies Quarterly*, 32 (1988), pp. 379–96.

15 Keohane, *International Institutions*, p. 393.

16 Kant, *Perpetual Peace and Other Essays*, trans. T. Humphrey (Indianapolis: Hackett Publishing, 1983), p. 341.

17 See "Polemics, Politics, and Problemizations," in *The Foucault Reader*, pp. 381–2. However, as I have argued elsewhere, this is not to support the kind of mushy, uncritical eclecticism that is found in much of the "contending approaches" school. See "Philosophical Traditions in International Relations," *Millennium*, pp. 189–93.

18 R. Keohane, "International Relations Theory: Contributions of a Feminist Standpoint," *Millennium* (Summer, 1989), p. 249.

19 On the debate between "French" and "American" varieties of feminism, see, for example, Toril Moi, "Feminism, Postmodernism, and Style: Recent Feminist Criticism in the United States," *Cultural Critique* (Spring, 1988), pp. 3–22. On the introduction of feminist theory into IR, see the Special Issue on Women and International Relations, *Millennium* (Winter, 1988); the conference report on "Woman, the State, and War: What Difference Does Gender Make," edited by V. Spike Peterson and Jane Jaquette (USC Center for International Studies, 1989); Christine Sylvester, "Reconstituting a Gender Eclipsed Dialogue" (1990 ISA Meeting paper); and Ann Tickner, *Feminism and International Relations Theory* (New York: Columbia University Press, 1992).

20 Stephen M. Walt, "The Renaissance of Security Studies," *International Studies Quarterly* (1991), 35, pp. 211–39.

21 Walt, ibid., p. 212.

22 Walt, ibid., p. 213.

23 S. Walt, *The Origins of Alliances* (Ithaca: Cornell University Press, 1987).

24 The political theorist William Connolly has also noted this tendency among international relations theorists, and refers to it as the "strategy of condemnation through refraction." See Connolly, "Global Political Discourse," *Identity\Difference: Democratic Negotiations of Political Paradox* (Ithaca: Cornell University Press, 1991), pp. 49–63.

25 Walt, "The Renaissance of Security Studies," p. 223.

26 A sample of forthcoming work in IR relying on poststructuralist or critical theory approaches would include: Richard K. Ashley and Heyward Alker,

Jr (eds), *After Neo-Realism: The Institutions of Anarchy in World Politics* (Columbia University Press); David Campbell, *Writing Security: United States Foreign Policy and the Politics of Identity* (Manchester University Press); Chris Hables Gray, *Computers as Weapons and Metaphors: The US Military and Postmodern War* (California University Press); William Chalowka, *Knowing Nukes: The Politics and Culture of the Atom* (Minnesota University Press); V. Spike Peterson (ed.), *Gendered States: Feminist (Re)visions of IR Theory* (Lynne Rienner); Nicholas Rengger and Michael Hoffman (eds), *Beyond the Inter-Paradigm Debate: Critical Theory and International Relations* (Harvester Wheatsheaf); Christine Sylvester, *Feminist Theory and International Relations in a Postmodern Era* (Cambridge University Press); Chris Hables Gray, Nicholas Rengger, Michael Hoffman, Christine Sylvester and R. B. J. Walker, *Inside/Outside: International Relations as Political Theory* (Cambridge University Press).

SPIES

2

INTELLIGENCE THEORY AND SURVEILLANCE PRACTICE

Simply put, intelligence is knowledge and foreknowledge of the world that surrounds us.
Intelligence: The Acme of Skill, CIA booklet

Every day I attach less value to intelligence.
Contre Sainte-Beuve, Marcel Proust

For many reasons — some valid, many not — intelligence is the least understood and most undertheorized area of international relations. It pervades and often subverts traditional statecraft; intelligence seeks to become, to quote the shadowy hero of Norman Mailer's *Harlot's Ghost*, "the mind of America." Yet IR theory gives it little mind.

This chapter and the next attempt to redress this theoretical lacuna, and to assess the value of intelligence for international relations. This chapter is a critical inquiry into the representation of intelligence and the practice of surveillance as a contest of visions of the Cold War and its demise. The next chapter undertakes an intertextual analysis of three forces within intelligence that have constituted the new antidiplomacy: alienation, surveillance, and speed.

THE GAME OF NAMES

A critical inquiry into intelligence immediately confronts recalcitrant problems of a terminological and theoretical nature. Unqualified, "intelligence" usually refers to the mental ability to acquire and retain knowledge. Historically, the modern association of the term "intelligence" with the collection of information necessary to the security of a state emerges in the diplomatic discourse of sixteenth-century France and England.[1] By the seventeenth century, spies are frequently referred to as "intelligencers," as are some of the weeklies — forerunners to the mass-circulation newspaper — which published accounts of the English Civil War and news of the Thirty Years War.[2] In both the eighteenth-century French *Encyclopedie* and Samuel Johnson's *Dictionary of the English Language*, the pre-eminent meaning remains a form of discovered news or "commerce of information" (Johnson). However, by the nineteenth century, common usage begins to shift back to the earlier, Latin (*intellectus*) connotation of an individual, mental *understanding*. And in our own century this usage of intelligence as a mental faculty takes a scientific turn: preceded by "artificial," it becomes a model for all cognitive processes; followed by "quotient," it is *the* standard to measure mental ability.

To add to the confusion, the contemporary "community of intelligence" has seemingly deemed the essential qualifier *foreign* as unnecessary, for reasons that might be quaintly archaic or self-evidently scientific — or perhaps both. Moreover, concise definitions of intelligence are rarely offered — except for the odd one "simply put." Perhaps there are policy benefits to be gained by a fuzzy definition. In a recent article, the CIA's Coordinator for Academic Affairs, Dr Michael A. Turner, admits that "There is a good deal of uncertainty about the definition of intelligence, contributing to controversy about what intelligence organizations should or should not be authorized to do."[3] He goes on to quote the relevant passage of the National Security Act of 1947 (Section 102(d), 50 USC Section 430(d)(1982)) which "defines intelligence in terms of what the CIA is empowered to do: advise the National Security Council; make recommendations to the NSA; correlate and evaluate intelligence; perform centralizing functions; and perform special activities."[4] It is interesting to note that Turner's preferred definition echoes the neutral eighteenth-century meaning, sanitizing intelligence into "information management: gathering raw information; analyzing it; and disseminating evaluated information to decisionmakers, some of whom have been elected to make national security decisions."[5]

To compensate for the historical lacuna, the new academic field officers of intelligence have begun to offer their own definitions, which tend to be long(winded) and composed in the language of social scientific rigor (mortis). For instance:

Accordingly, intelligence may be defined as knowledge, organization, and activity that results in (1) the collection, analysis, production, dissemination and use of information which relates to

any other government, political group, party, military force, movement or other association which is believed to relate to the group's
or government's security; (2) countering similar activities by other
groups, governments, or movements; and (3) activities undertaken to affect the composition and behavior of such groups or
governments.[6]

Anticipating an intelligent audience – and in the belief that a definition
should begin rather than pre-empt an argument – I offer at the outset a
definition that is openly hermeneutic rather than comprehensively
hermetic: *intelligence is the continuation of war by the clandestine
interference of one power into the affairs of another power.* To limn the
strategic and interventionist nature of intelligence, I have borrowed and
blended definitions provided by Clausewitz of war (the continuation of
political activity by an admixture of other means) and by Oppenheim of
intervention (the dictatorial interference in other states).[7] Clausewitz's
famous dictum has been purposely inverted to convey the presuppo-
sition that international politics is a continuation of conventional war
by alternative means; and Oppenheim's "dictatorial" has been expurgated to avoid a normative prejudgment of what constitutes legitimate
interference.
To be sure, intelligence in operation ranges widely from forcible to
non-forcible interventions; from purely analytical to violently "wet"
work; and from overtly persuasive to covertly manipulative forms of
influence. And, indeed, as the view within the community holds, intelligence can – by prediction, preparation, and, if necessary, pre-emption –
serve to prevent full-scale wars. But I believe a broad definition that
treats intelligence as a whole, rather than one that reduces it to its most
innocuous form of analysis – or, conversely, its most violent form of
secret warfare – will enhance the prospects for a judicious survey of a
field full of judgmental inclinations.
This chapter, then, seeks to widen the narrow horizon of traditional
inquiries with a counter-perspective, one that does not pre-view intelligence as either the guarantor of peace or the secret source of war, but as
the displacement and continuation of international conflict by other,
antidiplomatic means. Or, "simply put," intelligence is to wage war
without war – which, in the superpower stasis of a nuclear "peace,"
has made it, for a very long time, the only real game in town.[8] The
focus of this part will be on one mode of intelligence in particular which
I believe has emerged as the most powerful response to the estrangement
and accelerated pace of international relations: *surveillance,* the new
technostrategic force of normalization in world politics.

INTELLIGENCE THEORY

Such an inquiry requires a theory of intelligence, unless one holds that common sense is sufficient. As the economist John Maynard Keynes aptly points out in the conclusion to his *General Theory*, the pragmatist is usually – as well as unknowingly – in the grip of a defunct theory. A defamiliarizing theory can liberate the practitioner and thinker from the kind of political stasis and intellectual staleness that serve to defend against the effects of rapid historical change – at possibly great future costs.

If we take as a guide the CIA booklet, *The Acme of Skill* – cribbed from Sun Tzu's dictum, "To find security without fighting is the acme of skill" – then a theoretical inquiry into intelligence requires nothing less than a study of the knowledge and foreknowledge of the world: an intimidating thought that helps to explain the subject's atheoretical tendencies.[9] A more practical reason that is often mooted for the paucity of theory in intelligence is the lack of a set of *objects* for theory, conventionally defined as research materials. Official and unofficial secrecy acts on top of thirty-years' rules on archives *are* effective deterrents against scholarly investigations – and a sure guarantee that journalists, conspiracists, and propagandists will rush in where scholars fear to tread. I found an unexpected confirmation of this view from an unlikely source – Nikolai Yakovlev, a Soviet academic studying the US intelligence community who opens his book *CIA Target – The USSR* with a familiar complaint:

> Any analysis of Western secret services is bound to be difficult. It is like hewing one's way through a dark jungle of confusing, sometimes totally confounding, facts. The difficulty is both conceptual and functional, relating to search and selection of information. Though the subject is unquestionably autonomous, and at times, has its own motive forces, the work of secret services is ultimately no more than a continuation by other means of the policy of the governments concerned. In many cases, however, it is work that the governments will officially and vigorously disavow. That reason alone, to say nothing of the secrecy that shrouds the subject, makes the researcher literally gasp for air – for aren't facts the air the researcher breathes. What he often gets instead is poison vapour, because no other sphere of Western governmental activity resorts so freely to misinformation.[10]

Yakovlev's account of US intelligence, although informative about the particulars of some famous espionage cases, offers more of an infinite regression of mirror-opposites to American versions than any depth to the general theoretical questions of intelligence. This would include his perceptive claim that "the most tangible of Admiral Turner's innovations were the cynical paeans to the alliance of scholars and spies serving the interests of monopoly capital."[11]

Good reasons all, to explain the resistance of intelligence to theorization; reasons which have been, I should add, scanted by a fledgling group of Australian, British and North American academics trying to open up the field to study.[12] I believe, however, that there is a deeper reason to account for the lack of theory. There is the "classical" lament about the nature of international theory in general which aptly applies to the case of intelligence. In a rightly famous passage, Martin Wight ascribes the theoretical paucity and moral poverty in international relations to the necessitous demands of an anarchical system. It bears repeating:

> What I have been trying to express is the sense of a kind of disharmony between international theory and diplomatic practice, a kind of recalcitrance of international politics to being theorized about. The reason is that the theorizing has to be done in the language of political theory and law. But this is the language appropriate to man's control of his social life. Political theory and law are maps of experience or systems of action within the realm of normal relationships and calculable results. They are the theory of survival. What for political theory is the extreme case (as revolution, or civil war) is for international theory the regular case.[13]

I have attempted to show elsewhere how Wight is rewriting Hobbes, to make the claim that a total theory of IR would require a sovereign power.[14] However, this is not to identify both international relations and international theory merely as "a war of all against all." In the *Systems of States*, Wight goes into great historical detail to show how a cultural homogeneity, the mutual recognition of rights and obligations, and international institutions like the balance of power, diplomacy, and, indeed, even espionage have together yielded a modicum of order and intelligibility in international relations: in Hedley Bull's words, an anarchical society. His view of espionage is made in his usual, emphatic manner:

The *spy* deserves not to be forgotten. He is primarily a means of information, but sometimes of communication. In the modern West, the world of intelligence, counter-espionage and double agents provides a reverse image of the states-system: the dark underside of mutual interdependence.[15]

According to Wight, the error — and arrogance — of the moderns is to believe that the increase in transnational communication and the accumulation of knowledge will somehow transform international relations from a realm of repetition and recurrence into an working experiment for scientific progress.[16] In a sense, Martin Wight and Hedley Bull were "pre-mature" critics of "neorealism" in their attack on North American behavioralism as an attempt to accomplish in theory what could not possibly be achieved in practice: "man's control of his social life." Indeed, Bull found many of the tenets that would later be awkwardly subsumed under the rubric of "neorealism" to be, in fact, a form of "neoidealism."[17]

THE INTELLIGENCE OF THEORY

The putative problem of intelligence's resistance to theory is, I would like to suggest, further compounded by theory's resistance to intelligence. A brief genealogy of the coeval emergence of theory and intelligence can, I believe, make a credible proposition out of what admittedly sounds like a solecism. Of course, both theory and intelligence can be shown to have multiple chronological and diverse geographical origins; and when one steps outside of the dominant eurocentric historiographies, it becomes evident that other states-systems had extensive networks of intelligence — as well as theoretical accounts of their function and purpose — that pre-dated the Western experience. Sun Tzu's *Art of War* might come to mind for some students of intelligence, as it has, as we have seen, for the CIA. There is also the example of Kautilya's *Arthashastra*, in which the crucial role of intelligence for the Hindu state-system is clearly demonstrated by the fact that the duty of envoys earns a single chapter while the subject of spying extends over several. But lest the partiality of this inquiry be mistaken as yet another exercise in an unselfconscious eurocentrism, it is necessary to reiterate that it is the Western, techno-scientific models of intelligence *and* theory that have become — for better or worse — the global form.

Who then, were these supposed *ur*-theorists and *ur*-intelligencers, the

first agents, in other words, to form systems of knowledge in the service
of state power? I believe that the etymological and historical evidence
would point to the *theoros* and the *proxenos* of the Greek city-states.
Coming from *thea*, meaning "outward look," and *horao*, "to look at
something attentively," the *theoria* were individuals designated by Greek
officials to witness and later verbally certify the happening of an event
that was considered important for the polity.[18] Their *standing*, in both
a social and spatial sense, gave them the special status of detached
truth-tellers. A modern equivalent — at a much lower level of status —
would be a witness for a marriage, or to an execution. But in ancient
Greece, by position and perspective, the *theoria* were the institutional
voice of the public discourse.

The *proxenos* — meaning at first "one who stands before or protests,"
coming then to imply "guest-friend" or "foreigner" — was used throughout the Greek city-states as an *ad hoc* envoy who nonetheless enjoyed
various privileges and permanent residence in foreign city-states.[19] The
word incorporates the notion that they "stood in place" of their clients.
In spite of — or more likely because of — their special "guest-friendship"
status, the *proxenia* quickly turned into the primary institution of intelligence. In his book *Espionage and Treason*, Andre Gerolymatos documents close to fifty cases in which the *proxenia* saved their adopted
city-states from great harm — and inflicted some damage of their own.[20]

What, then, have the origins of theory and the forerunners of intelligence in common? Etymologically, both carry a sense of collecting
information at a significant distance. Epistemologically, both imply
a special power-knowledge derived from an authorized displacement.
Crudely, both can be said to have their origins in a kind of state-
sanctioned voyeurism. This is further borne out by the etymology of
intelligence itself, from *intelligere* (to see into, to perceive) and the early
synonymy of "intelligencer" and "speculator."[21]

What does this mean? As an alienated, speculative, perceptual knowledge of knowledge, *intelligence is theory* and *theory is intelligence*. It is
in their very resistance to pure *knowing* and their affinity for partial
seeing that both activities find their legitimation and standing. Mailer's
Harlot almost got it right: the duty of intelligence is to become the eyes
of the state.

Yet, the originary familiarity of theory and intelligence has bred a
modern, mutual contempt. This is the source of Proust's disdain for the
natural scientific corruption of theory and intelligence into a kind of
"literary botany."[22] The indeterminacies, subjectivity, and ambiguities
of life — the stuff of intrigue and literature — are disciplined by labeling,
classification, ordering. In the name of intelligence (that is, self-certain,

objective knowledge), the critic becomes taxonomist. In our own field, this contempt has been papered over on one side by the "pragmatic rationalists" who claim that "common sense" is sufficient to understand intelligence; and on the other side it has been scaffolded by the "hyper-rationalists" who try to "discipline" and neutralize a growing global disorder with organization and game theory, simulations of international conflict and cooperation, or rational choice models: in other words, to find in universal thought what can no longer be found in global practices.

It is not, then, a paradox but only logical that at a time when many of the conventional verities of world politics have come under sustained assault, the tendency toward grand theories and global explanations in IR should be matched by a disciplinary resistance against any form of critical pluralism.[23] All the more reason, I believe, to use theory to overcome the resistance that is theory; not to "master" resisting subjects — that is, international relations in general and intelligence in particular — but to liberate them from the inertia of academic practices through a self-conscious critique. This means that if one is to make sense of intelligence, a theory of theory as well as the intelligence of intelligence is needed. Or less simply put, a meta-theory to de-familiarize intelligence is called for.

What would such a meta-theory of intelligence look like? First, it must take into account, or more precisely, account for the fact that ambiguous discourse, not objective truth, is the fluctuating currency of intelligence: what was said or seen by whom when is the indeterminate exchange-value of the field. Further distanced from the "original" missile/battle/embassy/speech-site by encoding and decoding, disinformation and deception, the discourse of intelligence is short on truths (unless we share the Nietzschean definition of truths as "illusions whose illusionary nature has been forgotten"[24]) and long on what semiologists are wont to call free-floating signifiers. Second, a meta-theory must address — and attempt to redress — the current imbalance between *reason* and *rhetoric* in the study of intelligence. A rhetorical approach better serves intelligence because it assigns meaning to the status and capability of the reader, rather than the intentions of the author. It is attuned to this fundamental aspect of language: that often what is said is not what is meant, and what is meant is not what is said.[25] Hence, since intelligence is — probably more so than any other practice of international relations — a rhetorically conveyed and textually constituted field, an *intertextual* approach is called for.

INTERTEXTUALISM AND INTERNATIONAL THEORY

An *intertext*, defined by the semiologist Roland Barthes as "a multi-dimensional space in which a variety of writings, none of them original, blend and clash,"[26] aptly covers the field of intelligence, where there is no final arbiter of truth, meaning is derived from an interrelationship of texts, and power is implicated by the contingent nature and ambiguity of language and other signifying practices. There is as well a strategic sensitivity to intertextualism: theories are not judged as sovereign methods to order and verify facts but as part of an intersubjective process by which we create and promote political identities and differences. It recognizes that as surveillance intensifies, the truth becomes not clearer but more ambiguous, attenuated, removed from any material referent. In a polyphonic, multicultural, multipolar, three-ring world, we can no longer rely on the word of one *theoros*, one *proxenos* to convey the truth. "*At a certain moment*, therefore, it is necessary," says Barthes, "to turn against Method, or at least to treat it without any founding privilege as one of the voices of plurality — as a *view*, a spectacle mounted in the text, the text which all in all is the only "true" result of any research."[27] Intertextualism, then, inverts the power of the state by applying a surveillance practice to the intelligence text.

Intertextual theorizing is clearly not a process of scientific verification: nor, however, should it be construed as intrinsically anti-scientific. Rather, it takes a self-conscious step away from the dominant formalistic and ahistorical trends in international theory which "naturally select" hermetic, rational models over hermeneutic, philosophical investigations. Earlier criticisms of the theoretical closure apply here as well. Persistently, the various forms of the rationalist approach in international relations, from game theory to structural realism, have taken on the appearance of simulacra: appealing and persuasive in their modeled abstraction, but metaphysical and exclusionary in their hyperreal application. Even the most promising recent debate in international relations theory, between neorealists and their critics, told us much more about the politics of the discipline than about world politics. The issue was not how we, as theorists, think about the world, or even how others have thought about it in the past, but how we think others *ought* to think about it. Perhaps this is symptomatic of a degradation of theory, the effect of domesticating theory into a play for graduate students' minds and learned journals' pages. International theory continually confronts institutional pressures to conform, to reduce itself to the reigning dogma, to discipline insurgent antitheses. To keep intelligence theory from falling victim to similar perils, one must on occasion take on the role of *agent provocateur*.

Perhaps a dip into popular culture can help clarify these issues. Take, for instance, the new Miller Lite Beer advertisement. For over a decade Miller Lite Beer was sold by lining up two opposing sides of "Lite All-Stars" (composed of has-been comedians and retired athletes) in various locales, and having them shout at each other with increasing volume "Tastes Great!" and "Less Filling!". Saussure would recognize this as an identity structurally determined by a relation of binary opposites. There is no reference to external criteria, like a comparison to regular beer, or an analysis of the organic material that went to the making of the beer. We might call this a modernist or structuralist form of inter-textualism. This year Miller went for a postmodernist intertextualism. The ads consist of slogans like "Lite is what beer is today"; "It's the beer that beer's become"; and simply, "It's it." The last slogan is visualized by the "L" and the "e" dropping off the "Lite" sign on the side of a Miller delivery truck, parked in front of "The Original Irish Tap Room." The point? Identity becomes free-floating and self-referential as historical and material signifiers are radically appropriated or simply dropped.

We are still left, however, with the empirical question: where is the "beer" of intelligence, that is, the intelligence text? Facing similar lacunae in international theory, Wight turned to historical literature — the works of Thucydides, Machiavelli, Ranke, Wheeler-Bennett, Mattingly, and others — for it offers "a coherent structure of hypotheses that will provide a common explanation of phenomena," which certainly is not incompatible with scientific analysis, but "it does the job with more judiciousness and modesty, and with closer attention to the record of international experience."[28] However, intelligence, for reasons previously given, is bereft of such a respectable, commonly accepted corpus of knowledge. Its mysteries and paradoxes are not so easily rendered into univocal theories of coherence. The next best thing in the age of the New Ambiguity and the New Historicism?[29] I believe it is to be found in what many would consider to be the source of last resort in intelligence: the literature of international intrigue, intertextually interpreted.[30] What we need first is a clearer understanding of how a new surveillance regime has been intertextually constituted.

SURVEILLANCE: FROM PANOPTICISM TO TECHINT

Satellite, oh satellite,
Who sits upon our skies.
How deep do you see when you spy into our lives ...?
The The, "Good Morning Beautiful"

Within the utopian dream of the Enlightenment for the expansion of the social contract into a universal eternal peace, there lies a darker shadow, one that the rationalists of IR rarely note in their exaltations of modernity's promise. It is the perpetual dream of power to have its way without the visible exercise of will that would produce resistance. Readers of the Italian Marxist Antonio Gramsci have found evidence of a similar form of hegemonic power operating in international relations, but their focus has usually been limited to the state and class origins of this power.[31] To understand the technostrategic origins of the most pervasive power of intelligence in international relations, one must turn to the rupture point of the Enlightenment, the French Revolution, as does Michel Foucault, who sees in it ample evidence that modern politics would progress as war by other means:

> Historians of ideas usually attribute the dream of a perfect society to the philosophers and jurists of the eighteenth century: but there was also a military dream of society; its fundamental reference was not to the state of nature, but to the meticulously subordinated cogs of a machine, not to the primal social contract, but to permanent coercions, not to fundamental rights, but to indefinitely progressive forms of training, not to general will but to automatic docility.[32]

The French Revolution embodied both aspects of the Enlightenment: the high ideals of the Declaration of the Rights of Man coexisted with the power of terror, and both were promulgated by revolutionary wars that quickly took on imperial aims with the rise of Napoleon. These revolutionary tensions yielded changes over the battlefield, in the workplace, and in military institutions. In April 1794, for the first time, a company of *aerostiers* successfully used a balloon to observe the battle of Fleurus in Belgium; throughout the early 1790s "manufactories" were built according to principles found in the *Encyclopedie*, which called for close observation rather than coercion of the workforce; and in military schools, barracks, and hospitals a new architecture was developing, based on a monastic model of spatial distribution.[33] Looking first like a progressive, scientific reform, then playing a repressive, militarized role in the years of the *Ancien Regime*, and eventually flourishing in modern societies as a positive, seemingly benign form of social control and penal correction, a new power took hold which now pervades modernity – a disciplinary power based on surveillance.

The same Bentham who coined the name that graces our discipline provided a name and a blueprint for the architecture of the new disciplinary regime: the "panopticon." By now almost everyone in the social sciences is familiar with the concept of the panopticon, an annular structure with a tower in the center which contains – or might not contain – a guard to observe and through this observation indirectly, nonviolently control the behavior of prisoners, schoolchildren, hospital patients, military trainees, whomever finds themselves on the other side of the one-way gaze. In the final chapter of *Discipline and Punish*, after a detailed, critical historiography of the panopticon, Foucault elaborates a theory of *panopticism*. The prison is merely the extreme version, the most graphic model, the ultimate "pen" of our disciplinary society which inscribes the difference between normal and abnormal behavior, the good citizen and the delinquent. It is the ultimate sign of modernity's twin powers of normalization and surveillance. Put bluntly by the literary critic Maurice Blanchot: "If it weren't for prisons, we would know that we are all already in prison."[34]

Foucault does not take his acute analysis of modernity much beyond the borders of the prison-state. But I would like to extend his ideas to international relations, to suggest that it now faces similar developments in the field of intelligence. Obviously, in an anarchical society there is no central watchtower to normalize relations, no panopticon to define and anticipate delinquency. Historically, the great powers have reached relatively high levels of normalization by forging concerts of power, reciprocal codes of conduct, a body of international law. But this tenuous identity as a society was dependent upon a common diplomatic culture, *as well as* a collective estrangement from the "Anti-Christ Turk," the "colonial native," the "Soviet Threat," and the most recent pariah, the "international terrorist." In contemporary international relations the diminution of the Soviet threat under Gorbachev, the renunciation of terrorism by PLO leader Arafat, and the dissolution of the Warsaw Pact have removed critical points of collective alienation. Equally, the efferent forces of states seeking resources and security grow stronger as America's ability to assert a hegemonic position declines. What power (some might prefer "regime" or "institution") can maintain stability and re-normalize relations in this late modern state of affairs, with multiplying state and non-state actors contesting the sovereign powers and truths behind "Western domination" (Hedley Bull's "Third World Revolt"[35]), at the same time that the foundations of that domination are undergoing internal fragmentation and diversification?

That power is here and now, in the shadows and in the "deep black." It has no trouble seeing us, but we have had great difficulties seeing it. It is the normalizing, disciplinary, technostrategic power of surveillance. This modern panopticism takes many forms, but it is the communications intelligence (COMINT), electronic intelligence (ELINT), radar intelligence (RADINT), telemetry intelligence (TELINT), and photointelligence (PHOTOINT) – all operating under the 22,300-mile-high roof of technical intelligence (TECHINT)[36] – that constitute a new regime of power in international relations. Human intelligence (HUMINT) has played, and continues to play, an important role in normalizing relations through vigilance, but it lacks the ubiquity, resolution, and pantoscopic power of the technical intelligence system, as well as its apparent capability to provide value-free detailed information about the object of surveillance: "the picture does not lie." Indeed, much of its power lies in this aura of representational truth that surrounds the image, in spite of the interpretational debates – from the alarmist interpretation of Soviet civil defense bunkers by former head of Air Force Intelligence, Major General Keegan, in the early 1970s, to the supposed discovery of Soviet MIG airfields and "Cuban" baseball fields in Nicaragua in the early 1980s – that have marked the history of photoreconnaissance. Admiral Stansfield Turner, more than any other director of the Central Intelligence Agency, promoted this view of technical intelligence:

> What espionage people have not accepted is that human espionage has become a complement to technical systems. Espionage either reaches out into voids where technical systems cannot probe or double-checks the results of technical collection. In short, human intelligence today is employed to do what technical systems cannot do.[37]

My purpose is not to rant against the "machine in the garden," as Leo Marx put it; but neither is it to offer a paean to our new technogods. It is rather to point out a neglected problematic of the surveillance regime, and to consider *why* it has been neglected. There is the previously mentioned factor of secrecy and compartmentalized knowledge that surrounds the systems and the attendant issue of accountability that automatically politicizes any inquiry. Technical intelligence systems are considered so sensitive that a new security classification was devised: SCI, for Sensitive Compartmented Information.[38] Perhaps, then, one reason why the politics of surveillance has been understudied by the field of international relations is because there simply is no testable, scientific method to determine how it is controlled, used, and budgeted. These remain matters for historical investigation, intertextual interpretation, and open-ended speculation − not the usual methods and concerns of neobehavioralists or neorealists, but prime material for a poststructuralist inquiry.

The central problematic of the surveillance regime is that it normalizes relations by continuing *both* war and peace by other, technical means. The same satellite that monitors and helps us verify whether the Soviets are conforming to the INF treaty simultaneously maps the way for low-level, terrain-following cruise missiles. TENCAP (Tactical Exploitation of National Capabilities), using the latest generation of advanced KH-11 and Milstar satellites, was designed to provide field commanders with the real-time command, control, communications, and intelligence (C^3I) necessary to fight the war of the future − and perhaps to deter it, as immediate, local, *conventional* deterrence becomes a high priority with the prospects of a nuclear-free Europe.[39] Moreover, multiple perspectives and interpretations of international crises are on the horizon, as several nations take steps to develop their own spy satellite capability, including Britain, France, Italy, Japan, Spain, Israel, India, and South Africa. To avoid "political manipulation" by the superpowers, middle-level powers like Canada and Sweden as well as the Western European Union, the nine-nation security organization, have called for internationally controlled satellites that would verify arms control agreements and monitor troop movements.[40] Most recently, independent and commercial satellite surveillance sources have emerged. The first was the Swedish Space Media Network, which gained global attention when it scooped the Chernobyl disaster in 1986. Using images bought from the French SPOT system, American Landsats, and various weather satellites, and then boosting the resolution with a computer enhancement system, they have managed to uncover among other things Soviet laser installations, sites for Chinese missiles in Saudi Arabia, and new cocaine fields in Latin America.[41] More startling was what they failed to discover during the first few weeks of the Persian Gulf War: the massing of Iraqi forces on the Saudi borders that was used by President Bush to justify the immediate deployment of US troops to the region.[42]

Indeed, something of a paradox seems to be at work: the greater the transparency and the faster the response time of the new satellites (like the Lacrosse radar-imaging and Magnum communications-monitoring capabilities) that help provide C^3I, the greater the opportunity for deterrence to "work." At least that would seem to be borne out by one case — if it is to be believed — that Carter canceled a highly secret plan to attack Iran with 5,000 assault troops the autumn after the failed hostage rescue, because US satellites detected large Soviet troop movements (22 full divisions) heading toward Iran, a move made possible by the fact that the Soviets had gained access to US satellite-relayed messages — because the traitor John Walker had sold them the encryption key.[43]

THE PARANOIA OF CYBERSPACE

One policy implication of the new surveillance regime is that the great powers created a cybernetic system that displayed the classic symptoms of advanced paranoia: hyper-vigilance, intense distrust, rigid and judgmental thought processes, and projection of one's own repressed beliefs and hostile impulses onto the other. The very nature of the surveillance/cybernetic system contributes to this condition: we see and hear the other, but imperfectly and partially — *below* our rising expectations. This can induce paranoid behavior — that is, reasoning correctly but from incorrect premises — as happened with the participants in the well-known laboratory experiment at Stanford who unknowingly were subjected (through hypnosis) to a partial hearing loss: when placed in social situations, they assumed that people were whispering about them and soon took on the symptoms of paranoia.[44]

The pathological formation of the national security state takes on the characteristic of a feedback loop, constituting the need and the justification for surveillance systems which reinforces paranoid behavior. Some classic examples are the "bomber gaps" and "missile gaps" of the 1950s and 1960s, when Eisenhower and the CIA played superego to a warring military id that (ab)used the new U-2 photoreconnaissance to find bombers and missiles in every barn and silo of the Soviet Union.[45] Second, overclassification and overcompartmentalization of information in the national security state can lead to a form of overdetermined decision-making with policy outcomes based on a surfeit of "deep," discrete sources that resist corrective feedback. And third, the national security identity itself becomes constituted by the internalization of the fear of an external "other." Perhaps the best example of many that I have come across is a 1963 internal FBI memo, written the day after Martin Luther King delivered his "I have a dream" speech by the head of the Domestic Intelligence Division of the FBI, William Sullivan:

The Director [Hoover] is correct. We were completely wrong about believing the evidence was not sufficient to determine some years ago that Fidel Castro was not a communist or under communist influence. On investigating and writing about communism and the American Negro, we had better remember this and profit by the lesson it should teach us ... Personally, I believe in the light of King's powerful demagogic speech yesterday he stands head and shoulders over all other Negro leaders put together when it comes to influencing great masses of Negroes. We must mark him now, if we have not done so before, as the most dangerous Negro of the future in this Nation from the standpoint of communism, the Negro and national security.[46]

But what kind of feedback can possibly "cure" the modern cyber-paranoiac? At the level of great power politics, perhaps our best hope — and the best elevation — for understanding the other at the highest reaches remains the much-maligned "summit." To be sure, there are many historical examples and counter-examples — the exchange of threats by Kennedy and Khruschev in Vienna followed a decade later by bear-hugs between Nixon and Brezhnev — but a recent case sticks in my mind: President Reagan, who approached his first summit with his Soviet counterpart with visions of the "Evil Empire," came down from his third one saying (in something like Russian): "Trust, but verify."

Of course, it is dangerous to extrapolate lessons of the laboratory to the practices of power politics — the fetishization of the prisoner's dilemma game in International Relations theory is a case in point. But when hyper-rationalism combines with cyber-paranoia, an equivalent in international theory to the semiology of medicine — a study of the signs of illness — becomes even more expedient.[47] To that end, I offer an intertextual approach to the intelligence game and surveillance war.

Notes

1 Margery Sabin, "The Community of Intelligence and the Avant-Garde," *Raritan*, 4, no. 3 (Winter 1985), p. 2. To be sure, "intelligence" appears in *pre*-modern texts, like the Bible, and Sun Tzu's *Art of War*; see below.
2 Some examples would be the *Kingdomes Weekly Intelligencer* (published by the Parliamentary side, and according to its masthead, "Sent Abroad to prevent misinformation"), *The Publick Intelligencer*, and the European *Intelligenzblatt*. See Anthony Smith, *The Newspaper: An International History* (London: Thames and Hudson, 1979), pp. 10–12.
3 Michael Turner, "Understanding CIA's Role in Intelligence," *International Journal of Intelligence and Counterintelligence* (1991), 4, no. 3, p. 303.

4 Ibid.
5 Ibid., p. 296.
6 Roy Godson and Richard Shultz, "Foreign Intelligence: A Course Syllabus," *International Studies Notes of the International Studies Association*, 8, issues 3–4 (Fall–Winter, 1981–2), p. 5. There was an exception to the rule that I came across in Michael McKinley's highly informative and provocative paper, "The Alliance Intelligence Benefit and Australia: A Challenge to the Prevailing Orthodoxy" (Paper presented at the 1991 Annual Meeting of the International Studies Association in Vancouver). He quotes R. H. Mathams' definition of "strategic intelligence" as that "kind of intelligence a State must possess regarding other States in order to assure itself that its cause will not suffer nor its undertakings fail because its statesmen and soldiers plan and act in ignorance." See R. H. Mathams, "The Intelligence Analyst's Notebook," Working Paper no. 151 (Canberra: Strategic and Defense Studies Centre, Research School of Pacific Studies, Australian National University, February, 1988), p. 1.
7 See C. von Clausewitz, *On War*, trans. and edited by M. Howard and P. Paret (Princeton: Princeton University Press, 1976); and L. Oppenheim, *International Law*, vol. I (London: Longman, 1905).
8 "The art of deterrence, prohibiting political war, favors the upsurge, not of conflicts, but of *acts of war without war*." See Paul Virilio, *Pure War* (New York: Semiotext(e), 1983), p. 27.
9 Acting as commentator on a version of this chapter that was presented at the United States Institute of Peace, Paul Seabury informed me that the CIA got it wrong: it should be, "To subdue the enemy without fighting is the acme of skill." He attributed the mistranslation to misplaced peaceniks – like former Director Admiral Stansfield Turner – in the Agency.
10 Nikolai Yakovlev, *CIA Target – The USSR* (Moscow: Progress Publishers, 1982), p. 5.
11 Ibid., p. 134.
12 See, for example, the work of Christopher Andrew, Michael Fry, Michael McKinley, Wesley Wark, and other scholars, who can be read in two relatively new journals of intelligence: the *International Journal of Intelligence and Counterintelligence*, and *Intelligence and National Security*. See also the proceedings of "Espionage: Past, Present, Future?" (University of Toronto, 7–9 November 1991).
13 Martin Wight, "Why is there no International Theory?", in *Diplomatic Investigations*, edited by H. Butterfield and M. Wight (London: George Allen & Unwin, 1966), pp. 33–4.
14 See Der Derian, "The Boundaries of Knowledge and Power in International Relations," *International/Intertextual Relations*, pp. 3–10.
15 See Wight, *Systems of States* (Leicester: Leicester University Press, 1977), p. 30.
16 A notable exception is Walter Laquer, who offers a persuasive critique of efforts made by political scientists and other behavioralists to transform intelligence and its study into a scientific activity. See in particular "Craft or Science?", *A World of Secrets: The Uses and Limits of Intelligence* (New York: Basic Books, 1985), pp. 293–308.
17 Hedley Bull, notes from Oxford University Lecture on "The Neoidealists."
18 See J. Der Derian *On Diplomacy: A Genealogy of Western Estrangement*

(Oxford: Basil Blackwell, 1987), pp. 11–12; Wlad Godzich, "The Tiger on the Paper Mat," foreword to Paul de Man, *The Resistance to Theory* (Minneapolis: University of Minnesota Press, 1986), pp. xiv-xv; and the *Oxford English Dictionary*.

19　See Andre Gerolymatos, *Espionage and Treason: A Study of the Proxenia in Political and Military Intelligence Gathering in Classical Greece* (Amsterdam: J. C. Gieben, 1986); and Wight, *Systems of States*, pp. 53–6.

20　For example, Alexandros of Macedonia, a *proxenos* of Athens, supplied the Athenians with the Persian battle plan at Plataiai in 479 BC; and in 427 BC the Corinthian *proxenoi* in Corcyra arranged for the release of 250 Corcyrians imprisoned in Corinthos and then used them to subvert and overthrow the democratic government of Corcyra. See Gerolymatos, *Espionage and Treason*, pp. 110–115.

21　See Richard Wilmer Rowan, *Secret Service: Thirty-three Centuries of Espionage* (New York: Hawthorn, 1937).

22　Sabin, "The Community of Intelligence and the Avant-Garde," p. 7.

23　See J. Der Derian, "Introducing Philosophical Traditions in International Relations," *Millennium Journal of International Affairs*, xvii, no. 2 (Summer 1988), pp. 189–93. See also my account in Chapter 1 of theoretical effects induced by "the insecurity of security studies" (I owe the felicitous phrasing to Tom Biersteker).

24　de Man, *Resistance to Theory*, p. 67.

25　This borrows from one of the more recent – and certainly one of the richest – exchanges on the reason/rhetoric question between Jacques Derrida and John Searle on J. L. Austin's speech-act theory. See Searle, "Reiterating the Differences," *Glyph*, I (1977), pp. 198–208; and Derrida's reply, "Limited Inc abc," *Glyph*, II (1977), pp. 162–254.

26　"The Death of the Author," in R. Barthes, *Image–Music–Text*, trans. S. Heath (New York: Hill and Wang, 1977), p. 146.

27　"Writers, Intellectuals, Teachers," in *Image–Music–Text*, p. 201. Anyone who doubts the intertextual nature of intelligence should undertake a careful reading of the transcripts of the Senate Intelligence Committee hearings on the nomination of Robert Gates to be the next Director of the CIA. Consider just one incident: the textual appropriations, displacements, and strategies that surrounded the inquiry into the 1981 attempt on the life of Pope John Paul II. Ten texts are involved. Text 1 is a speech given by Secretary of State Alexander Haig the day after President Reagan's inauguration, in which he links the Soviet Union to international terrorism. Text 2 is a National Intelligence Estimate, commissioned by the State Department's Bureau of Intelligence and Research, which fails to find evidence that conclusively backs up Haig's charge. Text 3 is journalist Claire Sterling's book *The Terrorist Network*, which goes a step further and claims that the KGB is the mastermind behind practically every international terrorist act. Text 4 is the same text, aggressively waved in the face of authors of Text 2 by Director William Casey, who claims that he learned more from it than anything that the CIA analysts were providing. The analysts cite, to no avail, a very secret Text 5, a CIA disinformation campaign in Europe that was probably the hidden source of Text 3. In 1984 Text 6 appears, Sterling's *The Time of Assassins*, which argues that the KGB was indeed behind the papal plot, prompting Casey in 1985 to order Robert Gates to commission

Text 7, tendentiously entitled "Agca's Attempt to Kill the Pope: The Case for Soviet Involvement." Text 7, said by Gates in a cover memorandum to be the "CIA's first comprehensive examination of evidence of who was behind the attempted assassination of Pope Paul II," refutes the conclusions of Text 2, stating that "The Soviets were reluctant to invade Poland ... so they decided to demoralize [the Polish] opposition by killing the Polish Pope. Text 8 emerges in July 1985, when three senior CIA analysts note a political bias to Text 7 but absolve Gates of tailoring the report to satisfy pre-ordained conclusions. Text 9 comes from former CIA analyst Melvin Goodman, who testifies before the Senate Committee hearings that Gates personally rewrote Text 7 to confirm Sterling's Text 6, and excised a "scope" note that stated no effort had been made to weight arguments against Soviet involvement. Text 10 is Gates rebuttal of Goodman's charges before the Intelligence Committee: "Based on the evidence, the allegations that I drove this paper to its conclusions and then knowingly misrepresented it to policy makers is false." At the end of this war between texts and power, Gates − but not "the truth" − was confirmed. This account is drawn from videotapes of the hearings, and the edited transcripts of the hearings published by the *New York Times*, from 2 October 1991 to 5 October; David Johnston, "Documents Show CIA Debate over Whether Soviets Tried to Assassinate Pope," *New York Times* (2 October 1991), p. A19; Elaine Sciolino and David Johnston, "In Rebuttal to Senate to Senate Committee, CIA Nominee is Truthful but Incomplete," *New York Times* (13 October 1991); and Anthony Lewis, "Too Clever by Half," *New York Times* (October 1991).

28 Wight, "Why is there no International Theory?", p. 32.
29 By the "New Ambiguity" I refer to an historical period of uncertainty and unpredictability (as oft noted in speeches by President Bush); and by the "New Historicism" to the historical approach influenced by literary theory, ably demonstrated by Stephen Greenblatt, Jonathan Arac, Jean Franco, Hayden White, among many others. By the use of these terms I seek as well to highlight the new discursive power emanating from the *circulation* and *interpenetration* of historical "fact" and "fiction," best instanced in politics by the presidency of President Reagan (who drew many of his facts from movies); in history by Simon Schama (in, for example, *Dead Certainties (Unwarranted Speculations)*, New York: Knopf, 1991), and in fiction by Don Delilo (*Libra*, New York: Penguin Books, 1989). See also *The New Historicism*, edited by H. Veeser (New York: Routledge, 1989).
30 I have focused primarily on the written text rather than visual texts, not because of some literary purity but simply because of archival limitations. Indeed, it could be argued that the cinematic and video intertext of espionage is much more powerful. A case in point would be the shortlived television series "Under Cover," about a husband and wife team in the CIA (thinly fictionalized as the "National Intelligence Agency"). ABC decided not to broadcast one of the first episodes because it was deemed "too" timely: it involved an attempt to thwart an invasion of Kuwait by Iraq which was to include the deployment of chemical weapons and missiles. It seemed that the CIA and other US intelligence organizations lagged behind the "NIA's" assessment of the region by several months.
31 See Enrico Angelli and Craig Murphy, *America's Quest for Supremacy and*

the Third World: A Gramscian Analysis. (London: Pinter Publishers, 1988).

32 M. Foucault, *Discipline and Punish: The Birth of the Prison*, trans. by Alan Sheridan (New York: Pantheon, 1977), p. 169.

33 For three very different, very rich accounts of surveillance see Foucault's *Discipline and Punish*, P. Virilio's *Guerre et cinéma: Logistique de la perception* (Paris: Editions de l'Etoile, 1984), and W. Burrows's *Deep Black: Space Espionage and National Security* (New York: Random House, 1986).

34 M. Blanchot, *The Writing of the Disaster*, trans. by A. Smock (Lincoln and London: 1986), p. 66.

35 See H. Bull and A. Watson, (eds), *The Expansion of the International Society* (Oxford: Clarendon Press, 1984).

36 That is, unless one goes beyond the favored geosynchronous parking spots to include the US Vela spacecraft which watches for the double flash of a thermonuclear explosion from 60,000 miles out. See Burrows, *Deep Black*, pp. 19–20.

37 Quoted in Burrows, *Deep Black*, p. v.

38 Not that it prevented Christopher Boyce, employed in TRW's satellite program, and William Kampiles, a CIA watch officer, from stealing and selling to the Soviets detailed, comprehensive information about the Rhyolite and KH-11 satellite systems.

39 In chapter 8 on the new "cyberwar" we shall see whether it worked as planned in the Persian Gulf War.

40 See William Broad, "Non-Superpowers are Developing Their Own Spy Satellite Systems," *New York Times* (3 September 1989), p. 16.

41 Coming as a surprise to the Western intelligence agencies was the 1987 Soviet decision to enter the market of satellite photography, especially since it would appear that the photographs sold so far come from military satellites with a magnification power capable of discerning objects as small as 5 meters (the SPOT system resolves down to 10 meters, the Landsat 30 meters). It would seem that the exigencies of capitalism are greater than those of "national security," since the US is now reconsidering its long-held policy of total secrecy for military reconnaissance photographs. See William Broad, "Soviet Photos of U.S. Were for Spying," *New York Times* (30 January 1989); and Jeffrey Richelson, "The Future of Space Reconnaissance," *Scientific American*, 264, no. 1 (January 1991), 38–44.

42 This story was covered by the *St Petersburg Times* (6 January 1991), and reprinted in *In These Times* (27 February 1991), but largely ignored by the wire services and the national media.

43 See J. Barron, *Breaking the Ring* (Boston: Houghton Mifflin, 1987), pp. 24–5.

44 See W. Herbert, "Paranoia: Fearful Delusions," in the *New York Times Magazine*, pp. 62–3.

45 Burrows gives a good account of the inter-service rivalry and its effect on photo interpretation during this period. He quotes a former CIA officer who said that "To the Air Force, every flyspeck on film was a missile." See *Deep Black*, pp. 82–112.

46 Memorandum from William Sullivan to Alan Belmont, 30 August 1963, "Supplementary Detailed Staff Reports on Intelligence Activities and the Rights of Americans," Book III, *Final Report of the Select Committee to Study Governmental Operations with Respect to Intelligence Activities*

(Washington, US Government Printing Office, 1976), pp. 107–8.
47 But then IR theory might find it necessary to adopt the telling statement that I discovered in the fine print of a hospital release form: "The patient recognizes that medicine is an imperfect art, not a science."

3
THE INTERTEXTUAL
POWER OF
INTERNATIONAL INTRIGUE
—

Ye shall know the truth,
And the truth shall make you free.
John 8:32; inscription on the entry to the CIA

THE REPRESENTATIONAL POWER OF
INTELLIGENCE

Consider three reports on espionage cases between 1985 and 1989. The first is from the *New York Post*, 22 August 1985:

DEADLY RED SPY DUST

A State Dept. official said the US could not keep silent about the chemical dusting, even at the risk of imperiling the Reagan–Gorbachev talks. "It's not a fantasy. It's fact. It exists," he said.

The second is from the *New York Times*, 30 March 1987:

Marine Gave Conflicting Stories of Soviet Intrigue, Records Show

Sergeant Lonetree's statements, if true, do provide a picture of how a marine fascinated by espionage books and European Communism could be seduced by a young woman and initiated in espionage tactics in Moscow and Vienna.

And the third is from the *New York Times*, 16 July 1989:

Spy Trial Opens Today With Facts Like Fiction

An affable Turkish mechanic suspected by American officials of running a network of spies at one of this country's most valued eavesdropping posts in Europe goes on trial here Monday. The mechanic, Huseyin Yildirim, is at the center of a bizarre case with a plot line that seems more like pulp thriller than true life.

These excerpts suggest the thesis of this chapter: from the giddy days of the first and through the most morbid moments of the second Cold War, the popular culture, journalism, and academic study of international intrigue has been an important intertext of power and play in world politics. This intertext represents a field of ideological contestation where national security strategies, with their end-games of impossibly real wars of mass annihilation, can be played and replayed for mass consumption as a simulation of war in which states compete, interests clash, and spy counters spy, all in significant fun. It is, then, a complex space where various representations and representatives of the national security state compete to draw the boundaries and dominate the murkier margins of international relations. The intertextual arsenal is vast, but the preferred discursive weapon in the age of nuclear deterrence is the force of (official) "truth" which can convert mass (opinion) into power (politics).

In matters of intelligence, the force of truth is historically constructed and geopolitically specific, as borne out by the events captured by the excerpts above, and more recently by US Senate Intelligence Committee confirmation hearings on the nomination of Robert Gates to direct the CIA. For instance, when a chemical sensitive to ultra-violet light is wiped on a hand at a dance hall, it is an accepted form of crowd control; when 500 diplomats, journalists, and other foreign residents of Moscow are gathered at the American ambassador's residence and told that the chemical is being used to track them and that it might be carcinogenic, it is yet another incarnation of the "Soviet Threat." Or when overheated bees swarm in the summer and their droppings fall on New England farmers, they call it, as did my grandfather who was an apiarist, bee shit; when it falls on Afghan freedom fighters it is called "poisonous yellow rain."

Through intertextuality we can see how the American popular literature of international intrigue shares and privileges a narrative of the truth-sayers of the security state: beyond our borders the world is alien, complex, practically incoherent − an enigma but one which can be unravelled by the expert story-teller. Our interest in the practices and the genres of intelligence originates in this sense of insecurity and alienation; but it is the allure of puzzlement and the promise of resolution which sustains our fascination.

In the confusion and complexity of international relations, one particular realm of intelligence — espionage — becomes a discursive space where realism and fantasy interact, and seemingly intractable problems are imaginatively and playfully resolved. In an essay on Joseph Conrad's *Secret Agent*, Terry Eagleton remarks that "the spy-thriller inserts the fascination of the foreign into the sordidly routine world of *Realpolitik*; 'Dickensian' realism involves an imaginative caricaturing of the familiar."[1] Eagleton hits on one reason why espionage, right after science fiction, has become one of the most popular literary genres about world politics; and yet, along with science fiction, it is one of the least (seriously) studied elements of world politics. It may well be the case that espionage is too mythopoeic for sober study: like the gods' omniscience, the spy's secret knowledge confers a special kind of power which is mysteriously, even metaphysically appealing, but ultimately beyond our ken.

This difficulty is highlighted by the nature of the sources to which I referred earlier.[2] Any inquiry into espionage faces false leads, intentional errors, and the ever-ready lie. Because of official and unofficial Secrets Acts, the genre of *actual* spy stories is scant. There are the odd Senate and House Intelligence Committee reports; limited information gleaned from the US Freedom of Information Act; books by disaffected intelligence officers (Agee, Marchetti, Stockwell, McGehee, et al.); the rash of recent espionage court cases (Christopher Boyce, the "Falcon," and Daulton Lee the "Snowman;" the Walker menfolk; Richard Miller, Ronald Pelton, and Jonathan Pollard); and at the top of the heap, approved accounts from spies or spymasters still in or freshly out of the stable.[3] A notable exception has recently been published, *The Second Oldest Profession* by Phillip Knightley.[4] It is full of biting revelations of the escapades and follies of spies throughout history, but it is for the most part a journalistic history which tells us very little about the motivations, attractiveness, and most importantly, the narrative power of espionage.

It would be fairly easy to substantiate the impact of the revelations from these sources on the pop-lit of international intrigue of the 1970s, and to anticipate similar fictional developments from the contemporary spy scandals. Defections and blown covers have supplied many of the recurring characters. A particularly popular one is the "mole," usually an amalgam of the British spies Philby, Burgess, and Maclean, who is embodied by Bill Haydon in John le Carré's Smiley series, or Robin Darby, the Judas in Charles McCarry's *The Last Supper*. Then there are the mole-chasers, drawn from real spies like Peter Wright, formerly of MI5, or James Jesus Angleton, the CIA's counter-intelligence chief, who were sent out to pasture (in Wright's case, a stud farm in Tasmania) after their relentless investigations of Soviet penetration paralyzed their intelligence agencies. They appear, thinly disguised, as George Smiley in le Carré, Paul Christopher in McCarry, or, with the most tendentious verisimilitude, as Max Zimmer in Robert Moss's *Death Beam*. Post-Watergate revelations have also supplied much of the in-house language of the spy novel: "neutralization" and "extermination with extreme prejudice" for murder and assassination; "penetration" for placing agents inside hostile intelligence services; and "wet work" for violent covert action are a few examples.

Attributing influence in the other direction, from popular literature to the "real thing," is more difficult. There does not seem to be a clear-cut case similar to Arthur C. Clarke's science fictional antecedent to satellites in geosynchronous orbits. The language of espionage would seem to be a natural place to search for fictional influences; but even the most obvious example, John le Carré's conception of "mole" and the media's adaptation of it, is difficult to credit when one discovers that Francis Bacon several hundred years before similarly referred to an undercover agent in the enemy's camp. The most recent, if not necessarily the most plausible, evidence of spy "fiction" affecting spy "fact" can be found in the (t)rash of free enterprise espionage: for instance, Daulton Lee and Marine Sergeant Lonetree were reported to have consumed an inordinate amount of spy novels, and John Walker Jr. cultivated a James Bond image. For the FBI agents who searched Walker's house it must have been the *circularity* of influence which struck them: how were they to explain the discovery of a copy of *The Falcon and the Snowman* with a bookmark placed between the two pages recounting a 1975 meeting in Mexico City between a Russian KGB officer and Daulton Lee — a meeting which took place one week after a trip Walker made to Mexico? The FBI, understandably, chose not to publish its conclusions, and the press left the matter to public speculation. A curious circuitry of causality also surrounds the Sergeant Lonetree case. Lost in the sensationalism of the early accusation — later disproved — that he had been a night-time tour-guide for Violetta Seina and her KGB "uncle Sasha" at the Moscow embassy was Lonetree's own account of his motivations for engaging in espionage, which in one rambling interrogation he confessed to be "due to intrigue and his interest in intelligence matters." The final irony, or loop in the narrative, is that his interest was spurred by the books of John Barron, who later appeared as an "expert witness" at Lonetree's trial, and who was described by the *New York Times* as having "written extensive nonfiction works about the KGB" (as "nonfictional," one might surmise, as Claire Sterling's writings in the *New York Times* on terrorism).[5]

While frustrating to those who are engaged in the theoretical maintenance of the geopolitical borders of the states-system, the refusal of those lines to crystallize in the territory of espionage says something about the shadowy periphery of superpower politics: it cannot be reduced or abstracted to a controlled experiment, in spite of the best efforts of the disciplinary practices of, say, the *American Political Science Review*. Nor, as we have suggested before, is espionage a Hobbesian "war of all against all," for it is, after all, a game with rules and codes. As the pre-eminent truth-game of the state, espionage represents an epistemological as much as an ideological battle where the practico-inert of the history, economics, and military, that is, the *matter* of the state, is turned into the reason of a state through a confrontation with the anti-matter of the reason of another state.

The institutional ability to canalize and discipline the power that is produced by this encounter of alienated reason, without (too much) blood-shed, is an important source of legitimacy for the intelligence community. On occasion — and it seems with greater frequency — the intelligence community fragments and faces de-legitimation when the nature of the estranged relationship radically shifts and the matter of state proves irreducible to a single, uniform reason of state. This would appear to be the case in the transitional period from Stansfield Turner to William Casey when fundamental disagreements over Soviet economic and military strength spawned the independent "Committee B," pitted the Defense Intelligence Agency against the CIA, and turned the National Security Council against just about everyone in the State Department. Eventually, albeit briefly, Casey was able to reassert one voice, one text to the official discourse of intelligence. But how we apprehend dangerous others remained an imaginary intertext in the literature of intrigue.

Presently, we can detect signs of uncertainty and fragmentation in the intelligence community which are reminiscent of the period after Watergate and the Senate and House Intelligence Committee reports in the seventies. Glasnost, the Iran–Contra affair, and public hearings on narcoterrorism have surely contributed to the proliferation of competing facts, figures, and fictions. But no one seems to be rushing in, as did the *Washington Post* and *The Village Voice*, to chronicle the events. To be sure, the majority of journalists are neither fools nor angels: there are serious official obstacles and high costs which deter coverage of espionage. But something else seems to be at work. To call it a law of history is specious, but to call it a rule of journalism is perhaps more credible; the

Cold War the second time around generated more parodies than tragedies. Hence, much of the imaginative coverage of espionage takes place in the tabloids: finding parodic fiction to be as newsworthy and profitable as tragic fact, and demonstrating a broader definition of the "truth," they represent the grey market of the discursive economy of the national security state.

On the fringe lurks a new arrival, Bob Guccione's *Espionage*. Reinscribing the latest pornographization of the state by our spymasters, *Espionage* magazine stands out as a paragon of the espionage intertext. It declaims its comprehensiveness in large print:

> ESPIONAGE Magazine has everything: real-life adventures of national and international newsmakers, featuring their involvement in the espionage activities that are helping to shape the world in which we live; real life spy adventures of historical characters who were in part responsible for the world we've inherited; on-going reports of the major espionage activities taking place today; [and] exciting fiction depicting might-have-been and yet-to-be espionage activities possible. . . .

and disclaims in small print (at the bottom of the page) any essentialist truth-claims: .

> All data in ESPIONAGE magazine, technical or otherwise, is based upon personal experience, imagination, or on the spot reporting using specific products, equipment and components under particular conditions and circumstances, some of which cannot be verified. ESPIONAGE, its agents, officers, and employees disclaim any responsibility for all liability, injuries or damages.

Crudely, yet effectively, ESPIONAGE Magazine forces us to recognize that it is imaginative speculation — not causation — which underlies the relationship between the "real" spy world and its popular representation. This is not to refute the impact of espionage on national security, nor the serious claims of those who practice and who study espionage. By numbers — peaking at a record of 26 espionage convictions in the US during the 1986 "Year of the Spy — and by extreme (and slightly ludicrous) counter-measures — like Shultz having to discuss top secret issues in a Winnebago parked behind the Moscow embassy, or the Army setting up a hot line in 1985 to help catch spies (1–800-CALL SPY) — we can acknowledge the increased significance of espionage in the practice of international politics. In June 1986, former head of the

FBI and then director of the CIA, William H. Webster declared that "espionage is a bigger immediate danger to our national security than the various terrorist groups."[6] And, to put a truly official stamp on the issue, that same year the International Studies Association fully recognized intelligence studies as a sub-field.

How, then, might an intertextual inquiry into espionage help us to understand this putative surge? I have already stated that I believe there is some value to the common procedure of formulating definitions of espionage, making clear-cut distinctions between clandestine collection, counter-intelligence, covert action, and generating some data about the intelligence cycle.[7] I believe, however, that it would be more productive to use popular culture rhetorically — as Bakhtin used Rabelais, Barthes the strip-tease, or Derrida a postcard — to engage in some dialogic interpretations which might put into question some common assumptions about the relationship of espionage to international relations. What I suggest, then, is that for this textual moment we leave causation to the political scientists and the promulgation of monologic truths to the national security state courtiers, in favor of an intertextual approach which investigates how these two discourses — the fictive literature of international intrigue and the "factive" literature of national security and espionage — produce meaning and legitimate particular forms of *power* in their relation to each other.

Through an intertextual reading, I believe we can discern three kinds of power at work in espionage which have been neglected by the social sciences. The first is *alienation*, a power of delimitation which defines Cold War estrangement and the mutual struggle for recognition among states and state representatives. The second is *surveillance*, which, as the traditional diplomatic culture erodes, is increasingly becoming the most formidable power of normalization in global and domestic politics. And the third is *acceleration*, the power of speed which has become the essence of a permanent and pervasive race for arms and information. However, before modern intertexts can be confronted, some historical knowledge is necessary, for we must understand how earlier events of espionage were textualized before we consider how we inscribe our own.

A BRIEF HISTORY OF ESPIONAGE: ENCODING AND DECODING DIPLOMACY

The earliest accounts of spying are mainly about messages, and the travails of the messengers. But how far back should one go? To Hermes, the cunning messenger of the Greek gods? Or to Moses who sent out envoys to spy on the Canaanites, and Joshua who used two spies in the battle of Jericho? For our purposes, it is better to travel on historical rather than mythological ground. This is done not to insinuate an arbitrary border between the two, or to refute all myth as fallacious history; it is quite simply and frankly to limit the inquiry to fewer and more manageable texts. However, since this is a genealogical "history of the present" (in the Foucauldian sense of an interrogation of the past which might yield alternative possibilities for the present), it is important to establish how a "tradition" of espionage was written and what this entails for the modern literature.

When it comes to espionage, the classical texts for the most part are anecdotal and pedagogical. Herodotus, for instance, has a good story about the visit of Hystioeus to Persia. Buying time with Darius by a policy of appeasement, he decides the moment is approaching for a revolt against the Persians and seeks to inform his ally Aristagoras in Greece. But how to get the message out? By servant, of course; informing the servant that he has a cure for the man's poor eyes, Hystioeus shaves the man's head and imprints the message on the skull. He keeps the servant isolated until his hair grows back, and then tells him that a complete cure will result when he goes to Aristagoras for another haircut. Other stories are equally entertaining: messengers are disguised as beggars, hidden in coffins, dressed up as sea-monsters. By the time of Emperor Justinian secret messengers and spies are considered indispensable to the state. The sixth-century Byzantine historian Procopius writes:

> The spies were organized in the following manner: A number of men used to be supported at the State's expense, whose business it was to visit hostile countries, especially the court of Persia, on pretence of business or some other excuse, and to observe accurately what was going on; and by this means, on their return, they were able to report to the emperors all the secret plans of their enemies, and the former, being warned in advance, took precautions and were never surprised.[8]

In the West, as the suzerain Holy Roman Empire fragmented and reformed into an incipient system of states, a premium was placed on information about "jealous" neighbors. More than ever, secure lines of communication were sought. It is not surprising that one of the seminal modern works on spying was a handbook of cryptography. Written by Abbot Johannes Trithemius, *Polygraphia libri sex* was published and dedicated to Emperor Maximilian I in 1518. This work gained some notoriety, not only for its meticulous study of ciphers but also for the claim that it was a key for calling up and enlisting the aid of angels and demons of earth, time, and the planets. If all this sounds anticipatory of the modern slang for spy — "spook" — we should also note that Trithemius was greatly inspired by the famous Elizabethan spy, John Dee, who took the number 007 as his personal cipher. Judged to be diabolical, the book was burned. It was, however, republished in Darmstadt in 1621 under the title of *Steganographia*, and noted as an influence on Duke August of Brunswick's *Cryptomenytices et Crypto-graphiae* (1624) and the Jesuit G. Schott's *Steganographia* (1665).[9]

Texts on cryptography were followed by the first manuals on diplo-macy. Born out of the intrigues of Renaissance Italy, where a pentarchy of power required constant vigilance and frequent interventions, the art of diplomacy was barely distinguishable from the practices of espionage. As Machiavelli surely learned from his diplomatic missions for Florence, *raison d'état* countenanced force and fraud as often as it did peaceful negotiation. In shorthand, "proto-diplomacy" was practically inseparable from "crypto-diplomacy." However, as diplomacy made its way up through transalpine Europe it converged with a civilizing process coming out of the great courts of western Christendom. Codes of conduct, *courtoisie* and subsequently *civilité*, began to change the face if not the nature of the power political game. Texts such as the fifteenth-century *Book of Courtesye* by the English envoy William Caxton and the sixteenth-century *De civilitate morum perilium* by Erasmus contained the discursive rules which were to demarcate proper from improper behavior. Coupled with the highly panoptic court apparatus of the rising national monarchs, these refined codes of conduct signified the apparent separation of open diplomacy and covert espionage. While the diplomats were obligated by social constraints and rituals of power, they were privileged with the symbolic investiture of sovereign power and attendant political immunities. The spy could carry on unrestrained, but only in the shadows of — and, if caught, without — sovereign protection. Diplomats were still considered akin to spies, but by the time Abraham de Wicquefort wrote his manual *L'Ambassadeur et ses Fonctions* (1681), the diplomat was distinguished as an "*honorable spy.*" A few decades later, François de Callières repeated the definition in his better known guide, *On the Manner of Negotiating with Princes* (1716): "The ambassador has sometimes been called an honourable spy because one of his principal occupations is to discover great secrets; and he fails in the discharge of his duty if he does not know how to lay out the necessary sums for this purpose."[10] But Callieres makes it quite clear that the diplomat must distance himself from practices common to espionage if the interests of the state are to be served honorably and effectively. "It is a capital error," he writes, "which prevails widely, that a clever negotiator must be a master of the art of deceit."[11] And there is no place for a latter-day James Bond in Callières's practico-ethical universe: "If he is too fond of the gaming-table, of the wine-glass, and of frivolous amusements, he is not to be entrusted with the discharge of high diplomatic duty, for he will be so unreliable that at moments when he seeks the satisfaction of his ill-regulated desires he will be prepared to sell the highest secrets of his master."[12]

Even a cursory review problematizes the modern claim that espionage is a burgeoning enterprise and threatens the sanctity of diplomacy. Throughout the Cold War there were daily bulletins of diabolical Soviet schemes to infiltrate more KGB agents into the West through their embassies, trade organizations, or the United Nations. Most recently, the issue was the transformation of the new US embassy in Moscow into a massive listening device. One would have to be naive to doubt the conviction of the hostage-taking Iranians that embassies – all great power embassies – *are* "nests of spies." Not to take advantage of diplomatic immunities in this fashion would be unreasonable – and novel. This is not to say, however, that the history of diplomacy and spying is seamless or endlessly repetitive. After the establishment of resident diplomacy in the sixteenth century, crests and troughs of hostility enable one or the other temporarily to gain pre-eminence in the discourse of international relations. This is evidenced throughout historical upheavals like the Reformation, Counter-Reformation, and the Thirty Years War; the French and Russian Revolutions; and the first and second Cold Wars. Equipped with a limited historical awareness of the relationship between diplomacy and espionage, we can turn to the last cycle – and its possible recycling in the era of New Ambiguity – as it has been traced in the literature of national interest and international intrigue.

THE POWER OF ALIENATION: LORDSHIP, (JAMES) BONDAGE, AND ESPIONAGE

From a variety of sources – a glossy US Defense Department booklet on Soviet military power, Soviet Marshal Ogarkov's *History Teaches Vigilance*, a CIA "psy-op" comic book for the Contras – we can discern a shared theme of official superpower discourse and the best-selling intrigue literature: the state-system is demarcated by alienation. This means that *Realpolitik* rules, permanent vigilance is necessary, and the preparation for war constant. Since the early 1950s, the logic of nuclear deterrence and the ideology of the Cold War dictated that spying should continue as limited war by covert means.

With a multiplicity of socio-political factors and the complexity of the states-system, the alienation of states can only be understood as an overdetermined phenomenon. It is historically apparent that as Cold War tensions heightened, official mono-causal explanations of what constituted alienation in international relations predominated. Now, however, signs are multiplying of a thaw that is even beginning to penetrate the permafrost of the intelligence communities. While US Secretary of State Baker and Soviet Foreign Minister Shevardnadze meet at a pre-summit in the shadows of the Grand Tetons to negotiate intrusive inspections of nuclear and chemical facilities, the former head of the CIA, William Colby, and other US intelligence and terrorist experts meet with their Soviet counterparts to open the way to cooperation on antiterrorism. We shall see how similar fluctuations in superpower relations have been represented in the imaginative literature, from the bipolar views of Fleming in the fifties to Moss and de Borchgrave in the early eighties, split by the multipolar ambiguities of le Carré and McCarry in the seventies.

But the problem at hand — the historical complexity and ideological obfuscation of systemic alienation — makes meta-theoretical assistance necessary. For understanding the macro-alienation of state power, Machiavelli has been and continues to be a dependable guide. However, I believe Hegel and Nietzsche can provide a complementary, if partial, explanation of the source and character of the micro-alienation involved in espionage. For the global game is not simply a matter of power differentials: it has as much to do with the affirmation and negation of self-consciousness through alienation and *ressentiment*. A graph could be drawn that might illustrate the upward curve of state alienation and self-recognition. At the beginning a great power judges and proves itself by its relationship to other, alienated great powers. Self-consciousness of state power is affirmed, sometimes through diplomacy, more often through war. At the apex of its power, if a state should be able to take full advantage of its geopolitical strengths to overcome what Burke called the "empire of circumstance" and become a hegemon, self-consciousness starts to dissolve. At this point a great power indulges in doctrines such as *laissez-faire*, "invisible hands," Social Darwinism, and Manifest Destiny — in other words, unselfconscious doctrines — to explain its ascendancy. On the way down it is a different narrative: relationships of superiority-inferiority are recognized, but imaginatively *reversed*, and self-consciousness is negated by a collective resentment of the superior powers by those powers who now find but cannot acknowledge themselves in an inferior global position. It is in this period of "decline-denial" that the literature of international intrigue flourishes. While the national security state chronologically and mythologically distances itself from its own decline by an atavistic nationalism, the response of the spy novel, and the reader's response to it, resembles the *carnavalesque* of Rabelais: seeking to allay the fear and anxiety of nuclear annihilation and national *in*security, millions of readers engage in the playful escapism of the popular spy novel. Popularity in this instance cannot be class-defined: John Kennedy made no secret of the pleasure he derived from Fleming's James Bond series and Ronald Reagan enthusiastically endorsed Clancy's best-seller, *The Hunt for the Red October*.

An excellent study of how popular English adventure stories have represented this decline has been done by Tony Bennett.[13] At the height of English power, this tradition is rife with imperialist righteousness, class superiority, outright racism, and sexism — at best, with a dash of irony but usually without a hint of critical self-consciousness. After two debilitating world wars and with the advent of the Cold War, the erosion of England's global position and self-confidence begins to appear in the popular literature of international intrigue. However, acknowledgement of England's decline in power and prestige *vis-à-vis* the superpowers does not entail acceptance. Rather, the ideological thrust of the literature is to reassert in myth what has been lost in reality. Since the netherworld of intelligence organizations is so difficult to judge in terms of effectiveness, influence, and other power-relational standards, Her Majesty's Secret Service becomes the perfect stage for Bond's reconfirmation of Britain's superiority. Despite America's predominance in NATO and France's powerful position in Europe, it is always Bond who is giving orders to Felix Leiter of the CIA and Mathis of the *Deuxième Bureau*. The only concessions to American and French superiority would appear to be limited to technical equipment and champagne, respectively.

A reenactment of a kind is going on in American spy literature. Differences that exist have largely to do, generally, with what might be called the "law of uneven decline of national character." Just as US industrial and political development was "telescoped" by lessons learnt or forced home by the British experience, it is quite probable that US decline relative to other powers will skip certain stages, both in industrial and in literary production. The perceived and actual decline of US power and prestige after Vietnam and Watergate — and to speculate, perhaps after the Iran–contra affair as well — has manifested itself in different ways in the literature. At the lower level of pulp entertainment (such as the Nick Carter series, which easily outsells Fleming and le Carré), the individual spy embodies the imperialist ease and technological edge of recent American history; gadgets, such as the miniaturized bomb that Nick Carter keeps hidden as a third testicle, supplement athletic prowess in this capacity. At the upper level of "sophisticated" spy literature like McCarry or, in his better moments, Ludlum, the historical tension between isolationism and Manifest Destiny, between Teddy Roosevelt's bloody-mindedness and Wilson's legalistic moralism, are worked out between and sometimes within characters.

With McCarry this historical tension is acted out within families, and can be construed as a painful but necessary dualism for arresting the decline of the American family and nationhood. In *The Better Angels*, set in the near, terror-filled future, Julian Hubbard is the idealistic advisor to the President, while his brother, Horace, is the pragmatic counter-intelligence chief of the Foreign Intelligence Service (the replacement for the CIA after it had been dismantled for subverting the Constitution one too many times). Together they make a tidy Wilsonian–Machiavellian package which can combat Islamic terrorism and media irresponsibility (a prescient theme) on their own dirty ground without doing too much harm to American values. Of some interest for the decline theory is the British contribution to the struggle, which consists of a loutish, cynical spy, always ready to sell-out the Americans, and a flock of nubile "Old Etonians" who escape mass unemployment at home by working as butlers in America.

In Ludlum's thriller, *The Aquitaine Progression*, the male protagonist Joel Converse is accused by his estranged wife of being too legalistic and idealistic to realize that Americans are ready to accept fascist rule if that is what it takes to forestall America's decline:

> We're frightened; we're sick of the problems, sick of the *violence*. We want someone strong to *stop* it – and I'm not sure it even matters who they are. And if the men you're talking about push things any further – believe me they know what they're doing. They can walk in and be crowned, no votes required ...[14]

The usually unspoken assumption of the novels discussed and other works is that without this power elite group of super-spies – or in the case of Joel Converse, "normal" people propelled into overman status – America would be defenseless against Soviets, terrorists, and the vicissitudes of power politics in general. Sometimes it is brought up and defended with vehemence, as in the film *Three Days of the Condor*, when the renegade agent played by Robert Redford confronts the deputy director of the CIA with his discovery of an intelligence agency within the CIA that is planning assassinations and destabilizing nations in the Middle East in order to secure oil supplies in the future. The deputy director's reply is simple and to the point: would it be better to wait until Mr Middle America goes to switch on his lights or drive his car and finds he has no power? The message is the same as Ludlum provides through Valerie Converse – that espionage or crimes committed to maintain order and a high standard of living are not only tolerated but expected by the American public.

While C. Wright Mills on the power elite might be a good place to start in order to understand the power of micro-alienation which is pervasive in the national security state and its fictionalized depiction, I believe Hegel's theory of alienation offers some deeper, philosophical insights – notwithstanding Francis Fukuyama's recent provocative (yet strangely despairing) reading of Hegel to posit an "end of history."[15] Justification, indeed the necessity for plunging into such gnomic depths for such seemingly superficial material can be found in the Preface to the *Phenomenology of Spirit* where Hegel says:

> Quite generally, the familiar, just because it is familiar, is not cognitively understood. The commonest way in which we deceive either ourselves or others about understanding is by assuming something as familiar, and accepting it on that account; with all its pros and cons, such knowing never gets anywhere, and it knows not why.[16]

And in the following paragraph, Hegel provides a clue about what it is in espionage that both alienates and fascinates us:

> Death, as we may call that unreality, is the most terrible thing, and to keep and hold fast what is dead demands the greatest force of all. Beauty, powerless and helpless, hates understanding, because the latter exacts from it what it cannot perform. But the life of mind is not one that shuns death, and keeps clear of destruction; it endures death and in death maintains its being.[17]

Simply put, we are repelled and attracted by the liberty, if not the license, of the spy to kill and quite likely be killed. How much daring is invested in each death, not the body count, is what makes a spy novel appealing. The willingness and manner of facing death is what simultaneously separates the spy from the reader and makes an imaginative identification with the spy all the more desirable. Herein lies the crucial intertext, how the play of a particular text is related to a broader world-text, or more specifically, how the link between the power struggle of states and its secret agents is romantically forged by their enhanced relationship with death in an anarchical society. Great powers, said Ranke, do not die in bed; nor do spies — or at least as they are popularly represented they do not.

This is, of course, a rather loose application of Hegel's fundamental formulation of self-consciousness through alienation, the relationship of Lordship and Bondage. Other, much more obvious forms of alienation are now going on in spy literature: without recourse to and reinforcement of the Nazis or the Soviets as the evil Other, authors of the genre would suffer greatly reduced royalties. But Hegel has in mind a universal alienation, in which "self-consciousness exists in and for itself when, and by the fact, that it so exists for another; that is it exists only in being acknowledged."[18] How one becomes dominant ("recognized") and the other subordinate ("recognizing") is determined by the individual's willingness to risk death in the struggle for recognition, thereby achieving autonomy from others. Or in the words of Jacques Derrida (who is reinscribing Bataille's Nietzschean reading of Hegel):

> The servant is the man who does not put his life at stake, the man who wants to conserve his life, wants to be conserved. By raising oneself above life, by looking at death directly, one accedes to lordship: to the for-itself, to freedom to recognition. Freedom must go through the putting at stake of life. The lord is the man who has had the strength to endure the anguish of death and to maintain the work of death.[19]

The joke, however, or the "irony of history" is on the lord who remains dependent upon the bondsman for self-consciousness, whereas the bondsman has an alternative means: "The bondsman realizes," says Hegel, "that it is precisely in his own work wherein he seemed to have only an alienated existence that he acquires a mind of his own."[20]

The power of the espionage intertext lies in a series of constitutive (and iniquitous) oppositions, between empire and colony, West and East, male and female; but it is the liberating play between Bond the man and the bondsman in all of us which attracts a readership in the first place. To identify with but not take the risk of spies, vicariously to share the moral and psychological knowledge that comes with the defiance of death, to take part in a process of self-recognition through otherness at the level of micro-alienation, and to have the last laugh too — all this is a deeper current, in both the dangerous relationship between spymaster and his subjects, and the pleasurable relationship between reader and the espionage novel.

THE POWER OF SURVEILLANCE:
WATCHING THE SPIES WATCH EACH
OTHER

Hence the major effect of the Panopticon; to induce in the inmate a state of conscious and permanent visibility that assure the automatic functioning of power. So as to arrange things that the surveillance is permanent in its effects, even if it is discontinuous in its action; that the perfection of power should tend to render its actual exercise unnecessary; that this architectural apparatus should be a machine for creating and sustaining a power relation independent of the person who exercises; in short, that the inmates should be caught up in a power situation of which they are themselves the bearers.[21]

Until quite recently, the greatest gap between popular spy fiction and quasi-secret fact could be found in the area of technical intelligence-gathering. One searches fruitlessly through the novels of Ludlum, McCarry, Higgins, Deighton, and others for references to ACOUSTINT (Acoustic Intelligence), ARGUS (Advanced Rhyolite satellite), ELINT (Electronics Intelligences), FSINT (Foreign Instrumentation Signals Intelligence), FOSIC (Fleet Ocean Surveillance Information Center), RDSS (Rapidly Deployable Surveillance System), RORSAT (Radar Ocean Surveillance Satellite), SOSUS (Sound Surveillance System), acronyms *ad nauseam*. Some technological advances in surveillance have made it into the literature, such as the ubiquitous "bugs" and the odd nightscope, but the most common surveillance continued to be GSINT − Gumshoe Intelligence − to such a degree that in practically every Ludlum book the spy's first stop is to the shoe repair shop to have noiseless crepe soles attached. Even Robert Moss's *Death Beam*, billed as a "prophetic" novel about Star Wars, has very little to say about American satellite and anti-satellite technology − except to impress on the reader that it dangerously lags behind the Russians.

An intriguing exception would be Tom Wise's *The Children's Game*, which starts off as yet another mole-hunt but is actually full of revelations about the infamous "Halloween Massacre," the dismissal of 250 top-level counter-intelligence agents in October 1977 by Admiral Stansfield Turner, then Director of Central Intelligence. Reflecting Turner's disdain for cloak and dagger and faith in hi-tech, the book offers a rare glimpse into the development of highly technological methods of espionage.

On the other hand, what might be at work is a kind of literary lag. Judging from recent entries into the best-sellers lists, it would seem that a new generation of espionage literature is emerging, in which the spy's individuality is shaped not by his alienation (Smiley) or ironic amusement (Bond) from advanced technologies, but by his resourcefulness at using technological advantages not available to the other side. In Tom Clancy's *Hunt for the Red October*, a Soviet submarine commander's lost ideological faith is replaced by the belief that the radically innovative tunnel propulsion system of his *Typhoon*-class submarine, coupled with his considerable courage and skill, will allow him to defect to the West with a very appealing present. Possibly inspired by the actual attempt in 1975 of a Soviet *Krivak*-class missile frigate to make a run for Sweden, *The Hunt for the Red October* compensates for its cardboard characters with a remarkable display of technological expertise. In fact, aside from the early exposition of the decisions leading to the defection, human agency takes a back seat as submarines and SOSUS take on the roles of protagonists and antagonists. We shall see how Clancy, expanding into a wider spectrum of weapons-systems and a truly global stage, splices and thinly fictionalizes several Third World War simulations to the same best-selling effect in *Red Storm Rising* and later works.

Faith in the technological fix, often at the level of naive awe, also infuses a recent novel by Charles Robertson, *Red Chameleon*.[22] Cut and pasted together with factive newspaper accounts of the Star Wars debate, the narrative appears at first to aim toward an *Entzauberung*, a kind of Weberian "disenchantment" of the modern spy realm. But something entirely different is in store for the reader. The debunking of the shibboleths of espionage — assassination, penetration, conversion — occurs in order that a new deity, Prometheus II, can ascend. At once surveyor, destroyer, and protector, Prometheus II is the super-fast brain of a new space shield. However, Prometheus suffers from a tragic flaw, not Greek but Judeo-Christian in character: a KGB mole has penetrated the Silicon Valley and suborned the guilt-ridden, pacifistic scientists who fear that Prometheus is an aggressive rather than — as billed — a defensive deity. One of the Judas-scientists has managed to whisper into the program of Prometheus a glitch which will shut the system down in the event of a Soviet first-strike. The ending is as predictable as a morality play: as both superpowers go to a full war alert, a combination of accident, technological ingenuity, and individual bravery allows the US to debug Prometheus, and the USSR, blinking rather than striking first, undergoes a domestic upheaval which leads to a new moderate leadership.

Finally, there is *Sight Unseen*, a first novel by Dan Gilroy. The hero is a reconnaissance satellite specialist who discovers something he was not meant to, a sunken submarine off the coast of California that has Soviet markings but later turns out to contain dead American sailors. Unlike the early Clancy novels, the author blends techno-speak with human intelligence.

Just from the plethora of acronyms to be found in the new spy novels – and in the intelligence community – it should be clear that a bureaucratization as well as the technologization of surveillance espionage is taking place. In fact, the majority of modern spy scandals has involved low- or middle-level bureaucrats from the CIA or military intelligence – and now even low-ranking Marines and Navy men – passing on secrets about hi-tech surveillance equipment. One of the first was William Kampiles, a CIA bureaucrat who walked out of the Langley headquarters with a manual for one of the United States' most advanced spy satellites, the KH-11, and sold it to the Soviets for the rather paltry sum of $3,000. One explanation for the low pay-off might be the emergence of a buyer's market: Christopher Boyce, a former employee of TRW, had been convicted in 1977 for selling satellite secrets to the Russians, among them a close description of a satellite resembling the KH-11. More contemporary – and more sinister in its significance for control of the press – was the arrest in October 1984 and recent conviction for espionage of naval intelligence analyst Samuel Morrison for passing to a British publication classified photographs taken by a KH-11 surveillance satellite. Three other naval intelligence technicians, John and Arthur Walker, and Jerry Whitworth, were accused in the spring of 1985 of providing the Soviet Union with important information on submarine detection. In November 1985 Ronald Pelton, a communication specialist, was charged with giving the Soviets top-secret information about his former employer, the National Security Agency, which uses photoreconnaissance satellites and long-range eavesdropping to provide more than 80 percent of America's intelligence. More recently, Army Warrant Officer James W. Hall was convicted in 1989 of selling information about electronic intelligence to Warsaw Pact powers.

What we also witness in these contemporary cases is the recommercialization of spying. It would appear that a significant number in the sub-hierarchies of the surveillance industry have been immunized against the ideological fever of the first Cold War (the fifth column impetus behind the espionage of that period) and the ideological chill of the second (the ineffective deterrent to current espionage), and – with the New Ambiguity in great power relations – are ready to deal. As the love and fear of Stalinism have receded chrono- and geopolitically to the peripheries of the great powers' spheres of decreasing influence, spying has once again become a "rationalized" business. The Walker brothers provided important information on missile submarine deployment and surveillance not out of any ideological affinity to the Russians or a moral cause (John Walker voted for Reagan and was supposedly a member of the John Birch Society) but for money and perhaps to add some excitement to their lives. Although the reasons behind the theft and selling of "crypto" information about spy satellites by Christopher Boyce and Daulton Lee are more ambiguous, with a vague anti-establishment sentiment at work, it does seem that money was the bottom line. And the rash of spy scandals in 1987, which might well challenge 1985 for "The Year of the Spy," had a pecuniary (and often hints of a sexual) motive behind it.

Many experts have noted how the shift from traditional to modern forms of surveillance has transformed espionage. I would also argue that this transformation is at least partially responsible for the popularity of the spy genre. The technologization, bureaucratization, commercialization, and — not least — the computerization of surveillance has profoundly affected everyday life. In banks, shopping malls, airports, the workplace, and even public toilets, we are being watched as we have never been watched before. In advanced electronic states, the identity and claims of employees can be confirmed or denied by polygraphs, voice stress analysis, and even retinal eye patterns. This is no longer solely the stuff of fiction and spying; it surrounds, intrudes in, and softly controls our lives. In the literature of international intrigue we find confirmation (and perhaps some comfort) that indeed permanent surveillance is needed, for those that appear most innocent, those that we trusted the most are, under intense scrutiny, usually exposed as the mole, the traitor, the spy.

Of the earlier generation of spy novels, one does stand out on its treatment of surveillance, and the style in which the subject is presented. The *Miernik Dossier*, by former CIA agent Charles McCarry, is remarkable for several reasons. As the title implies, it is a dossier, composed of 89 documents submitted to an intelligence agency committee. There is no attempt to "novelize" it into chapters or to cast it into a monological authorship. From the opening pages we learn that the dossier includes:

> (a) agent's reports, including those of intelligence services other than our own;
> (b) written communications exchanged by the principals outside security channels;
> (c) transcripts of telephone conversations and of other conversations that were recorded by listening devices;
> (d) certain other documents, e.g., surveillance reports, diary entries, biographical sketches;
> (e) footnotes supplied by our Headquarters.[23]

Recounting an event that "could have happened in 1959," the dossier begins with an internal communication from the "World Research Organization," a specialized agency of the United Nations which is heavily infiltrated by a large number of intelligence operatives from various countries. The first document relates to a request from the Polish government that their representative at the organization, Tadeusz Miernik, return to Poland. Suspicions are aroused on all sides when Miernik attempts to evade the recall for fear of execution or imprisonment. The puzzle for all the operative· is whether Miernik is genuinely preparing to defect, become a double-agent, or do something entirely unexpected – like lead a communist revolt in the Sudan. From the multiple documents describing single events comes an extremely ambiguous – politically, morally, even sexually – portrait of Miernik and espionage in general. The critical role of surveillance is implicit in the style of the novel, but the explicit theme is how surveillance reduces human values to a single exchange-value: information, as the alienated commodity of the intelligence market-place. In an aside to Paul Christopher, the US operative, Miernik links his objectification by surveillance to his eventual death:

> They know things about me even I don't know. They are artists, these secret police. They make a file. Into it they put their suspicions. To justify one suspicion they must find another, and another. The file gets fat. A thousand lies equal one great truth, just like a novel. When the dossier is fat enough, they send the man to the butcher.[24]

The piling up of documents does not lead to the truth: with the accumulation of evidence comes great doubts, more impenetrable enigmas, and – at least for the agent who is not merely an "operative" of *Realpolitik* – complex moral dilemmas. Meanwhile, bureaucracies compete to supply the greatest amount of information, in the hope of influencing the decision-makers and maintaining or expanding their status in the hierarchy of the national security state. But as with Miernik, rather than a qualitative leap in intelligence there is a quantification of the truth which adds up to the dominant bureaucracy's unconscious (for they do not risk death like the operative in the field) expectations. Hence, document #87, a report by Christopher's case officer:

> The officer notes, not in criticism but as a matter of observation, that Christopher is more than usually prone to believe that his understanding of this operation is more accurate than that of the

case officer, the station, or the country desk at Headquarters. The
death of Miernik made a vivid impression on him, and he gives it
undue weight in his estimate of the overall value of the operation.[25]

From different texts a backlash against the technologization of
espionage can be detected. In a review of recent non-fictional spy
literature, Andrew Cockburn derides the modern spy as a "techno-
bureaucrat" who uses sophisticated machines, complex bureaucracies,
and a grab-bag of acronyms to screw his respective citizenries.[26] Not
quite so articulate is Rambo's rampage against the heavily techno-
bureaucratized spook who is ready to abandon the MIAs and Rambo
for politically expedient reasons. Lost in all the racialism and glorification
of superior American firepower is the fact that Rambo's last (at least
until Rambo III hit the screen) violent gesture is to wipe out the banks
of computers, listening devices, and radar which through the power of
surveillance were meant to control and to entrap him. And preferring
an arched eyebrow and amused expression over a hyper-Luddite rage,
Bond deconstructs the technical fixes and gadgetry of "Q" with a
carnivalesque flair.

A literary lag also seems to be at work in other technological areas.
Only in a cursory way has the literature dealt with the growing contradiction between national sovereignty and its technological obsolescence.
When ICBMs and SLBMs can penetrate a nation's air-space in minutes,
information and commodities flow through nation-states, and satellites
can overfly and inspect every square inch of foreign territories, it becomes
more difficult to exalt national security as the maintenance of impermeable borders. Ludlum does explore the globalization of militarism
and its links to transnational corporations in *The Aquitaine Progression*;
his conclusion, however, seems to be that rugged, talented individuals
brought in from outside the security apparatus will save the democratic
nation-state from itself. In some ways, this is to recognize that there is
an international convergence going on in the realm of espionage: in the
future only outsiders will challenge a growing condominium of power
through total surveillance, and only a supra-state actor like BCCI will
add some excitement to what has become the increasingly boring occupation of watching the spies watch each other. Indeed, according to FBI
counter-intelligence agent George Mozingo, the real goal *is* boredom:

> [We try] to occupy as much of their time as we can and appear
> to satisfy the needs of their bureaucracy for information. They
> can use the remaining time on their tour to visit the restaurants
> and see the sights. If both sides are busy and nothing is being
> passed ... we are winning.[27]

THE POWER OF ACCELERATION: TIME, SPEED, AND TERROR

This is why the airport has become the new city ... People are no longer citizens, they're passengers in transit ... The new capital is no longer a spatial capital like New York, Paris or Moscow, a city located in a specific place, at the intersection of roads, but a city at the intersection of practicalities of time, in other words of speed.[28]

International airports have become the premier library and setting for espionage. Like the literature itself, there exists the ubiquity of threat, intrigue, and death, all out of proportion to statistical reality. Imagined menace is made immediate by extensive security systems: luggage is X-rayed, bodies are electronically scanned, bags are "sniffed" for explosives, and at various choke points, surveillance cameras swivel and zoom. Although no bells might be triggered by our presence, a psychological, almost reflexive response is common. A heightened sense of visibility acts as a constraint on our behavior, and simultaneously awakens our own powers of surveillance. Fellow passengers are compared to mental identikits of terrorists supplied by pages and hours of media and government hyperbole. Each of us contributes an extra pair of eyes to the panoptic grid. And yet, all this pales when compared to what lies ahead after Beirut and Malta, the Vienna and Rome airport massacres:

Airport '85 would be a blend of sophisticated gadgetry and tight procedures — what experts call "tactical technology." Ideally, it should be isolated and surrounded by a guarded barbed-wire fence. Inside the terminal passengers would funnel through a few controlled checkpoints under constant surveillance by video cameras, guards on overhead catwalks and armed security forces.[29]

Once in, you can't get out — as is true with most popular literature of the airport, the spy novel. "The inertia of the city of the future," says Virilio, "is not the inertia of immobility, but the dictatorship of movement ..."[30] The covers of spy thrillers speak of "breathless plots" and "fast-paced action," much of which seems to take place in and between airports. The characters from Ludlum's recent book, *The Aquitaine Progression*, seem to be in permanent competition for Frequent Flyer points. The novel opens with Joel Converse in Geneva ("the city of inconstancy") — but not for long: a Swissair flight to Athens and then a smaller Olympic plane to Mykonos, all in the same day, starts the race to prevent the global take-over by the fascistoid generals. Enlisted in the

cause by Joel, his estranged wife Valerie surpasses him in airport hopping:
from Amsterdam's Schilpol Airport to JFK, a brief slowdown for a cab
to LaGuardia, a cancelled flight to Boston after a night in an airport
hotel and then off to Las Vegas and Nellis Air Force Base where an
uncorrupted general is willing to help her. When the general dies after
his F-18 crashes, hope rests with his adjutant, Colonel Metcalf, who
decides to out-airport his pursuers. Fifty pages later the reader catches
up to him:

> — At nine o'clock yesterday morning I drove south out of Las
> Vegas to Halloran and from there I began a series of cross-country
> flights a computer couldn't follow, from airport to airport under
> more names than I can remember.
>
> — "You're a frightened man," said the captain.
>
> — "If you're not, I'm talking to the wrong person."[31]

What has them frightened and traveling at air-speed most of the time
are the words first uttered by the Israeli general, Chaim Abrams (any
resemblance to actual generals is, of course, disavowed by Ludlum), in a
careless slip:

> "You do not take into consideration the time element!" cried
> Abrams defiantly, for the first time raising his voice. "*Accumulation*,
> Converse! Rapid *acceleration*!"[32]

Several countries and corpses later, Converse realizes the significance of
the words:

> All they need is that initial wave of terror, a tidal wave of killing
> and confusion. "Key figures" were the words they used. "Accumu-
> lation" . . . "rapid acceleration" — chaos. Powerful men cut down
> as riots break out in half a dozen capitals and the generals march
> in with their commanders. That's the scenario, right from their
> own words.[33]

In Ludlum we confront two themes of modernity which recur in the
intrigue literature: speed and terrorism, often entwined. But what constitutes "modernity" in this context? In conventional war it can be
defined by new levels of surprise and destruction: the Stuka dive-
bombers over Madrid, the dawn attack at Pearl Harbor, the *Blitzkreig*

through Europe, the acceleration of death by new technologies of genocide; in other words, the advent of a new strategical dimension to
warfare which transgresses traditional constraints. In war — including
wars by other means like terrorism and espionage — how are we to
assess modernity, evaluate its effects? Speed is a neglected factor. It is
speed which made the First World War the last traditional and first
modern war: the slowness with which the Archduke Ferdinand's carriage
wheeled around in front of the startled anarcho-terrorist Princip; the
inertial and ponderous movement of the mobilizations, locked into the
time-schedules of trains; the unrefined lethality of gas, determined by
the slowness of wind currents and the quickness of an unprotected
breath. For the first time, the creeping, mechanical pill-box, the tank,
appears on the battlefield; and from the observation balloons to the first
fixed wing aerial attacks, war becomes three-dimensional.

To be sure, it is not *only* speed — or the lack of it — which defines the
First World War as pre- or proto-modern. But speed certainly shapes
our perceptions of the First World War: it was the last war in which
technology limited its representation to less than 24 images per second.
In other words, we now must take into account not only the impact of
speed on events but also on our senses. In modernity, with little *time* for
legitimating practices, violence blurs into terror, is fixed at the speed of
light by cathode ray tubes, and then disappears with barely an after-
image. Purveyed by cinematic and televisual media, the intertext of
espionage becomes a speeded-up shadow-play, for the most part dimly
back-lit by leaks in the national security state, occasionally in silhouette
when a spy is caught and exposed (one thinks of Alec Leamas in *The
Spy Who Came in from the Cold*, frozen by searchlights and ready to
die at the Berlin Wall), and always already to be obliterated by the
incandescent glare of the ultimate expression of speed and violence,
instantaneous nuclear annihilation.[34]

Of course, these are fleeting impressions of a transition which cannot
be *proven* by a review of espionage literature. The transformation can,
however, be instructively limned by two works, one an exquisite study
of espionage at the turn of the century — "before the lights went out all
through Europe" — and the other a trashy exemplar of the modern
high-velocity spy novel.

Before Thomas Pynchon entered the pantheon of high literature,
he wrote "Under the Rose" a short story which appeared in an
"O. Henry" collection: hence, a fairly credible claim of popularity can
be made for a writer whose other major works, *V* and *Gravity's Rainbow*,
are more frequently cited than read. Set before the Fashoda crisis which
presaged the coming of the First World War, the story pits the improb-

ably named English spy, Porpentine, against his German counterpart, Moldweorp, in a surrealistically slow scramble for power and prestige across North Africa. With fatalistic dedication, Porpentine tries to slow the race to apocalypse with the only brakes that the spy possesses — the rules of the game. But just as the master eventually recognizes that he has become the recognized in his relationship with the slave, Porpentine realizes that even a "veteran spy" such as himself is losing lordship over events and time, now "that history was being made no longer through the *virtu* of single princes but rather by man in the mass":

> Or possibly because now, with a century rushing headlong to its end and with it a tradition in espionage where the playing-fields of Eton had conditioned (one might say) pre-military conduct as well, the label [of veteran spy] was a way of fixing identity in this special *haut monde* before death — individual or collective — stung it to stillness forever.[35]

In the end, after a moonlit horse-carriage chase to the Sphinx, Porpentine faces his antagonists: younger, quicker, rule-less spies who carry modern revolvers against Porpentine's single-shot. Porpentine, who "felt as always an alien," knew that the "apocalypse would surely begin at Fashoda if for no other reason that he felt his own so at hand."[36] The lumbering and defensive Porpentine ("porcupine") loses out to the blindly aggressive Moldweorp ("mole"), but he dies willfully, preferring the inertia of death to the acceleration of mass violence.

Jack Higgins's *Exocet*, a pulp portrayal of speed as violence, is at the other end of the transition; however, with the seemingly eternal recurrence of apocalyptic threat, one might interpret the literature as having gone full circle. The action — and reading — rate is very high:

> They swept in over the mountains of West Falkland as dawn came up, as close to the ground as they dared because of the missiles, and turned into Death Valley barely sixty feet above the water. It happened incredibly fast as always. First the mountains, then Falkland Sound with the ships of the Task Force and more in San Carlos Water. Montera was aware of the Skyhawk on his right sinking desperately, a Rapier missile on his tail. There was an explosion, a ball of fire.[37]

A shifty arms dealer works with terrorists and the Russians to supply the much-needed Exocets (the "fire-and-forget" air-to-surface missile which nearly turned the tide in the Falklands/Malvinas war) to the

Argentinians but is thwarted in the end by British counter-terrorists. The rest of the novel is perpetual movement without any progress of plot. Although a novel about intelligence and counter-intelligence, intelligence *per se*, even at the lower level of mental agility, is rarely displayed as a virtue. Most of the thinking seems to be done by the weapons-systems. *Exocet* stands out as a precursor of the second-generation spy novels, infused with a kind of techno-Ramboism where the machines of destruction supply most of the brains and brawn, and the protagonists the reflexes and willpower. We shall see in the final chapter how the genre provided in the Gulf War the highest intertext of late modern warfare: *cyberwar*.

THE FUTURE OF THE INTELLIGENCE INTERTEXT

What lies ahead for intelligence? In keeping with my attempt to apply *critical* intelligence to the topic, my conclusions can only be speculative and skeptical: a *precis* of the gravest dangers, not a list of policy suggestions, is the best I can offer, and the most that the evidence can support as history continues to accelerate.

With the Second Cold War now a backdrop for MTV videos (the falling Wall and toppling Lenins playing as loop videos), and a hot regional war in the Persian Gulf proving slow to cool, there is little doubt that US intelligence will begin to change its focus – and little hope that there will be a decline in its (roughly) $30 billion budget.[38] Resources will be reallocated, industrial espionage will heat up, satellite orbits shifted, and new regional, multiple intertexts of intrigue will emerge to replace global, bipolar ones. However, still smarting from the underestimation of social and economic problems in the Soviet Union and overestimation of the staying power of Communist regimes in Eastern Europe, the CIA is working hard to convert an intelligence failure into a bigger budget.[39] The two messages most often delivered by the Director of Central Intelligence William Webster before he retired were that arms control agreements under negotiation will require "staggering" amounts of surveillance (that is, money), and that more and better intelligence (that is, money) will be needed in a world that "may be more dangerous because it has become less predictable."[40] Senator Boren, the chairman of the Senate Intelligence Committee, also weighed in on the side of budgetary increases as the Cold War winds down, stating in one interview that "It's an irony, but it's true: as Star Wars winds down, spy wars are escalating."[41] And during the Robert Gates hearings, various new priorities for the CIA were mooted. Alongside the traditional roles of arms control verification and surveillance of nuclear weapons proliferation were placed new efforts to stem narcotics trade and terrorism, to locate new energy sources, and to improve economic analysis and to monitor pollution and global warming (the CIA goes Green?).

Meanwhile in the once-East, many intelligence officers find themselves out of work, and worse, the butt of jokes. The one I heard most frequently during a 1990 tour of Central Europe was that only names needed to be given to taxi drivers, because the drivers were all former Stasi who already knew their passengers' addresses — and those of their friends as well. In the same region old intelligence archives are being excavated and appropriated for new political purposes. The "true" confessions of former KGB officers compete for space in US supermarket tabloids, the new Bulgarian intelligence officers promise to share clues of the assassination attempt on the Pope with US intelligence, and McCarthyism makes an appearance in Prague when Parliament members — including some like Jan Kavan with impeccable dissident credentials — face accusers waving papers from old intelligence files. And now former Soviet spies are discovering the merit and profit of intertextuality: two defectors, Stanislav Levchenko and Alexandra Costa, have written their own spy novel for Random House. According to Ms Costa, a factual autobiography was eschewed because there are "events that strain credibility . . . it is much easier to write about them in a novelistic way."[42] This is surely only the beginning: at the end of *the* history comes a thousand, newly reinscribed ones.[43]

To return to the claim of the introduction, the most promising way to assess the status and future of intelligence is to focus on its shift from an identity constituted by the Soviet Other to forms of estrangement more fragmented and less monotonic in nature. Originary moments of such a shift are impossible to identify, except by an historical sleight of hindsight. Reagan and Gorbachev exchanging toasts and jokes over dinner might well have been the first date of a post-Cold-War relationship, but it will take a new joint surveillance regime to consummate it. Twenty-five years after Eisenhower proposed in Geneva an "Open Skies" policy, the greatest hopes and greatest obstacles for a new intelligence identity remain in the promise of new verification and surveillance technologies and the threat that it would pose to traditional sovereign identities. We can contrast the hopes raised by the experimental flight of a Canadian C-130 transport plane flying over Hungarian and Soviet military bases in February 1990, and the recent resolution of long-standing differences over missile factory inspections and the encryption of missile test flights that had stymied a Start agreement on limiting long-range nuclear weapons.

Should one promote, can one even imagine, a global surveillance system? The collateral damage to liberties of all kinds is obvious. Think back to the absurdist drama of the new American chancery in Moscow. Designed to be a state-of-the-art embassy, and built at a cost of $23 million, the building turned out to be one big listening device; the Soviet builders had managed to incorporate surveillance systems into the steel girders and concrete walls. The Soviets were stupid enough to think that the surveillance equipment would go undetected; the Americans arrogant enough to think that they could detect inferior Soviet technology at the outset. Both were wrong. After several expert studies, the State Department concluded "that razing the building and constructing a new one in its place would cost less, be less physically dangerous, and take less time than neutralizing the listening systems in the uncompleted building."[44] The best-case scenario is that the end of the Cold War will return a level of diplomatic civility that might balance the desire for total transparency. However, given the value and quest for total information in late modernity, the citizen, like the diplomat, must maintain a level of counter-vigilance commensurate with the power of the global cyber-paranoids and voyeurs of the future.

But an intertextual analysis helps us to plot a different reformation, or just as likely, *deformation* of the intelligence identity. An earlier fictive and factive result of the diminution of the Soviet Threat was the political recombinant of Russians and international terrorists into a new super-alien Other. This development was first evidenced in the spy literature during a thaw in the First Cold War, when the Soviet SMERSH was replaced by SPECTRE (Special Executive for Counterintelligence, Terrorism, Revenge, and Extortion). By the high-point of detente, Carlos-clones were a ruble a dozen, and subject to literary and cinematic exaggeration. Claire Sterling and other Cassandras of the "Bulgarian Connection" did their journalistic best to revivify this triple threat of the communist–terrorist–spy. Much has been made of the latest development of how the Bulgarians themselves offered "open archives" to the US. Enjoying less media attention was the May 1989 Moscow meeting of Secretary of State Baker with Gorbachev to discuss among other pressing issues the sharing of intelligence data on international terrorism; five years earlier the two would not have been able to come up with a common definition of "freedom fighter" and "terrorist."[45]

As the Soviet threat declined, the threat of international terrorism increased as a matter of national and literary interest.[46] Capable of inhuman crimes and daily defiance of death, armed with low visibility and high mobility, and prepared to launch high-speed surprise attacks, international terrorism and its official counterpart, low-intensity conflict, became the popular intertexts of the eighties. We shall see in the chapters ahead how the intertext expanded to include renegade Third World countries and "state-sponsored terrorism." But the spy would live on, perhaps deeper in the shadows, higher in space, faster in time, but still providing intrigue if not intelligence for the reader and the state.

Notes

1   T. Eagleton, *Against the Grain* (London: Verso, 1986), p. 24.
2   See chapter 2, pp. 19–26.
3   See A. Dulles, *The Craft of Intelligence* (New York: Harper and Row, 1963); W. Colby, *Honorable Men: My Life in the C.I.A.* (New York: Simon and Schuster, 1978); K. Roosevelt, *Countercoup: The Struggle for the Control of Iran* (New York: McGraw-Hill, 1979); M. Copeland, *The Real Spy World* (London: Sphere, 1978); V. Walters, *Silent Missions*, (New York: Doubleday, 1978). To illustrate the difficulty of obtaining "factual" stories, the first CIA document to be declassified and transferred to the National Archives was a 1,000 page official history of the CIA: it was completed in 1953 and not released until 1989. See "CIA's History Sheds Light On Fighting Over Authority," *New York Times* (27 November 1989); and Peter Karlow, letter to the *New York Times* (6 December 1989).
4   P. Knightley, *The Second Oldest Profession: Spies and Spying in the Twentieth Century* (New York: Penguin, 1986). Other useful accounts of the mixing of spy fact and fiction can be found in John Atkins, "The Real and the Fictional," *The British Spy Novel: Styles in Treachery* (London: John Calder, 1984), pp. 119–30; and *Spy fiction, Spy films and Red Intelligence*, edited by Wesley Wark (London:)
5   *New York Times*, 29 March 1987. Perhaps the two best documented instances of spy fiction influencing fact are the cases of two British novelists, William Le Queux and Hector Bywater. Le Queux wrote sensationalist spy novels at the beginning of the twentieth century; these so convinced the English that there were German spies in every flower garden that the British parliament established a secret service in 1909.
    Bywater's case is more interesting. There is a theory that has been bruited since the early 1980s, freshly documented in William Honan's *Visions of Infamy*, that the British novelist and part-time spy may have supplied the inspiration and strategic plans for the Japanese attack on Pearl Harbor in 1941. In 1925 Hector Bywater wrote what could best be described as a war fantasy, *The Great Pacific War*, outlining a surprise attack by Japanese carrier forces on US territories. Honan compiles a persuasive amount of evidence to argue that Isoroku Yamamoto, the archi-

tect of the Pearl Harbor attack, read the book while a naval attaché in Washington, and reported it to his superiors in Tokyo. (See William Honan, *Visions of Infamy: The Untold Story of How Journalist Hector L. Bywater Devised the Plans that Led to Pearl Harbor* (New York: St Martin's Press, 1991).

It is also interesting to note that former KGB director Vladimir Kryuchkov summoned the works of the British spy — and "novelist" — Sidney O'Reilly from the KGB library when he became head of KGB foreign intelligence (according to Christopher Andrew, University of Toronto conference on Espionage, 7–9 November 1991).

  6 *American Legion Magazine*, June 1986, p. 16. The magnitude of the threat was reiterated by Robert Gates (then Deputy National Security Advisor to President Bush) in an interview published in the *US Naval Institute Proceedings*: "Over the past three years [1985–1988], we have discovered more penetrations of the US defense and intelligence communities than at any time in our history." See N. Polmar and T. Allen, "The Decade of the Spy," *US Naval Institute Proceedings* (May 1989), pp. 104–8.

  7 Two good examples of this genre would be the *Central Intelligence Factbook* (April 1985), and the multi-volume series edited by Roy Godson, *Intelligence Requirements for the 1980s*.

  8 J. Thompson and S. Padover, *Secret Diplomacy: Espionage and Cryptography 1500–1815* (New York: Frederick Ungar, 1963), p. 15.

  9 Ibid.

 10 F. de Callières, *On the Manner of Negotiating with Princes* (Washington DC: University Press, 1963), p. 27.

 11 Ibid., p. 31.

 12 Ibid., p. 34.

 13 T. Bennett, "James Bond as popular hero," in *Politics, Ideology, and Popular Culture* (Milton Keynes: Open University Press, 1982).

 14 R. Ludlum, *The Aquitaine Progression* (New York: Bantam, 1983), p. 504.

 15 See Francis Fukuyama, "The End of History," *The National Interest* (Summer 1989), pp. 3–35.

 16 G. Hegel, *The Phenomenology of Spirit* (Oxford: Oxford University Press, 1979), p. 18.

 17 Ibid., p. 19.

 18 Ibid., p. 111.

 19 J. Derrida, "From Restricted to General Economy: A Hegelianism without Reserve," *Writings and Difference* (London: Routledge, 1978), p. 254.

 20 Hegel, Ibid.

 21 M. Foucault, *Discipline and Punish* (New York: Vintage, 1979), p. 201.

 22 C. Robertson, *The Red Chameleon* (New York: Bantam Books, 1985).

 23 C. McCarry, *The Miernik Dossier* (New York: Signet, 1973), p. 9.

 24 Ibid., p. 67.

 25 Ibid., p. 20.

 26 *Harper's Magazine*, April 1985.

 27 *New York Times*, 6 January 1985.

 28 P. Virilio, *Pure War* (Semiotext(e), 1983).

 29 *Newsweek*, July 8, 1985.

 30 Virilio, *Pure War*, p. 35.

 31 Ludlum, *Aquitaine*, p. 607.

32 Ibid., p. 288.

33 Ibid., p. 616.

34 For three provocative accounts of the interdependent relationship between the war and media, see P. Virilio, *Guerre et Cinéma 1: Logistique de la perception* (Paris: Editions de l'Etoile, 1984); P. Virilio, *L'inertie polaire* (Paris: Christian Bourgeois Editeur, 1990); and Friedrich Kittler, "Media Wars: Trenches, Lightning, Stars," *1—800*, 1 (Fall, 1989), pp. 5—9.

35 T. Pynchon, "Under the Rose," in *Slow Learner* (New York: Bantam, 1985), p. 96 and p. 90.

36 Ibid., p. 120.

37 J. Higgins, *Exocet* (New York: Signet, 1983), p. 278.

38 Since the budget is secret, all such figures are very rough estimates. Contrary to the popular view, the CIA receives just over a tenth of the overall intelligence budget (in 1990, around $3—$3.5 billion annually), while the technological ears and eyes of the community, the National Security Agency and the National Reconnaissance Office, receive the bulk of the amount (about $5 billion and $8 billion, respectively). See Michael Wines, "Washington is Tiring of Supporting All Those Spies," *New York Times* (4 November 1990), p. E—5.

39 This is not an idle concern: after the failure of the intelligence agencies to predict the 1973 Yom Kippur war, the Deputy Secretary of Defense ordered budget cuts of 25 percent. The CIA was spared, but not those agencies under Pentagon control, including the National Security Agency. See Stephen Engelberg, "Pressure Grows for Cuts in Intelligence Spending," *New York Times* (28 November 1989); and "US Intelligence in the Gulf and into the 1990s," *Security Intelligence Report* (25 February 1991), p. 2.

40 See William J. Broad, "US Adds Spy Satellites Despite Easing Tensions," *New York Times* (3 December 1989); and Michael Wines, "It's Still Business as Usual for Spies, Even as the Eastern Bloc Rises Up," *New York Times* (31 December 1989), p. 15. During his tenure William Webster also used the theme of Soviet industrial espionage to justify the continuation of a high budget for US intelligence agencies. But with the common enemy gone, we should also expect more spying among friends, as was the recent case of French intelligence trying from 1987 to 1989 to recruit agents in IBM, Texas Instruments, and other computer companies. See Michael Wines, "French Said to Spy on US Computer Companies," *New York Times* 18 November 1990), p. 4.

41 See Stephen Engelberg, "Senator Faults US Effort to Deter Espionage," *New York Times* (30 July 1989).

42 See Barbara Gamarekian, "Two Defectors from Soviet Marry and Turn to Writing about Spies," *New York Times* (15 July 1988).

43 Some are less tendentious than others: see, for instance, Christopher Andrew and Oleg Gordievsky, *KGB: The Inside Story* (New York: Harper Collins, 1990).

44 See Elaine Sciolino, "The Bugged Embassy Case: What Went Wrong," *New York Times* (15 November 1989), p. A12.

45 See Thomas Friedman, "US May Tell Soviets: Let's Share Some Secrets," *New York Times* (21 April 1989), p. 5.

46 See Sam Meddis, "CIA's future may be found in its Past," *USA Today* (25 April 1991), p. 1; and chapters 4 and 5 below.

TERROR

4

READING TERRORISM AND THE NATIONAL SECURITY CULTURE

—

Security is Mortals cheefest Enemie.
William Shakespeare, _Macbeth_

The first item on the agenda of the first meeting of the National Security Council under President Reagan was international terrorism. On the very next day, 27 January 1981, President Reagan issued a public warning: "Let terrorists be aware that when the rules of international behavior are violated, our policy will be one of swift and effective retribution." To punctuate the point, Secretary of State Alexander Haig announced the following day at his first press conference that "international terrorism will take the place of human rights" as the number one priority of the Reagan administration. A decade later George Bush, who as Vice President headed the Task Force on Combating Terrorism which formulated US policy, proclaimed in his Inaugural Address that terrorism and drugs would be the two primary targets of his administration. And Robert Gates, in his opening statement before the Senate Intelligence Committee, listed "international drug cartels" and "regional conflict and its terrorist stepchildren" as two of the five most important issues for the future of US intelligence.[1]

The relationship of national security and terrorism is often considered as a purely modern phenomenon, the product of a new alchemy of fanatical beliefs, deadly weapons, easy targets, and media manipulation, that is antithetical to traditional diplomacy. But a longer view disturbs this conventional one: security is born out of a primal terror and estrangement which diplomacy has historically sought – and often failed – to mediate.[2] This chapter and the next challenge many of the conventional beliefs about terrorism by undertaking first, a genealogy of security and terror; second, a deconstructive reading of the contemporary national security culture; and third, a constructive theory of the current knowledge and practices of terrorism. Together they challenge some of the conventional beliefs about national security and terrorism by taking what I believe to be a necessary first step: a genealogy which disturbs the onto-theology of security; that is, the a priori argument that proves the existence and necessity of only one form of security because there happens to be a widespread, metaphysical belief in it. This genealogy is admittedly thin on analysis and thick on description. But its intention is to provoke a new way of thinking about security issues, and to suggest that there is more than an historical basis for the acceptance of a security that is less coherent and dogmatic, and more open to the paradoxical and contingent nature of international politics. By showing how the historical meanings of security exceed our current beliefs, I hope to open up some alternative possibilities and intelligibilities for the study of national security and the politics of antidiplomacy.

A GENEALOGY OF SECURITY AND TERROR

In its earliest use, "security" traveled down a double track, and then, somewhere at the turn of the nineteenth century, one track went underground. Conventionally understood, security refers to a condition of being protected, free from danger, safety. This meaning applied in the great power diplomacy of the modern states-system. In 1704, the *Act of Security* was passed by the Scottish Parliament, which forbade the ascension of Queen Anne's successor to the throne of Scotland unless the independence of the Scottish kingdom was "secured."[3] In 1781 Edward Gibbon conveyed a specifically geopolitical meaning when he wrote in *The History of the Decline and Fall of the Roman Empire* that "the emperor and his court enjoyed ... the security of the marshes and fortifications of Ravenna."[4] However, coeval with the evolution of security as a preferred condition of safety was a different connotation, of security as a condition of false or misplaced confidence in one's position. In *Macbeth* Shakespeare wrote that "Security is Mortals cheefest Enemie."[5] In a 1774 letter Edmund Burke impugned "The supineness, neglect, and blind security of my friend, in that, and every thing that concerns him."[6] And as late as 1858 the *Saturday Review* reported that "Every government knew exactly when there was reason for alarm, and when there was excuse for security."[7]

Clearly the unproblematical essence that is often attached to the term today does not stand up to even a cursory investigation. From its origins "security" has had contested meanings, indeed, even contradictory ones. Certainly the tension of definition is inherent in the elusiveness of the phenomenon it seeks to describe, as well as in the efforts of various users to fix and attach meanings for their own ends. Yet there is something else operating at the discursive level: I believe there is a talismanic sign to security that seeks to provide what the property of security cannot. The clue is in the numerous citations from sermons found in the *Oxford English Dictionary*. They all use security to convey the second sense; that is, a careless, hubristic, even damnable overconfidence. The excerpts range in dates from the sixteenth to the nineteenth century: "They ... were drowned in sinful security" (1575); "This is a Reflection which ... should strike Terror and Amazement into the securest Sinner" (1729); "It is an imaginary immortality which encloses him in sevenfold security, even while he stands upon its very last edge" (1876).[8]

Mediating between these two senses of security is a third. In the face of a danger, a debt, or an obligation of some kind, one seeks a security, in the form of a pledge, a bond, a surety. From the 1828 *Webster*: "Violent and dangerous men are obliged to give security for their good behavior, or for keeping the peace."[9] In Markby's *Elementary Law* (1874), the word is given a precise financial meaning: "I shall also use the word security to express any transaction between the debtor and creditor by which the performance of such a service (one capable of being represented in money) is secured."[10] A security could also be "represented" in person. Shakespeare again, from *Henry IV*: "He said, sir, you should procure him better Assurance, the Bardole: he would not take his Bond and yours, he lik'd not the Security."[11]

This is not, as President Bush would say, a mere matter of semantics. It is rather to relink the etymology of security with its ontology, in order to dismantle the a priori argument based on *doxa*, that proves the existence (and necessity) of one form of security over against a plurality of others based on *paradoxa*. The paradox is this: in security we find insecurity. Originating in the contingency of life and the certainty of mortality, the history of security reads as a denial, a resentment, and finally a transcendence of this paradox. In brief, the history is one of individuals seeking an impossible security from the most radical "other" of life, the terror of death, which, once generalized and nationalized, triggers a futile cycle of collective identities seeking security from alien others — who are seeking similarly impossible guarantees. It is a story of differences taking on the otherness of death, and identities calcifying into a fearful sameness.

Nietzsche's interpretation of the origins of religion can shed some light on the paradoxical origin and transvaluation of security. In *The Genealogy of Morals*, Nietzsche sees religion arising from a sense of fear and indebtedness to one's ancestors:

> The conviction reigns that it is only through the sacrifices and accomplishments of the ancestors that the tribe *exists* − and that one has to *pay them back* with sacrifices and accomplishments: one thus recognizes a *debt* that constantly grows greater, since these forebears never cease, in their continued existence as powerful spirits, to accord the tribe new advantages and new strength.[12]

Sacrifices, honors, obedience are given but it is never enough, for "the ancestors of the *most powerful* tribes are bound eventually to grow to monstrous dimensions through the imagination of growing fear and to recede into the darkness of the divinely uncanny and unimaginable: in the end the ancestor must necessarily be transfigured into a *god*."[13]

Is this not what we have experienced, yet failed to give semantical and theoretical significance to, in the modern reincarnation of "security"? For instance did not the debt of US citizens to the Founding Fathers grow "to monstrous dimensions" with the "sacrifices" − many noble, some not − made in two World Wars? Did not the collective identity, once isolationist, neutralist, and patriotic, become transfigured into a new god, that was born and fearful of a nuclear, internationalist, interventionist power? The evidence is in the reconceptualization: as distance, oceans, and borders became less of a protective barrier to alien identities, and a new international economy required penetration into other worlds, *national interest* became too weak a semantic guide. We found a stronger one in *national security*, as embodied and institutionalized by the National Security Act of 1947.

The story that follows is an excessive reading of an extreme interpretation of the law − "to perform such other functions and duties related to intelligence activities affecting the national security as the National Security Council may from time to time direct" − as well as the spirit of the national security state.[14] In its excess we might find both the necessity and the means to reconsider the concept of security.

ARMS, HOSTAGES, AND THE IMPORTANCE OF SHREDDING IN EARNEST

The social intervention of a text (not necessarily achieved at the time the text appears) is measured not by the popularity of its

audience or by the fidelity of the socioeconomic reflection it contains
or projects to a few eager sociologists, but rather by the violence
that enables it to *exceed* the laws that a society, an ideology, a
philosophy establish for themselves in order to agree among themselves in a fine surge of historical intelligibility. This excess is
called: writing.

> Roland Barthes, *Sade/Fourier/Loyola*

Deciphering the contemporary culture of the state requires excessive
writing, to offset academic silences and to reclaim the subject from the
official scribes, but also to overcome prevailing problems of estrangement.
How do we define what defines us, what separates Us from Them, what
draws symbolic boundaries between order and disorder, what distinguishes meaning from meaninglessness in international relations?
There is the temptation to ape traditional diplomatic history; that is, to
sift through the archival accretions which define and constitute a national
culture. But if the reader/writer travels to the borders of the national
security culture, instead of definitions they find fences of arcane classifi-
cations surrounding the most significant archives. And when they finally
gain entry through freedom of information actions or by public dis-
closures, worse news awaits them:

"When did you shred them, sir?"

"My answer, Mr Nields, is that I started shredding documents
in earnest, after a discussion with Director Casey in early
October ... Director Casey and I had a lengthy discussion about
the fact that this whole thing was coming unraveled and that
things ought to be cleaned up. And I started cleaning things up."[15]

Thus on the first day of his testimony at the Iran—Contra hearings,
Lieutenant Colonel Oliver North informed the American people of the
importance of shredding in earnest, of sanitizing the messy margins of
the national security culture. Perched on the edge of this culture, Oliver
North offers a special perspective on its most significant and deconstructive activity: terrorism. He first dogged President Reagan's heels
when he carried the "football" containing the codes for launching
nuclear terror; in 1981 he was brought into the National Security
Council "to handle easels and carry the charts" (according to Richard
Allen, the first of President Reagan's five national-security advisers);
and he eventually worked his way up to the post of Assistant Deputy
Director for Political—Military Affairs at the NSC, from which he
directed US counter-terrorism policy while secretly managing the aid

program for the Contras and the negotiation with Iran of arms for hostages.

In this shadowy corner of the state, North is our compass point, a guide to traverse the terrorist-etched boundaries of the national security culture. This is not to say that the "nature" of this "culture" would be revealed if the "truth" about North's story could be pasted, or pastiched, together again; nor is it to claim that he represents or is the incarnation of the national security culture. These were the faulty presuppositions of many members of the media and of the House and Senate Select Committee investigating the exploits of North; they also acted as impediments to any politically meaningful revelations, because the true North — magnified and globally projected by television — proved *to be* the magnetic North. In this sense, North was the living simulacrum of a national security culture: more real than the reality the Committee sought to uncover, more seductive than anything the polymorphous, acephalous Committee could reconstruct, North's truth was like the CIA outside the CIA that he and William Casey sought to create — an "off-the-shelf, self-sustaining, stand-alone entity" — the perfect agent for constructing and combating a hyperreal terrorism.[16]

This means that a cultural reading of terrorism requires much more than an inquiry into the state's archival accretions: we must seek out its most sensitive *secretions*. The way in which they leak out and then reappear as public narratives, in the news, fiction, and film, provides us with a map of a particular *cultural economy*, by which I mean a flow and exchange of valorized symbols. But once obtained, how might we read the archive of the "high" (political) culture of the national security state — that is, the official currency of discursive practices which circulates, accumulates, *piles up* around the great power, with the techno-bureaucrats of the state on one side, the deconstructive forces of terrorism on the other, and in the moat between, Oliver North and his crypto-military? The penumbra of the Iran—Contra case certainly provides some immediate material, but the West's "first" hostage crisis in Iran illuminated, and in the process revealed chinks in, the modern national security culture. Some artful investigative techniques were generated by, among others, the Iranian Revolutionary Guard who used ancient weaving techniques to create politically sensitive tapestries from the shredded documents of the US embassy in Teheran, and then published them as a 54-volume set of the Great Satan's hitherto unknown sayings.[17] Now, however, the most relevant and revealing archives of the NSC are pulverized or cross-cut (rather than linguini-shredded) and burnt. The only recourse for a critical inquiry, it seems, would be an epiphenomenology of terrorism, a study of the smoke rising from the "burn bags" of the Executive branch.

But let us pretend for a dialogical moment that Marx was on epistemologically solid ground when he wrote in the Preface to the *Critique of Political Economy* that "mankind always sets itself only such tasks as it can solve, since it will always be found that the task itself arises only when the material conditions for its solution already exist or are at least in the process of formation." Lt Colonel North shredded in earnest and retyped letters with a doctored IBM golfball; Ms Fawn Hall surreptitiously removed documents and erased incriminating floppy disks with a vengeance; and Director of Central Intelligence William Casey conveniently died with his secrets. Yet an electronic archive was preserved and discovered, for the magnetic tracks of the now infamous PROF notes lived on in the memory of the computers. As all hackers know, you must *overwrite* a file to obliterate it.

The problem confronting all inscriptive readers and semio-critical writers of this story is how are we, armed with this resurrected data, excessively to reinscribe this story of arms, hostages, and terrorism without overwriting the disorder which gave rise to it?[18] This is not just a figurative concern, for the media transformation of violence into a news event has magnified and distorted the terrorist threat, further reducing the possibility of any meta-critical *and* ethico-political response to it. From a safe distance the commentator might condemn terrorism, but the camera zooms in to fascinate us with the fear and spectacle of death which usually attend acts of terrorism.[19] Further complicating the problem of media reinscription is the proliferation of terrorist "experts" who appear *ad nauseam* in the media: we hang on the words of national security "consultants" who speak and write to compensate for the fact that we cannot hang the international terrorist (or more reasonably, *deter* through internationally legalized homicide), for nations cannot agree to a common definition of terrorism, let alone a common power to enforce sanctions against it. That would require the discipline of a universal law and order, and there can be no law where there is no sovereign, as Thomas Hobbes said and Oliver North pleonastically embellished: "it is very important for the American people to understand that this is a dangerous world, that we live at risk and that this nation is at risk in a dangerous world."[20]

It would seem that outside the cultural economy of national security the non-military options for responding to terrorism are severely limited — semantically, epistemologically, ethically, practically. Is it possible to write/read about terrorism without a teleology, without trying, self-consciously or unselfconsciously, to make terrorism "safe" — safe for definition, criminalization, or even legitimation? Or is the only other option to remain silent/blind, as we do in the face of "natural" disasters like Armenian earthquakes, Bangladeshi floods, and

Ethiopian famines, when no rational explanation or response can possibly encompass the meaninglessness and contingency of catastrophic deaths?[21]

Wandering in intertextual and international relations, between post-modernity in thought and what looks like a neo-medievalism in practice, I can make no privileged claims for an explanatory or analytical reading of terrorism and the national security culture. The best I can offer here — and the best I believe the material will provide — is a *descripting*. In effect, this means a melding of the reconstructive technology of the Iran–Contra hearings with the palimpsest technique of the Middle Ages. In the next chapter I shall attempt a constructive theory of terrorism. But the first step — I believe a necessary step — is an inquiry into the national security culture behind the official documents, inside the "erased" electronic files, within the sub-texts of violent hyperrealism, all of which maintain the immaculate esplanade between the dark wood and the castle, terrorism and counter-terrorism.[22]

FACT, FACTOIDS, AND THE FACTOTUM OF TERRORISM

Just as Nietzsche alleged the precession of meaning to facts, North — the factotum of terror and counter-terror — preceded the factoids of terrorism. To be sure, there are some commonly accepted "facts" about international terrorism, many of which will be subject to scrutiny in the next chapter. But for now, a skim of Rand Corporation documents reveals the ones relevant to the decade leading up to the Oliver North Story: terrorists seized over 50 embassies and consulates; held the oil ministers of 11 states hostage; kidnapped hundreds of diplomats, businessmen and journalists; made several hundred million dollars in ransom money; assassinated Lord Mountbatten and President Sadat and the former premier of Italy; and attempted to assassinate the President of France, the Pope, and Alexander Haig (a near miss with a rocket launcher when he was supreme allied commander of NATO). Terrorist incidents and their severity *did* increase over those ten years, but most terrorist actions involve few or no casualties: they are symbolic acts of violence. Compared to the ruthlessness and destructiveness of states, or even to natural disasters, terrorism is a mere nuisance. Yet it is cause for crises of state, media spasms on a seismic scale, and the hyper-production of institutes, conferences, and books on terrorism.

Why is this? International terrorism does represent a crisis, but *not* in terms of body-counts or a revolutionary threat to the states-system. On

a political level, the simulacrum of terrorism — that is, the production
of a hyperreal threat of violence — anticipates a crisis of legitimation.[23]
What this means is that international terrorism is not a symptom nor a
cause nor an effect of this systemic crisis: it has become a spectacular,
micro-cosmic simulation. International terrorism simulates a legitimation
crisis of the international order; conversely, counter-terrorism is a
counter-simulation, an attempt to engender a new disciplinary order
which can save the dominant legitimacy principle of international
relations.[24] On a representational level, the spectacle of terrorism displaces — and distracts us from — the signs of a pervading international
disorder. As a result, much of what is read and written of terrorism
displays a superficiality of reasoning and a corruption of language
which effects truths about terrorism without any sense of how these
truths are produced by and help to sustain official discourses of international relations. This was repeatedly evidenced by the proceedings
and documents of the Iran—Contra hearings, in which our reason of
state was exposed as ideological expediency and redressed as principled
policy.

If the reader of terrorism is to break out of the dominant cultural
economy, in which each of us acts as a factotum of factoids — that is, a
transmitter of official truths — then some critical interpretive skills must
be deployed. Along with an empirical study of the salient sources of
disorder around us, we need a genealogy of our knowledge of international terrorism and legitimacy, of how consumers in this cultural
economy arrive at some shared assumptions about the exchange-value
of both. One goal, then, of a cultural reading is to reach a better understanding of whether these assumptions or constructions of terrorism
and legitimation serve to preserve principles and practices beneficial to
the international order, or whether they forestall the knowledge necessary
to deal effectively with an increasing fragmentation, a diffusion of
power, and a sustained challenge to the sovereign state's once-natural
monopoly of force: in short, the neo-medievalism alluded to earlier.

What this entails — and what this chapter attempts — is a critical
preface to a text that each reader of terrorism must "write." Having
asserted the precession of meaning in terrorism, I do, however, recognize
the need to address the definitional factoids of terrorism. In the following
chapter I will review some of the definitional distinctions that have been
useful, and some that have not, to the study of terrorism. But as noted,
confusion over definitions arises not just because of terrorism's multiple
sponsors and forms, but because of the cultural efforts to tame its
arbitrary nature, unpredictability, and chimeric character. Rigorous or
broad, rigid or sloppy, definitions are in themselves an important dis-

cursive practice of the terrorism industry. Often they appear to be yet
another weapon in the vast arsenal of counter-terrorism, aiming to re-
establish order and meaning in international relations practice and
discourse at a time when both are undergoing extensive and intensive
assaults.

Is it possible to recognize the battlefield of contending definitions
without getting bogged down in it, to stand at the edge of the political
fray, to launch "truth"-seeking missives which might clear the ground
for a new reading of terrorism? Probably not. In an age of surveillance
and speed, the ultimate strategic power of terrorism and counter-
terrrorism is not the quantity and secure *siting* of weapons/targets —
that is, geo-politics — but the velocity and timely *sighting* of them —
that is, chrono-politics.[25] In other words, a different strategic game
requiring a different cultural analysis is being played out: to match the
opacity rendered by Stealth technologies, the transparency achieved by
satellites and ELINT (Electronic Intelligence), the targeting ("illuminating") power of radar and laser, a new cultural reading is needed.
Hence, the best I can offer is a deterrent de-scription rather than a pre-
emptive definition, a view of the boundaries of the national security
culture drawn by terrorism from two elevations which might yield a
parallax advantage over the conventional one-dimensional definitions.
In high orbit and at low resolution, I see terrorism as does the social
critic Jean Baudrillard, historically "initiated by the taking of hostages
and the game of postponed death"; but in a lower orbit, at higher
resolution, on the screen, I view it as do others — as a televisual
strategic simulation choreographed by violence and staged for a fearful,
captive global audience.[26]

A POSSIBLE TEXT FOR THE PREFACE

So far, I have established some of the important problems of reading/
writing about terrorism that need to be examined in the next chapter.
First, the question of legitimacy: how we signify statements and discursive
practices in international relations as reasonable, justifiable, verifiable,
or authorized determines in part who are the victims and agents of
terrorism, the legitimate and pariah states and non-state actors.[27]

Second, this signification is difficult enough within the borders and
security of the state, but outside the state, with no sovereign authority
(in both the juristic and linguistic senses) to rule on legitimacy, we
cannot establish facts which will bring an end to terrorism.

Third, there is an historiographical problem to contend with. Histories of terrorism are rare: rarer yet is a history of how terrorism has been read, or interpreted.[28] What usually stands in for a history of terrorism is a televised factive, sometimes fictive narration of 30 seconds to 3 minutes. Of course, there is always the option of acquiring information from the proliferating Institutes of Terrorist Studies. For the most part, though, what they provide is simply learned repetition of what can be heard on *ABC Nightline*.[29]

Fourth, this is not so much a crisis in the legitimation process as it is a crisis of representation, in which the once-dominant state's construction of legitimate political violence, now competing with terrorism's fragmentation of power and globalization by the media, is reduced to a pure simulation of terrorism and counter-terrorism.[30]

Fifth, this evokes an ethical and political dilemma: how do we reconstruct a reading of terrorism which critiques the maintenance of an order favorable to the dominant interests of the great powers while recognizing the imperative of ensuring the internal and external security of citizens who face natural and "artificial" disasters in an international, quasi-anarchical society?

There is always the temptation, prompted by the more vulgar forms of poststructuralism, to end with this summation and critical interrogation, to leave it to the reader to construct an alternative history of terrorism out of the "fragged" remains of the body politic. But this would highlight the worst aspects of poststructuralism, its propensity for the extremes of gaming or despairing when confronted by the seemingly implacable problems of modernity. In international theory we must demonstrate something more than what Nietzsche referred to as "the strength to forget the past," by which he meant forgetting the kind of history that neatly adds up past events to rationalize our present condition. Otherwise we leave a void, a vacuum of knowledge and power in which others engaged in a different kind of "positive forgetting" – most notably political leaders who preside over the past through a process of selective senility – can install metaphysical visions of terrorism. For counter-terrorism, then, I suggest a counter-history: instead of the flash-bang grenades of anti-terrorist rhetoric which have blinded and deafened us to past struggles of international political violence and legitimacy we need a study of the relevant *archives*, in the Foucauldian sense of the "play of rules which determines within a culture the appearance and disappearance of statements."[31] In other words, we must come to some understanding of how our knowledge of terrorism has bestowed it with an antidiplomatic power.

THE SANITATION OF TERROR AND THE CONSTITUTION OF SECURITY: PLEDGE-MAKING AND HOSTAGE-TAKING

The cultural archive of security and terrorism eternally recurs with the making and breaking of pledges: the loyalty oath of feudal warriors, the first contracts of the traders, the compact for a commonwealth, the *pacta sunt servanda* of the fledgling system of states; all founded on promises — some kept and many broken — to move from an anarchic terror to a ruled order.[32] A skimming of some of the exemplary thinkers of the rationalist episteme discloses the anti-terrorist role of the pledge in reason and history. Although Thomas Hobbes's prescription of a one-sided pledge to the Leviathan for security in the permanent "war of all against all" has dominated modern thinking about international relations, there have been significant challengers to this realist paradigm like Hugo Grotius and Samuel Pufendorf, the foremost jurists of the seventeenth century, who saw in the promise a cultural mechanism through which natural law and a mutual alienation of interests could provide rules for an international society.[33]

In the grip of microeconomic, neorealist paradigms, we have "forgotten" how the pledge/promise acted as a vehicle for ordering societies, juristically and discursively, but also theoretically through social contracts (Rousseau), the confederation of states (Kant), the universalization of Spirit (Hegel), and the solidarity of a class (Marx). But now, in a society fragmented and nuclearized by terrorism and the balance of terror, there are no authors, no subjects, only hostages — actual and potential — for the international pledge. The anonymity of mutual assured destruction, the indiscriminate exchange of hostages by terrorism, the requisite secrecy of counter-terrorism, act as an ellipsis in international relations. Held hostage to a pledge which is significant for everyone but signed by no one, inscribed by a death sentence that makes no juristic or grammatical sense outside of the official context, the subject is predicated — "disappeared" — with the terrorist ellipsis.

In the Iran–Contra hearings Oliver North filled the ellipsis and became a "heroic" subject to the extent that he was able to assert a pure identity (the counter-terrorist/victim) against an evil difference (the terrorist/criminal). In contrast to the threats of master-terrorist Abu Nidal, Iranian fanatics, and "totalitarian Sandinistas", the issues of a free security system for his home, missing travelers' checks, and Swiss bank accounts seemed insignificant. For North, moving from his rule-less world of counter-terrorism to the litigious stage of the hearings, the only pledge of importance became the one against perjury:

> *Sullivan*: Well, what is your question, counsel?
> *Nields*: Have you forgotten the question?
> *Sullivan*: Well I have and I have to make objections, so you ask it again and I'll –
> *Nields*: You did and it was over-ruled and the question stands. I'd like the witness to answer it, if he remembers it.
> *Sullivan*: Could we – he obviously doesn't remember it, he just asked you to repeat it. May we have –
> *Nields*: You did, you did, he did not. Sir, do you remember the question?
> *North*: My memory has been shredded. If you would be so kind as to repeat the question.[34]

I have previously made note of the modernist attempt to resurrect the historical relationship between the pledge and security, terror and freedom made by Jean-Paul Sartre in his much-maligned but rarely read *Critique of Dialectical Reason*.[35] His theoretical distillation of the pledge and alienated group dynamics offers an interpretive conduit for plotting the historical transformations of the modern national security culture:

> But *this* is precisely what a pledge is: namely the common produc-tion, through mediated reciprocity, of a statute of violence; once the pledge has been made, in fact, the group has to guarantee everyone's freedom against necessity, even at the cost of his life and in the name of freely sworn faith. Everyone's freedom demands the violence of all against it and against that of any third party as its defence against itself (as a free power of secession and alienation). To swear is to say, as a common individual: you must kill me if I secede. And this demand has no other aim than to install Terror within myself as a free defence against the fear of the enemy (at the same time as reassuring me about the third party who will be confirmed by the same Terror). At this level, the pledge becomes a material operation.[36]

How would a history of the "material operation" of the pledge read? There is no text to turn to, really only fragments, but the best pieces come, I believe, from the erudite writings of the two British "classical" international theorists, Martin Wight and Hedley Bull.[37] Wight's

sweeping inquiry into the development of principles of international
legitimacy offers a panoramic view of how violence was made safe for
the society of states. This story of the sanitation of political violence,
what could be called "the hygienic of terror", begins with the establishment of the dynastic principle and ends with the popular principle of
legitimacy:

> By international legitimacy I mean the collective judgment of
> international society about rightful membership of the family of
> nations; how sovereignty may be transferred; and how state
> succession is to be regulated, when large states break up into
> smaller, or several states combine into one. Until the French Revol-
> ution, the principle of international legitimacy was dynastic, being
> concerned with the status and claims of rulers. Since then, dynas-
> ticism has been superseded by a popular principle, concerned with
> the claims and consent of the governed.[38]

It is a long story, which cannot be retold here, of the formation of
hierarchies and rituals of power in Latin Christendom (the Holy Roman
Empire, papacy, national monarchs, fiefdoms, principalities, and city-
states) based on precedence and prescriptive rights. What concerns this
inquiry is a counter-plot, how a series of challenges in the seventeenth
and eighteenth centuries to the dynastic principle of legitimacy – the
republicanism of the Dutch revolt; the theories of political and social
contract; and the English, American and French Revolutions – shifted
pledge-making from dynastic rulers to popular politics; and how from
the American Revolution to the imperialism of the French Revolution
the principle of legitimacy underwent a sea-change, from all men are
created equal and have inalienable rights to the idea of *national* self-
determination. "The rights of man", says Wight, "gave way to the
rights of nations."[39] With this alienation of obligations, the nation-state
takes on the pledge, or contract, of security. But it is the sub-plot of the
counter-plot which informs this modern reading of terrorism: that is,
the emergence of a neo-medieval hostage-taking to enforce, and increasingly displace, a newly challenged national security pledge.

For those more materially or neorealistically inclined in their global
analysis, these may seem like "paper" issues in a *kapitalpolitik* world
where trade and microchips, if no longer blood and iron, seem to rule.
But from the first chanceries of the early middle ages to the modern
national security archives, the "text" has always preceded the state. It is
the chancellor, or *cancellarius*, "keeper of the barrier," who by his
accumulation of official diplomas inscribed the first boundaries of the

early Holy Roman Empire that Charlemagne only fleetingly and tenuously secured by sword. It is the statutory power of the National Security Act of 1947 ("to perform such other functions and duties related to intelligence affecting the national security as the National Security Council may from time to time direct") that so effectively redrew the reach of the American Empire after its military troops had come home.

To be sure, as we have witnessed in the Persian Gulf, war as the *ultima ratio* of the state still counts, but in nuclear and cybernetic times it counts for less. It was the *sign* of war — the uniform, the silver and bronze stars and purple hearts, the ramrod posture — that protected North from the media glare and committee probings. North took a hostage — our concept of patriotism. And it was the war of signs, not a presidential pardon or judicial prestidigitation, that would determine North's future. Having subpoenaed the President, President-elect, and other high government officials, and having demanded over 30,000 classified documents, North took the ultimate hostage: the secret archive of the national security state. Already hampered by its inability to use North's Congressional testimony, the judiciary eventually conceded to North's superior accumulation of sign-power.

We probably will never learn of the pledges (let alone their legality) made and broken in this particular campaign of terror and counter-terror because we — or some counterfeit "we" that bought into the cultural economy of the national security state — pledged not to. We can, however, use this reconstruction of the relationship between the pledge and terror to ask broader, critical questions about the future of an antidiplomatic order. Will the fragmentation of state-power, the pervasiveness of the nuclear and chemical terror, the rise of a new international disorder void the international contracts of the dominant powers and once again "legitimate" the taking of hostages? Are we returning to a practice institutionalized when Europe was evolving from a suzerain system to a states-system, where only a physical pledge was sufficient to maintain order? At best, can we hope for a recurrence of the mutual exchange of elite hostages as a commitment to keep a pledge, as Spain and France exchanged hostages — one of them William I of Orange — to enforce the Treaty of Cateau-Cambrésis in 1559? For control of nuclear terror, should the US not have offered the Soviets Abraham Sofaer (the controversial legal advisor to the Department of State) as insurance for maintaining the "narrow" interpretation of the Anti-Ballistic Missile Treaty? Now that intermediate (and if tactical) nuclear weapons are removed from Europe, will American troops be sufficient hostages for NATO? And could more extreme hostage-takings be institutionalized, such as guaranteed air-time on *ABC Nightline* for the year's most popular terrorist and counter-terrorist, to follow Abu Nidal and Oliver North in split-screen?

PENULTIMATUM

I will leave it for the following chapter to consider whether modern terrorism, the break-down of the pledge, and the taking of hostages are harbingers of a new medievalism, or morbid symptoms of a Gramscian moment where the old is dying and the new cannot yet be born. My final speculation returns instead to the critical link between international terrorism and the balance of terror, where everyone, combatants and noncombatants alike, is conceivably a hostage. At the polemical level, the most effective anti-terror tactic would be to attack the stasis of a global insecurity that presently privileges great powers and marginalizes lesser powers, that perpetually postpones a negotiated settlement in the Middle East, that ensures an opportunistic rather than serious commitment to general disarmament. But this begs an expanded interpretation of the international cultural economy which might allow us to reinscribe broader, looser borders to the national security culture; to deconstruct institutions like the balance of terror which we have created but seem beyond ultimate control; and of no lesser importance, to be less earnest when reading/writing/shredding the archive of terrorism.

Notes

1 For a breakdown and explanation of terrorist incidents from 1980 to 1988, see *Patterns of Global Terrorism: 1988* (Department of State Publication, March, 1989), pp. 1–11 and 85. See also "Excerpts from Committee's Hearings on the Gates Nomination," *New York Times* (17 September 1991), p. A16.
2 See J. Der Derian, chapter 4 on "Mytho-diplomacy," and chapter 7 on "Anti-diplomacy," *On Diplomacy*, pp. 47–68 and 134–67.
3 See *Oxford English Dictionary*, vol. 9, p. 370.
4 Gibbon, *The Decline and Fall of the Roman Empire* (1781), xxxi, III, p. 229, quoted in *OED*, vol. 9, p. 370.
5 W. Shakespeare, *Macbeth* (1605), III, v. 32, quoted in *OED*, vol. 9, p. 370.
6 E. Burke, "Letter to Marquis of Rockingham," quoted in *OED*, vol. 9, p. 370.
7 *Saturday Review* (17 July 1858), p. 51, quoted in *OED*, vol. 9, p. 370.
8 *OED*, vol. 9, p. 370.
9 Quoted, ibid.

10 Quoted, ibid.
11 Quoted, ibid.
12 F. Nietzsche, *On the Genealogy of Morals*, trans. and edited by W. Kaufmann (New York: Random House, 1967), pp. 88–9. See also *On Diplomacy*, pp. 53–6, for a fuller account of how the reciprocity of this relationship between the living and the dead is projected as a mytho-diplomatic mediation between alien peoples.
13 Ibid.
14 *Compilation of Intelligence Laws*, US Congress, House Permanent Select Committee (Washington, DC: US Government Printing, 1981), p. 7.
15 *Taking the Stand: The Testimony of Lieutenant Colonel Oliver North* (New York: Pocket Books, 1987), pp. 26–7.
16 "Abstraction today is no longer that of the map, the double, the mirror or the concept. Simulation is no longer that of a territory, a referential being or a substance. It is the generation by models of a real without origin or reality: a hyperreal." From J. Baudrillard, *Simulations* (New York: Semiotext(e), 1983), p. 2.
17 Entitled *Documents From the U.S. Espionage Den* (*not* readily available at $248.00, but selected volumes can be found at the National Intelligence Book Center and the National Security Archive in Washington, DC), the collected work contains intelligence reports on Iran, Pakistan, Kuwait, Turkey, the Soviet Union, and other Near and Middle Eastern countries. Of special interest is a 170-page study of international terrorism which claims that Syria "sponsored" many of the incidents of Middle Eastern terrorism in the 1970s.
18 On semio-criticism, see earlier reference to Roland Barthes, "To Write: An Intransitive Verb?," in *The Rustle of Language*, trans. by R. Howard (New York: Hill and Wang, 1986), pp. 11–12, quoted in chapter 1 above.
19 "Is it the media which induce fascination in the masses, or is it the masses which divert the media into spectacle? Mogadishu Stammheim: the media are made the vehicle of the moral condemnation of terrorism and of the exploitation of fear for political ends, but, simultaneously, in the most total ambiguity, they propagate the brutal fascination of the terrorist act." From Jean Baudrillard, "The Implosion of Meaning in the Media," in *In the Shadow of the Silent Majorities* (New York: Semiotext(e), 1983), pp. 105–6.
20 *Taking the Stand*, p. 12.
21 Two provocative studies of how cultures of terror subvert order and meaning, and how disasters compel silence or dissimulation, are Michael Taussig's *Shamanism, Colonialism, and the Wild Man: A Study in Terror and Healing* (Chicago and London: The University of Chicago Press, 1987), and Maurice Blanchot's *The Writing of the Disaster* (Lincoln and London: University of Nebraska Press, 1986).
22 "There is no distinction possible between the spectacular and the symbolic, no distinction possible between the 'crime' and the 'repression.' It is this uncontrollable eruption of reversibility that is the true victory of terrorism." From J. Baudrillard, "Our Theater of Cruelty," in *In the Shadow of the Silent Majorities*, pp. 115–16.
23 See Jean-François Lyotard's *The Postmodern Condition: A Report on Knowledge* (Minneapolis: University of Minnesota Press, 1984), particularly the foreword by Frederic Jameson, pp. vii-xxi.

24 Two seminal writings which anticipate Baudrillard's study of simulation
and hyperrealism as legitimating forces for political order – one on the
"culture of distraction" and the other on the "society of the spectacle" –
are Siegfried Kracauer's *Das Ornament der Masse* (Frankfurt A. M.:
Suhrkamp Verlag, 1963), forthcoming as *The Mass Ornament*, translated
and edited by Thomas Y. Levin (Cambridge, MA: Harvard University
Press); and Guy Debord's *Society of the Spectacle* (Detroit, Michigan:
Black and Red, 1983).

25 See P. Virilio, *Pure War* (New York: Semiotext(e): 1983), and *Speed and
Politics* (New York: Semiotext(e): 1986); and J. Der Derian, chapter 8 on
"Techno-diplomacy" in *On Diplomacy*.

26 Baudrillard supplies the theoretical base for this definition, and the major
television networks" production standards for coverage of terrorism provide
an empirical foundation.

27 These questions presuppose if not confirm a legitimacy crisis in international
relations; or it would appear so, if we share a view of inquiry into
legitimacy with "the owl of Minerva," whose wings stretch from Hegel to
Habermas to Frederic Jameson who says soothly in the Foreword to
Lyotard's *Post-modern Condition* that "legitimation becomes visible as a
problem and an object of study only at the point in which it is called into
question" (p. viii).

28 For its narrative style and absence of scientific pretensions, Walter Laqueur's
Terrorism (and his anthology on terrorism) stands out as an exception to
the ruling policy-oriented material on the subject. See in particular his
preface to the Abacus Edition, where he states that "the failure of political
scientists to come to terms with the terrorist phenomenon cannot possibly
be a matter of legitimate dispute ... Historical experience, it is said,
cannot teach us much about terrorism; but what else can?" From *Terrorism*
(London: Sphere Books, 1978), pp. 7–8.

29 I wonder, after watching some of these pundits (like Michael Ledeen) who
are wheeled out as impartial commentators on terrorism, whether the best
counter-terrorism action would be a surgical airstrike on some of those
institutes (but then again, it might miss and hit the Institute of Policy
Studies).

30 For the transformation of political representation into simulation, see
Baudrillard's *Simulations*, pp. 11–13 ("Whereas representation tries to
absorb simulation by interpreting it as false representation, simulation
envelops the whole edifice of representation as itself a simulacrum."); and
for its elision through the balance of terror into a "mutual simulation," see
Virilio's *Pure War*, pp. 159–72.

31 M. Foucault, "Réponse au cercle d'épistémologie," *Cahiers pour l'analyse*,
9 (Summer, 1968). This is of course only a sketch of Foucault's historiographical technique. On the difficult task of plumbing our own archive,
"the general system of the formation and transformation of statements,"
see the introduction and chapter 5 of Foucault's *The Archaeology of
Knowledge* (London: Tavistock Publications, 1972); and on his recuperation
of the genealogical approach, "gray, meticulous, and patiently documentary," see his seminal essay, "Nietzsche, Genealogy, History," in *Language,
Counter-Memory, Practice: Selected Essays and Interviews*, edited by D. F.
Bouchard (Ithaca: Cornell University Press, 1977).

32   For a related view on the function of the promise and contract in both the
     domestic and international order, see chapters 1 and 2 of Hedley Bull's *The
     Anarchical Society* (London: Macmillan, 1977); and the introduction by
     Bull to *The Expansion of the International Society*, edited by H. Bull and
     A. Watson (Oxford: Oxford University Press, 1984).

33   See T. Hobbes, *Leviathan*, edited by M. Oakeshott (Oxford: Basil Blackwell),
     pp. 85−7 and 112; H. Grotius, "Of Promises," in *De jure belli ac pacis*,
     trans. W. Whewell (London: John Parker, 1835), vol. II, pp. 35−6;
     S. Pufendorf, "Of the Nature of Promises and Pacts in General," in *Of the
     Law of Nature and Nations* (Oxford: Clarendon, 1935), pp. 390−401;
     and I. Kant, "Second Section Which Contains the Definitive Articles for
     Perpetual Peace Among Nations," in *Perpetual Peace and Other Essays*
     (Indianapolis: Hackett Publishing, 1983), p. 111.

34   *New York Times*, 8 July 1987, p. 8.

35   See *On Diplomacy*, pp. 40−1.

36   For Sartre, then, terror is not an anomalous feature of modern society, but
     fundamental, as is scarcity, to the formation of societies: "The origin of the
     pledge, in effect, is fear (both of the third party and of my self) . . . Terror . . .
     is common freedom violating necessity, in so far as necessity exists only
     through the alienation of some freedom" (Sartre, *Critique of Dialectical
     Reason*, pp. 430−1).

37   See M. Wight, *Systems of States* (Leicester: Leicester University Press,
     1977); and *Power Politics* (Middlesex: Penguin, 1979).

38   Wight, *Systems of States*, p. 153.

39   Wight, *Systems of States*, p. 160.

5

THE TERRORIST DISCOURSE: SIGNS, STATES, AND SYSTEMS OF GLOBAL POLITICAL VIOLENCE

—

**Why is it, that anything on this Earth we do not understand,
We are pushed onto our knees to worship or to damn?**
The The, "The Violence of Truth"

From the 1978 news photograph of the kidnapped Italian Prime Minister
Aldo Moro sitting under the banner of the *Brigate Rosse*, to the 1989
videomurder of Lieutenant Colonel William Higgins by the Organization
of the Oppressed on Earth in Lebanon, terrorism has attracted much
public attention, a great deal of media commentary, and very little
critical theory. After the 1980s, a decade marked by a rising number of
incidents, the proliferation of terrorist studies, and the escalation of
rhetoric by US Presidents, terrorism remains as resistant to comprehension
as it is to remediation.[1]

This is not for the lack of intellectual effort. To explain the terrorist
predicament, a welter of articles, academic books, professional reports,
and special news programs have been produced. The predominant focus
of the expert field has been on the psychological and organizational side
of terrorism – its often fanatical motivations, unpredictable nature, and
twisted techniques – resulting in models that range from complex and
insightful to the crude and identikit.[2] Another group, popular in both
journalistic and literary circles, has sought out – presumably for the
purpose of retaliation and extirpation – the invisible hand that supplies
and controls terrorism. Especially vocal are the counter-terrorist conspiracists, who see behind every Carlos, Agca, Abu Nidal (or the latest

terrorist exemplar) the Soviet Union, Libya, Iran (or some other pariah state), acting as the central command of international terrorism.[3] Found somewhere between these camps are the liberal commentators, who study the particular features of democracies — an aversion to the use of naked force, an unrestrained media, hand-tying checks and balances — that make them appealing and vulnerable targets for terrorism. Generally more astute about the various religious, social, and economic causes of terrorism, the liberal theorists vacillate between remedies like better law enforcement and selective use of anti-terrorist forces.[4]

THE MATTER OF METHOD

For all the academic, professional, and journalistic efforts of the 1980s, we seem far from a general theory of terrorism and further yet from any credible or generally acceptable plan for eradicating terrorism in the near future. To be sure, the "terrorist specialists" are not the only nor the most culpable party. Our ability to think and make judgments about terrorism has suffered from a corrosive mix of official opportunism, media hype, and public hysteria. The essential link between detached analysis and policy-making has become as attenuated as a fuse wire, ready to blow at the mere *threat* of a terrorist attack.

It is fairly easy — that is, politically expedient — to single out particular individuals as responsible for this state of affairs. Current candidates would include the political leader preoccupied with the "wimp-factor," the media magnate with an eye on profit-margins, or the think-tank courtier eagerly working the space between. But such an assessment of blame is to mimic the very cardboard construction of terrorist identities that presently pre-empts any serious attempt to comprehend terrorism.

It is more difficult — and certainly less popular — to assess the intellectual and structural obstacles blocking an inquiry into terrorism. The first obstacle is *epistemological*: even the most conscientious and independent student of terrorism faces a narrowly bounded discipline of thought. During the 1980s terrorist studies became a fortress-haven at the edge of the social sciences, a positivist's armory of definitions, typologies, and databases to be wielded as much against the method-ological critic as the actual terrorist who might call into question the sovereign reason and borders of the nation-state. The second obstacle is *ideological*: to gain official entry into the terrorist debate one must check critical weapons at the door, and join in the chorus of condemnation — or risk suspicion of having sympathy for the terrorist devil. What this means is that following a rash of terrorist incidents — at the moments of highest tension when sober thinking is most needed — responses other than instant excoriation and threats of retaliation are seen as "soft," or worse, collaborationist. As others have noted, this is very reminiscent of the regimentation of critical thinking by threat-mongering that marked Cold War I in the 1940s and 1950s and the most morbid moments of Cold War II in the early 1980s. Let Oliver North remind us once again: "It is very important for the American people to understand that this is a dangerous world, that we live at risk and this nation is at risk in a dangerous world."[5]

However, as Gorbachev worked hard to improve relations with the United States, and as the Soviet bloc began to disintegrate, it proved increasingly difficult to find, let alone maintain the credibility of an alien, uniform, foe. In the future, there will indeed be external dangers, but it is US *national identity*, not the United States as nation, that it is truly at risk. Here lies the third, *ontological*, reason for the intractability of terrorism: it has been subsumed by the traditional gambit of defining and unifying a national identity through the alienation of others. In spite of the odds that we are more likely to die from a lightning strike, an automobile accident, or even a bee sting, many have come to accept the ubiquity of the terrorist threat as well as take on the identity of the victim.

Yet, even in polls taken immediately after a terrorist strike, the majority of Americans are reluctant to endorse military retaliation.[6] Common sense probably plays a conservative role: if polled, most Americans would probably not (for similar reasons) endorse surgical air-strikes on automobile plants or bee colonies to lessen the chances of an unlikely death. But I suspect something beyond common sense is at work. Reflecting the diverse and highly individualistic forces behind terrorism, we are not — nor can we be — of one mind, of one identity, or of one course of action when it comes time to think and act collectively *against* the terrorist threat. What the polls probably reflected is that after Vietnam (and before another Lebanon debacle), many preferred the *non*-identity of a silent but safe majority when it comes to taking on an enemy that is fearsome but faceless, anywhere and nowhere.

This is not to claim that one must sympathize with terrorism in order to understand it, although this chapter does attempt a better understanding of the terrorist *in situ*. Nor is it to pretend that a total comprehension of terrorism is possible, remedial, or even preferable, although this chapter does try to reconstruct our knowledge and to critique current practices of terrorism and anti-terrorism. Rather, it is to argue at the outset that any productive reading of terrorism requires a difficult, even contorted feat, of stepping outside of the one-dimensional identities that terrorism and the national security culture have implanted in both sides of the conflict.[7]

For some, this kind of intellectual activity might be considered subversive. Indeed, former Secretary of State George Shultz in a major policy address on terrorism stated that the US cannot effectively respond to terrorism unless Americans are of one mind on the subject: "Our nation cannot summon the will to act without firm public understanding and support." Without such a consensus we risk becoming, in Shultz's words, "the Hamlet of nations, worrying endlessly over whether and how to respond."[8] I believe, however, that it is time to take up a position of detachment towards terrorism that Hedley Bull approvingly referred to as "political nihilism."[9] After all, "when times are out of joint," as they were for Hamlet and as they appeared to be for the USA as the 1980s took a radical turn, we might find in Hamlet — who through his passionate yet intellectual introspection discovered just how rotten the declining state could be — a better guide than, say, Henry V — who, "because he did not know how to govern his own kingdom, determined to make war upon his neighbors."[10] We might also discover that there are more things in heaven and earth than are dreamt of in the official terrorist discourse, perhaps even the uncomfortable truth that there is some of the terrorist in us, and some of us in the terrorist. My response, then, to Shultz is more diplomatic than politic: the new *antidiplomatic* estrangement of international relations *requires* that we endlessly mediate the terrorist act and the response to it with a deeper and broader knowledge of *all* practices of global political violence. Otherwise, the will to act becomes inseparable from the will to know, and terrorism becomes indistinguishable from counter-terrorism.

Moreover, an alternative approach is needed because the problem of terrorism is implicated by a profound predicament that now confronts advanced societies. Call it late capitalism, post-modernism, post-warring, or, as I prefer, neo-medievalism, it is a disturbing, anxiety-inducing condition in which traditional modes of knowledge and formations of identity no longer seem up to the task of representing, let alone managing international relations. Nation-states never enjoyed a true monopoly on the use of force, but now more than in any other post-Westphalian time — and certainly at an accelerated pace — the legitimacy of that monopoly has come under serious challenges from social, economic, technical, and military changes. Interdependent economies, global ecological concerns, penetration by surveillance and media technologies, the three-dimensionality and nuclearization of warfare – they have all been recognized as growing antidiplomatic forces undermining the sovereign privileges and obligations of the territorial state.[11]

Less noticed and understood is the emergence of a *terrorist discourse*, by which I refer to a global semiotic activity where violent powers and insurgent meanings clash.[12] With a nuclear stalemate curtailing super-power, and a global information economy boosting sign-power, it is increasingly in the discursive realm of terrorism that the "crises" of political legitimacy, national identity, and practical knowledge are being played out. Simultaneously brutalizing, repugnant, and fascinating, the terrorist repertoire – kidnapping, hijackings, and assassination – cannot alone account for its rise to the singular status of international crisis. In terrorist discourse a less visible battle is being fought – most desperately between the vanguards of aspiring powers and the reatguards of great powers – to reinscribe the boundaries of legitimacy in international relations.

In short, four important yet neglected theoretical points are being made here. In the study of terrorism, method matters: but very little critical consciousness of just how much it matters has been demonstrated in the field. Second, method *is* matter: given the symbolic practices of terrorism, the limitations of physical anti-terrorism, and the simulacral projection of terrorism by the media, the representations of terrorism have taken on a powerful materiality. Third, because of changing con-figurations of power that rival traditional claims of international legit-imacy, new critical methods are called for. Fourth, method alone cannot substitute for an ontological step that anyone seriously seeking truths about terrorism must take: questioning how our own identity is impli-cated and constituted by the terrorist discourse must precede any study of terrorism.

These critical considerations inform the analysis of modern forms of terrorism that follows. Taking into account the sheer volume of the terrorist archive, I can make no claims for comprehensiveness. My strategy is deconstructive *and* reconstructive: to provide a method which might displace, critique, and historicize received accounts of terrorism and, simultaneously, to present an alternative primer for reading terrorism in its multiple, de-territorialized forms.[13] What I wish to avoid is the subtextual ploy found in much of the terrorism literature where the theoretical organization of an inchoate body of thought pretends to reconcile the differences and contradictions of terrorism, thus "taming" rather than interpreting a heavily conflicted field.[14] At best, I hope to leave the reader with a critical method and the minimal amount of historical knowledge necessary to distinguish the politically dispossessed from the violently possessed, and to imagine possible forms of coexistence with the former, while galvanizing collective action against the latter.

RITES OF PASSAGE

First, we must make the diversion promised in the preceding chapter. Entry onto the grounds of the terrorist discourse requires an initiating ritual of purification — otherwise known as definition. It is a difficult ritual, given that much of the semantic confusion as well as the urge for terminological purity is enmeshed in the discursive operations of terrorism and anti-terrorism. How are we to distinguish the terrorist from the bandit, criminal, or freedom fighter? What sets terrorism off from other forms of violent conflict? Why is one state's violence considered terrorist, while another's is anti-terrorist?

On the violence spectrum, terrorism is clearly somewhere between a rumble and a war. Or is it? In 1985 Secretary of Defense Weinberger called the TWA 847 hijacking and hostage-taking "a war and it is the beginning of war."[15] What could appear to be a logical trap — if terrorism is war, why isn't war terrorism? — or at the very least a chronological distortion — does terrorism precede its beginnings? — could also be interpreted to be a calculated definitional maneuver to invoke the strategies of war for a phenomenon that *by* definition resists such strategies. By first making terrorism discursively if not logically identical with war, Weinberger attaches justification for a military response, and then seeks to add credibility by declaring "it is the beginning of war." If the taking of the hostages becomes identical to war, then it also is the "beginning of war," because the US can and will use military force in retaliation for a form of conflict that, in fact, defies "traditional" beginnings, in the sense of hostilities with an extended duration or an official declaration between belligerents. Faced by the spasmodic immediacy of terrorism, Weinberger — who much preferred the *threat* of retaliation to the real thing — equates the terrorist discourse with war in the desire to install a compensatory, *deterrent* strategy.[16]

Other sources of confusion intrude. War clearly has its terrorist element: Dresden, Hiroshima, My Lai, Afghanistan all testify to the ability of states in an age of total war to sanction the killing and maiming of large numbers of civilians. Conversely, many terrorist groups employ the nomenclature of war (The Red *Army* Faction, the *Armed Forces* of National Liberation, the Red *Brigades*, the Provisional Irish Republican *Army*, the Holy *War*), *communiqués* full of military jargon, and many of the tactics of war, like tactical surprise, diversionary attacks, and psychological operations.

But ultimately, I believe, the definitional distinction between war and terrorism holds, which is why it should it be studied as an antidiplomatic discourse rather than a paramilitary form. War is a form of organized violence conducted by states, with commonly accepted (if not always observed) rules against bombing, assassination, armed assaults, kidnapping, hostage-taking, and hijacking of civilians — the type of actions that make up 95 percent of what is most often described as "terrorism."[17] Terrorism, moreover, relies on unpredictable, randomized violence to achieve its various objectives.[18] However, the nature or type of violence utilized by terrorists does not provide sufficient criteria to define terrorism. Outgunned, outmanned, and outlawed by states, terrorists rely more on the intangible power of menacing symbols than on techniques of physical violence to achieve their goals. So, typologies and definitions of terrorism perform much like the airport security systems that seek to prevent terrorism: finely calibrated, they alert the reader to dangers that can prove to be so much loose change; crudely set, they might miss entirely the non-ferrous, free-floating, *immaterial* threats that make up much of the terrorist arsenal; but regardless of the setting, they are supposed to work as much through deterrence as through detection.

This chapter eschews the intellectual equivalent of an anti-terrorist security system. It does not seek to define or detect, to stereotype or deter "the" terrorist. It takes an alternative route of plotting the many philosophical, historical, and cultural differences that have made the multiple forms of terrorism so difficult to understand and so resistant to remedy. To this end, I have interpreted terrorism as a strategy of intimidation and violence which can be delimited into eight formations: mytho-terrorism, anarcho-terrorism, socio-terrorism, ethno-terrorism, narco-terrorism, state terrorism, anti-terrorism, and pure terrorism. These formations should be read as an *array*: like soldiers on parade, this intellectual marshalling does not pretend to reproduce or capture the horror, uncertainty, and savagery of terrorism — it just temporarily represents and gives some order to it for the purpose of a critical review.

MYTHO-TERRORISM

The first (if not primal) form is mytho-terrorism. At the root of much terrorism lies fear, desire, and violence — all the makings of myth.

There is the reciprocal fear that comes from a relationship in which the less powerful simultaneously need and feel alienated from the more powerful. There is the desire for national, class, or simply *more* power to make a different world than the one inherited. And there is the violence that erupts when the desires of the alienated confront each other in mimesis and can no longer be negotiated, displaced, or ritualized away.[19]

Mythology and terrorism fuse when imagined solutions to intractable problems are pursued through new or unconventional rituals of violence. Mytho-terrorism has similar characteristics to other forms of ritual violence, like wars or general strikes, that bind together the deprived, the weak, the resentful, the repressed, or just the temporarily disadvantaged in a violent encounter with more powerful others.[20] The difference however — and this is the difference that both gives mytho-terrorism its power and anticipates its failure — is that its targets are identified by others as innocent victims, not guilty surrogates. What is tactically effective against the more powerful is strategically disastrous because terrorism's mythical justifications are sufficient to arouse the fears and anti-terrorism of the authorities, but not to assure the support of the mythical "people" in whose name the terrorist strikes. Executed in the name of an imagined group-identity, looking backward to a prior Golden Age, or anticipating a future utopia, mytho-terrorism can undermine an order through violence but is unable on its own to generate the necessary ritual substitutes for violence (in contrast, for instance, to the Eucharist, diplomacy, or jurisprudence).

The most potent forces behind mytho-terrorism are usually eschatological and millenarianistic: that is, they join redemption, social change, and cathartic violence in the pursuit of a new era. The eschatological millenarianism of the Crusades, the *jihad*, the Anabaptist insurrections of the sixteenth century, and indeed, the more radical forms of Catholic liberation theology and Islamic fundamentalism of today have inspired or sanctioned mytho-terrorism. The attempt to construct the Kingdom of Heaven on Earth has been marked by assassinations, violent uprisings, and all kinds of martyrdom. Understandably, many historians have turned once again to the Middle East to study possible transhistorical links between myth and terrorism.[21]

Even a superficial scan clearly shows that no one nationalist religion or religious nationalism has had a monopoly on mytho-terrorism. From the random killings of the messianic Zealots in their first-century struggle against the Romans, to the Assassin *fidayeen* seeking to purify Islam in the twelfth and thirteenth centuries; from the terrorist attacks of the mid-twentieth century, of the Jewish Irgun blowing up British occupiers, to more recent cases of Christian Phalangists massacring Palestinians, and Islamic Hizballah car-bombing American and French soldiers; all have appealed to myth and resorted to violence to attain their other-worldly aims. Indeed, in the US's own back yard, such groups as the Order, the Covenant, and the Sword and the Arms of the Lord (CSA) have targeted American judges and FBI agents for assassination in their apocalyptic pursuit of a second Christian millennium.

In mytho-terrorism as well as the other types of terrorism that follow, there is no clear-cut boundary of motivation or targets. Obviously, social, ethnic, ideological and other factors weigh heavily on any consideration of why people turn to terrorism. A short history of the Provisional Irish Republican Army would be a case in point. But it is important to recognize the power of the mythological element that binds and motivates a variety of terrorist groups with multiple grievances – and how this might handicap a purely reasonable inquiry or reaction. In the modern states-system, the pale of power is marked by mytho-terrorism, the boundary where legitimate, rational use of violence to attain goals comes up against the illegitimate, irrational use of violence. On this borderline, the intelligibility of terrorism is more likely to be discerned by a mythical reading than a rational analysis.

ANARCHO-TERRORISM

A statement reprinted in the *New York Times* underscores the spreading threat posed by yet another form of terrorism:

> It was soon recognized at the Rome conference that very little could be done in the matter by diplomatic means. I, therefore, took the earliest opportunity in the course of the conference of proposing that the sixteen chief officers of police of different nations who were present or their representatives should be formed into a special committee secretly to consider with closed doors and without minutes or written reports what steps could most advantageously be taken.[22]

These uncomfortably familiar remarks were made by Sir Vincent Howard, Great Britain's representative at the Rome Anti-Anarchist Conference – convened in 1906. The assassination of Tsar Alexander II by the *Narodnaya Volia* (the People's Will) in 1881, the Haymarket

Square killings in 1886, an assassination attempt on H. C. Frick of Carnegie Steel by a Russian anarchist in 1892, the murder of the President of France by an Italian anarchist in 1894, the King of Italy assassinated in 1900, President McKinley shot by a follower of Emma Goldman in 1901, the assassination of the Empress Elizabeth of Austria: this is just a sampling of the rise of a new kind of international political violence, the amalgamation of anarchism and terrorism, or *anarcho-terrorism*.

Captured by the rapidly growing mass dailies, the anarchist archetype of the nineteenth-century terrorist — eyes borderline mad, revolver in one hand, bomb in the other — lingers long after its ideological origins have been forgotten, its technology antiquated. Certainly any elision of anarchism and terrorism risks simplifying the subject of a major political debate among some very heavy thinkers of nineteenth-century radicalism — including Proudhon, Bakunin, Marx, and Kropotkin — and furthering the modern slide into the false equation of anarchism = communism = terrorism. But at least a cursory knowledge of the originary forces behind anti-state political violence is needed if we are to understand much of the history of Euro-terrorism, for the anarchist message was to resonate in the discourse of, among others, the German Red Army Faction, the Italian Red Brigades, and the French Direct Action. Moreover, the anti-anarchist reaction at the beginning of the twentieth century certainly found its echo in the anti-terrorism summit conferences of the 1980s.

The common element of anarchism is violence against the state. The politics of reform is not an option, for its instruments of debate and persuasion are too weak when confronted by the cloaked violence of the state. Words are corruptible and ambiguous: violent deeds are pure and to the point. While vengeance, hate, and despair might secretly reside in the anarchist's heart and motivate his or her actions, there is an open and often overlooked archive of the destructionist intent of anarchism.[23] Most notorious is Sergey Nechaev's 1869 *Catechism of the Revolutionist*. In 21 points he constructs the identity of the anarcho-revolutionary: "a doomed man . . . an implacable enemy of this world . . . he knows only one science, the science of destruction."[24] Anarchist manifestos proliferated in this period, but it is in the series of increasingly vehement debates between Nechaev and Bakunin against Marx and Engels that we can locate the heroic, individualist terrorist ethic that was rejected by socialists yet persists in the anarcho-terrorism of the modern Euro-terrorist groups like the small but deadly French Direct Action and Belgian Communist Combatant Cells.[25]

SOCIO-TERRORISM

Terrorism acquired its modern meaning in the French Revolution, when Robespierre, St Just and other Jacobins advocated the use of systematic social violence "to make right and reason respected" – and to get rid of some factional enemies in the process.[26] Originally a word with some positive social connotations, the heavy use of the guillotine and the internationalization of the French Revolution radically transformed the term. By 1795 "terrorist" had entered the lexicon as a clearly pejorative term when Edmund Burke referred to the "thousands of those hellhounds called terrorists."[27] Ever since, the word has been part of a socio-political game – a kind of "pin-the-term-on-the-class" – to condemn some forms of social violence and legitimize others.

The debate over who were the "real" socio-terrorists, those who endorse and conduct class warfare, erupted again in France in 1871. It is an important debate because it had a profound influence on future socialist and Marxist–Leninist positions on terrorism. After workers of the Paris Commune were charged by the British press with terrorist "incendiarism", Marx countered with cases of when the "British troops wantonly set fire to the Capitol at Washington and to the summer palace of the Chinese emperor," and "the vandalism of Haussmann, razing historic Paris to make place for the Paris of the sightseer."[28] But Marx's major concern was not explicating the class character of pyromania or urban planning. He was attempting to rebut the accusation that a revolutionary party in power was inherently terrorist, as was suggested by the Communards' execution of 64 hostages, including clergy and the Archbishop of Paris. Marx's reply bears quotation, not only because it is a seminal statement for future socialist positions on terrorism, but also because it makes short shrift of the out of context, *Reader's Digest*-ation of Marx that went on in the 1980s to prove that Communism equals Terrorism.

Marx first historically establishes that revolutionary socialists and colonial subjects have never been protected by the rules of war:

> The bourgeoisie and its army, in June 1848, re-established a custom which had long disappeared from the practice of war – the shooting of their defenceless prisoners. This brutal custom has since been more or less strictly adhered to by the suppressors of all popular commotions in Europe and India; thus proving that it constitutes a real "progress of civilization"!

In the disputed case of the Communards, Marx claims they were responding in kind to others, like the Prussians and the French statesman
Thiers, who initiated the taking of hostages. Moreover, the Communard's
efforts to negotiate a hostage-exchange were rebuffed, which Marx
believed to have exposed "the unscrupulous ferocity of bourgeois
governments":

> The real murderer of Archbishop Darboy is Thiers. The commune
> again and again had offered to exchange the archbishop, and ever
> so many priests in the bargain, against the single Blanqui, then in
> the hands of Thiers. Thiers obstinately refused. He knew that with
> Blanqui he would give to the Commune a head while the archbishop
> would serve his purpose best in the shape of a corpse."[29]

Future theorists of socialism would draw on Marx's analysis to both
condemn terrorism and to justify the extreme occasions when the use of
terror against terror is necessary. At the height of the Russian civil war,
Leon Trotsky, as head of the Red Army, wrote:

> The revolution "logically" does not demand terrorism, just as
> "logically" it does not demand an armed insurrection. What a
> profound commonplace! But the revolution does require of the
> revolutionary class that it should attain its end by all methods at
> its disposal − if necessary, by an armed rising; if required, by
> terrorism.[30]

Trotsky's defense of terrorism comes across as a *realpolitik* mix of
Marx, Clausewitz, and Bismarck. Terrorism in itself is "helpless" as a
political instrument unless adopted as a temporary measure against a
reactionary class. "Intimidation," says Trotsky, "is a powerful weapon
of policy, both internationally and internally"; and "War, like revolution,
is founded upon intimidation."[31] The niceties of morality do not obtain
in such extreme moments; or as he coldly puts it, "we were never
concerned with the Kantian-priestly and vegetarian-Quaker prattle about
the 'sacredness of human life'." However, Trotsky is not one to make a
virtue out of a necessity. The expedient use of terrorism must not
obscure the higher aims of Marxism: "To make the individual sacred
we must destroy the social order which crucifies him ... and this
problem can be solved only by blood and iron."[32]
  Lenin was just as straightforward in his attitude towards terrorism.
Early in the fight against Czarism, Lenin sought to distance the social

democratic movement from the *Narodnaya Volia* as well as other popu-
lists and anarchists who were advocating or practicing terrorism and
assassination against Czarist officials (often successfully, with the 1881
assassination of Czar Alexander II the most notable). Writing for the
party paper *Iskra* in 1901, Lenin criticized the growing wave of terrorism:

> In principle we have never rejected, and cannot reject, terror.
> Terror is one of the forms of military action that may be perfectly
> suitable and even essential at a definite juncture in the battle, given
> a definite state of the troops and the existence of definite conditions.
> But the important point is that terror, at the present time, is by no
> means suggested as an operation for the army in the field, an
> operation closely connected with and integrated into the entire
> system of struggle, but as an independent form of occasional
> attack unrelated to any army ... Far be it from us to deny the
> significance of heroic individual blows, but it is our duty to sound
> a vigorous warning against becoming infatuated with terror, against
> taking it to be the chief and basic means of struggle, as so many
> people strongly incline to do at the present.[33]

But once in power and besieged by war and famine, Lenin finds
terrorism defensible. In August 1918 he writes a "Letter to American
Workers" for *Pravda*:

> How humane and righteous the bourgeoisie are! Their servants
> accuse us of resorting to terror ... The British bourgeoisie have
> forgotten their 1649, the French bourgeoisie their 1793. Terror
> was just and legitimate when the bourgeoisie resorted to it for
> their own benefit against feudalism. Terror became monstrous and
> criminal when the workers and poor peasants dare to use it
> against the Bourgeoisie![34]

A few years later, Lenin was attacking the actions of the Social Revolutionary Party as anarchist and terrorist.[35] And Trotsky, exiled by a man
who would make wide and brutal use of both internal and international
terrorism, soon found himself in the position of defending his earlier use
of terrorism against Stalin's.[36]

What does this prove? Only a minimal amount of the writings and
history of socialism is required to dismiss the accusation that Marxism
is identical to terrorism. A slightly more sophisticated if specious charge
is that Marxism promotes the kind of relativism that condones terrorism.
A more accurate, and I believe realistic, assessment would be that

Marx, Lenin, and Trotsky endorsed an historicist perspective to make difficult and complex judgments on the effectiveness and justifiability of terrorism. It is another question, begged by Stalin's unchecked use of terrorism, whether they got it right. But this analysis of terrorism on a historical and social level can, I believe, contribute a better understanding of the motivations and actions of modern counterparts like the Farabundo Marti National Liberation Front (FMLN) in El Salvador, the New People's Army (NPA) in the Philippines, and the Sendero Luminoso in Peru who exploit (and are exploited by) the ambiguous boundary between social revolutionary and terrorist politics.

ETHNO-TERRORISM

The pursuit of honor and justice, wealth and territory have been recurrent and seemingly eternal causes of violence in the history of the states-system. But from the dynastic rights of the "prince" to the popular rights of the nation there has been an evolution in the legitimacy of violence. The multiple, sometimes conflicting, even extra-terrestrial loyalties of medieval feudatories, and the "jealousies" and often capricious alliances of the royal houses made for unpredictable, unaccountable, or what today we would refer to as "irrational" political violence. It might be historically dubious — as well as morally specious — to consider it a sign of progress that when push comes to legal shove in the contemporary international system, a peoples' war is more likely now to determine the outcome than, say, individual trial by combat. But the tandem rise of the principles of national self-determination and non-intervention with the rights of war has brought a degree of *formally* democratic benefits to the international order.

Ironically, they have also abetted the rise of *ethno-terrorism*: the violent efforts of a national, communal, or ethnic group to acquire the status of a state. There are many nations or groups acting in the name of a nation, still pursuing the legitimacy and protection of statehood, like the Kurds or the Palestinians. There are nation-states which have lost — or have failed to fully acquire — the rights of self-determination because of enduring conditions of suzerainty that the great powers have installed at one time or another, as has been the case at different times in Central America and Eastern Europe. And the history (and still unfinished process) of de-colonization in which social and ethnic forms of terrorism merge into a violent prelude for state formation has been well documented.[37] Indeed, some radical analysts, like Franz Fanon writing of the Northern African case in *The Wretched of the Earth*, consider terrorism to be an essential element of de-colonization, both to liberate the physical territory and to free the colonized subject from years of psychic repression.[38]

The next explosion of ethno-terrorism, however, is more likely to be on the peripheries of the former Soviet Union than in the Western or developing regions of the world. Lost in the anti-terrorist din of the 1980s is the fact that it has been over five years since a major terrorist group has emerged in North America or Europe (the Combattant Communist Cells, or the CCC in Belgium). In the meantime, the potential for ethnoterrorism in the disintegration of the Soviet bloc had been willfully neglected by those on the right who persistently viewed the Soviet Union as an unchanging totalitarian monolith, as well as by those on the left who considered the United States to be the only imperial power of significance in the post-war system. The ingredients for a violent combustion are plentiful: 104 discrete nationalities in 15 republics, 20 autonomous republics, and 18 national districts have been radically reconfigured after the collapse of the Soviet Union; and at the fringes of power, mass movements in Latvia, Lithuania, Estonia, Moldova, Georgia, Armenia, Azerbaijan, Ukraine and other regions where expectations for autonomy and democracy have come up against great economic hardship. The prospect for outbreaks of ethno-terrorism in this area — whether by impatient minority groups (particularly in the Islamic republics) or newly subordinated majorities (like Russians and Gagauzians in Moldova) — has yet to be seriously studied.

It must be acknowledged that these positive developments — the breaking up of a monolithic Marxist–Leninist system (which had created conditions of totalitarian terrorism), the repudiation of the Brezhnev Doctrine (which had provided *ex post facto* justification for Soviet intervention into Czechoslovakia), the open rejection of the secret pro-tocols of the 1939 Nazi–Soviet pact (which had led to the annexation of the Baltic Republics) — have a darker side. Alongside — and sometimes within — the display of progressive nationalism in the Baltic, Georgian, Azerbaijani, and Armenian Republics there lies an atavistic chauvinism. For instance, at the same time that Estonians declared their virtual sovereignty, they disenfranchised a sizeable portion of their Russian population, prompting widespread strikes and increased tensions. Christian Armenians and Muslim Azerbaijanis killed each other over their claims to the Autonomous Region of Nagorno-Karabakh, resulting in martial law. And in the Republic of Georgia, Soviet troops used shovels and toxic gas against nationalist protestors who were taking seriously Gorbachev's slogans of perestroika and glasnost. Elsewhere, in

Rumania, Yugoslavia, Bulgaria, Uzbekistan and the Ukraine, the volatile ingredients for ethno-terrorism − territorial disputes (between Rumania and Hungary), economic disparities (in Yugoslavia between political, religious and ethnic groups), cultural differences (between Slav and Turk in Bulgaria) − have also begun to surface after many years of repression.

Full of historical disparities, the experiences of the Jews, Basques, Irish, Sikhs and others who waged long campaigns of ethno-terrorism against hegemonic powers nonetheless offer some insights for what might lie ahead for the former Soviet Union and its neighbors. Why some terrorist groups succeeded in their bids for statehood while others failed seems linked to their ability to mobilize and subsume social cross-sections of native populations against occupying or dominant powers that have lost the will and/or the way to rule. The mytho-terrorism of the Jewish Irgun, the anarcho-terrorism of the Serbian Black Hand, or the socio-terrorism of the Irish Republican Army alone were not sufficient to achieve their respective goals. It is ethno-terrorism, once legitimized as a stage in the transformation of nations into states, that has the best historical record among terrorist movements in achieving its goals.

However, this very ability to mount and sustain a long-term campaign of political violence makes ethno-terrorism a favored target of external manipulation, as well as a potential trigger for *systemic*, inter-state violence. Throughout history, ethno-terrorist groups have acted − sometimes as the vanguard, at other times as proxies − for *trans*national rivalries that have ended in global conflicts, such as the friction generated by pan-slavic and pan-germanic terrorism in the Balkans before the First World War, and the racial supremacist violence that fueled Italian, Japanese, and German fascism before the Second World War. Parallels could be drawn with the hydra offshoots of pan-Shiism like the Revolutionary Justice Organization, Organization of the Oppressed on Earth, and other groups under the umbrella of Hizballah that have proven their ability to light fuses that stretch far beyond the Middle East.

NARCO-TERRORISM

It is difficult to pin a date on the origins of *narco-terrorism*, the violent blending of illicit drug trade and political intimidation. In the early eighties, Peruvian officials began to popularize the term by linking the Sendero Luminoso (Shining Path) insurgency to the narcotics trade; soon after the military arm of the Medellin drug cartel was similarly labeled. The war *against* narco-terrorism is better marked, with Nancy and Ronald Reagan in 1986 sitting on a sofa somewhere in the White House, giving the American public the first high-level, televised debriefing of the "war on drugs." At a time when Gorbachev seemed intent on unilaterally calling off the Cold War, and Khaddafi preferred to sulk in his tent rather than execute his threat to bring terrorism home to the United States, narco-terrorism moved up the ranks to become the most immediate and dire foreign threat to the US. The charges flew: Columbian cartels were using drug profits to suborn left-wing guerrillas, the Syrians were growing opiates in the Bekaa valley to fund Palestinian militias, the Nicaraguan Sandinistas were providing transshipment for cocaine and using the money to back El Salvadoran rebels and General Noriega of Panama was brokering protection deals between Castro and the Medellin cartel. US popular culture was selling a similar narrative, although the good guys and bad guys were often reversed: *Miami Vice*, *Lethal Weapon* and *Above the Law* took the first step in this reversal by dredging up the drug-running forays of the CIA-proprietary Air America in Southeast Asia, and reinstating their clandestine operations to Latin America.[39]

The discursive tactic of "just say no" quickly proved inadequate in the war against the new public enemy number one. A volatile combination emerged: internal terrorism in US cities, led by Jamaicans, Columbians, and the expansionist gangs of Los Angeles, the Crips and the Bloods; international terrorism, by the Mexican *narcos* who killed DEA (Drug Enforcement Agency) agents and the Medellin "Extraditables" who assassinated Columbian judges and other officials; and media over-representation, topped by the video *vérité/simulé* of *Cops* and *America's Most Wanted*. US national security *and* the American way of life now being at risk, narco-terrorism took on the qualities of a synergistic threat. In response, then Mayor Koch of New York advocated an air attack on Medellin, and Daryl Gates — the chief of the Los Angeles Police who had become infamous for his anti-drug sweeps of the city with helicopters and armored vehicles — out-did Koch by calling for an outright invasion of Columbia. Military AWACS began to patrol the Caribbean; the State Department was supplied with over 150 fixed wing aircraft and Huey helicopters for use in Columbia, Bolivia, and Peru; the Customs Service and Coast Guard set up a Command, Control, Communications and Intelligence Center (C^3I) in Miami, and lined the Mexican border with radar-equipped blimps; and the Green Berets set off to train paramilitary forces in Latin America for the war against narco-terrorism. It was only a matter of time before Stealth technology was introduced, as a front page article from the *Arizona Republic* reported that "National Guardsmen in Texas could be fighting the war on drugs dressed as cactuses, sneaking up on smugglers under the cover of night and prickly needles, according to a proposal submitted to the Defense Department."[40]

How did narco-terrorism come to claim precedence over all other forms of terrorism? One history, the official history, is made up of what President Reagan once referred to as "stupid facts," by which he meant of course the stubborn facts that US users spend between 100 and 150 billion dollars a year on narcotics, creating a demand that – according to the State Department's 1989 *International Narcotics Strategic Control Strategy Report* – over 56 countries are ready to service in the capacity of growers, manufacturers, traffickers, or money launderers.[41] Again, we should not allow the data to obscure the most important fact, that illegal drugs ruin and kill people. But we have heard all this so often that they have become not stupid but stupefying facts: they incur an inertia of helplessness, a mass mood that accepts the official view that only the experts, the police, the forces of law and order can handle the drug problem. But the problem clearly exceeds the capabilities of the best trained "TNT" (Tactical Narcotics Team) units which sweep a neighborhood clean of dealers one week, only to lose it the next, or the DEA, which was recently forced out of Medellin, Columbia. The problem is that the cultural economy of the day has so valorized the logistics, demonized the agents, and devalued the victims of the drug problem that we have lost sight of its all too human face.

To compensate, some alternative facts and histories are needed. Tobacco, an addictive drug, kills over 300,000 people a year, alcohol kills 100,000 (including those killed by drunk drivers), while the use of all illegal drugs combined – cocaine, heroin, marijuana, angel dust, LSD, etc. – accounted for less than 4,000 deaths in 1987.[42] From the latest available figures (1989), the use of illegal drugs in the United States is declining. Yet the war on drugs continues to escalate. This can be explained, I believe, only in the larger context of past examples of when US strategic interests intersected with the interests of the drug trade. Some would claim that the US became entangled in the drug web; others that we helped spin it.[43] The web-spinning theorists claim that we not only inherited the Vietnam war from the French, but also the opium trade which the French intelligence service, SDECE, had used to finance and win the support of Hmong tribesmen from the Vietnamese highlands in the struggle against the Vietminh guerillas. Even earlier, from 1948 on, the CIA had supposedly used drug smuggling routes and trade in the Golden Triangle to disguise intelligence and paramilitary operations against the Chinese Communists. It is also claimed that some of the players who later showed up in the Iran—Contra affair first perfected the guns—drugs—secret-warfare matrix in Laos in the 1960s, when Theodore Shackley was station chief of the CIA in Ventianne, General John Singlaub was chief of the SOG (Studies and Operations Group) which carried out secret raids into Laos, and Thomas Clines, also of the CIA, worked with (then) Lt Colonel Secord to run covert air-supply missions. The Iran—Contra hearings also revealed other drug connections, with the DEA involved in the hostage ransom attempt in Lebanon, and the CIA use of the Santa Elena airstrip in Costa Rica for the transshipment of illegal drugs and weapons.[44] There is a substantial body of evidence that leads one to conclude that agencies of the US government have at various times colluded with narcotics trafficking. At the very least, since about 1960 narco-terrorism has been mainly perceived as a minor strategic threat and as a sometime ally in the battle against (what was seen then as) the much larger danger of communism.[45]

My own suspicion is that narco-terrorism was finally taken seriously — if not hysterically — because it had taken on characteristics of a major transnational conglomerate rather than primitive capitalism, with a commensurate increase in political power.[46] In Columbia, the source of 80 percent of the cocaine that reaches the United States, right-wing paramilitary squads, Marxist guerrilla groups, and two major drug cartels have used drug profits to build up power bases that seriously challenged the sovereignty of the Columbian government. We have heard much of how the *narcotraficantes* have killed over 300 judges and court employees since 1981, and more recently, assassinated several candidates for president. Less often reported is the number of jobs, homes, health services, soccer fields, earthquake relief, and schools supplied by the *narcos* — amenities that the state cannot provide.[47] For many peasants they provide a cash crop, and more importantly, a transportation system that can get the "produce" to its far-flung markets. The *narcos* do not — could not — rule by terror alone: their notorious option of "plomo or plato" (lead or silver) captures this dual strategy. As war is for most states, terrorism is for the *narcos* the *ultima ratio* of their burgeoning agribusiness empire. Providing a relatively lucrative living for everyone from the subsistence farmer to the ghetto dealer — along with bribes for the underpaid police or military officer — is as important a source of power as the threat or use of terrorism. That many of the amnestied Columbian "druglords" have been able to set themselves up in well-appointed "prison-haciendas" attests to this power.

Hence, the much ballyhooed solution of beating narco-terrorism by anti-terrorism is certain to fail, as are schemes to make interdiction and eradication the top priority.[48] The same plan was used with marijuana, which simply resulted in an increase in domestic production as well as in the potency of the marijuana supply. There are already signs that the other Columbian drug cartels, like the Cali combine, are feeling the heat, and moving operations into Brazil, Bolivia and Ecuador. And even if we could someday develop the equivalent of a Narcotics Defense Initiative to shield the United States from foreign-produced narcotics, designer and synthetic drugs could quickly fill the void.[49] Narco-terrorism will not be stopped until the supply *and* demand of illegal narcotics are stopped, which means that the US must provide treatment and education, substitute businesses and jobs in the American cities, and crop alternatives to coca as well as an infrastructure of credit and roads in the Latin American countries. For political and economic reasons, that is unlikely to happen in the near future. The worst-case scenario, then, would be for incarceration, the preferred drug treatment program in the US, to be exported as foreign policy. The legal principle of *posse comitatus* against the military making arrests as well as taking on policing duties will be further eroded as actions are taken, through sanctions, surveillance, and even perhaps blockades, to imprison "criminal" nation-states.

STATE TERRORISM

If one were to parachute back into the early 1980s, attend a White House briefing, sit through a State Department news conference, or read Robert Gates's testimony (but not his critics') in the *New York Times*, one could walk away with the impression that terrorism was a violent activity orchestrated, supplied, and executed by a semi-permanent coterie of pariah states, among them Libya, North Korea, Iran, Syria, and the Soviet Union. In this period, "terrorism," over-used and lacking rhetorical sufficiency, had begun to show all the signs of semantic bleaching. Conservative spokespersons like Jeane Kirkpatrick, main-stream word-smiths like Claire Sterling, and White House spin-masters reissued and circulated a new term: *state terrorism*, by which they meant – among many other things – "premeditated, politically motivated violence perpetrated against noncombatant targets by clandestine state agents."[50]

What got lost in this ideological/semantical shuffle was a long history of state rule by terror: in modern times, Hitlerite Germany, Stalinist Russia, Suharto's Indonesia, Argentina's "Dirty War," Idi Amin's Uganda, Pol Pot's Khmer Rouge ... the list goes on. And today, South Korea, South Africa, and the People's Republic of China stand out as examples of how states − communist or capitalist in their economy but politically dictatorial − regularly resort to violent intimidation and political murder to maintain and further their power. Enhanced by a security, police, or military apparatus, internal state violence − or what we might generally call *endo-terrorism* − has achieved a much higher body count than any other form of terrorism. But Kirkpatrick and Antiterrorism, Inc., have a different form of terrorism in mind: state *exo-terrorism*. Defined as state-supported kidnapping, hostage-taking, or murder by proxy terrorists, state exo-terrorism is for the most part seen as a Middle Eastern continuation of war by condemnatory means: the motivations and actions of the terrorist groups that bombed the "Labelle" discotheque in Berlin, seized the cruise ship *Achille Lauro* and killed Leon Klinghoffer, hijacked TWA Flight 847 and killed Navy diver Robert Stethem, and kidnapped and killed Marine Lieutenant Colonel Higgins are defined and countered through their links to Libya's Khaddafi, Syrian intelligence, Iranian fundamentalist leaders, or with Moscow in the background. Secretary of State Shultz put it bluntly in a policy address: "States that support and sponsor terrorist actions have managed in recent years to co-opt and manipulate the terrorist phenomenon in pursuit of their own strategic goals."[51]

But if we stick to the strict definition of state exo-terrorism, would we not also need to include US sponsorship of the Contras, the delivery of missiles to the mujahideen, the 1985 mid-air "hijacking" by F-14s of the Egyptian airliner carrying the *Achille Lauro* terrorists, the 1986 "assassination" attempt on Khaddafi by US F-111s, the 1987 "kidnapping" of suspected terrorist Fawaz Younis in international waters off Cyprus?[52] Is it only a matter of scale that separates legitimate state violence from illegitimate state terrorism? The official position is that US violence is defensive, retaliatory, and − hopefully − deterring. But can a mere prefix − the *anti* before "our" terrorism − support the distinction?

ANTI-TERRORISM

The construction and maintenance of an unambiguous boundary between terrorism and anti-terrorism has become a preeminent function of the modern state. In the 1985 policy address, an indefinite "we" are told by Secretary of State Shultz that the distinction is self-evident, once "we" settle on "our" definition of terrorism:

We cannot afford to let an Orwellian corruption of language obscure our understanding of terrorism. We know the difference between terrorists and freedom fighters, and as we look around the world, we have no trouble telling one from the other.[53]

If the definition of terrorism is the primary semantic battlefield in the struggle for international legitimacy, the delimitation of terrorism from anti-terrorism has became its bloodiest strategic site.[54] The official side of this struggle is embodied in the proliferation of anti-terrorist forces. Just about all of the major as well as many of the smaller powers have developed such elite anti-terrorist units: the Israeli *Sayaret Matkal*, the German *Grenzschutzgruppe 9* (Border Protection Group 9) or GSG9, and the British Special Air Service or SAS, are among the more successful ones − if we are to judge by the movies made of their hostage rescues in Entebbe, Mogadishu, and London.[55] So far, however, Hollywood has shown little interest in the exploits of the US anti-terrorist unit, Delta Force, which gained the wrong kind of publicity in Operation Eagle Claw, the 1980 rescue attempt in Iran that ended in a calamity of malfunctioning helicopters, colliding aircraft, eight dead − and no one rescued.[56]

But a closer, colder scrutiny of the terrorist/anti-terrorist distinction reveals an ambiguity that both sides of the divide have sought to eliminate. This has been most tragically borne out in the killing ruins of Beirut, where all the violent players − state, anti-state, and non-state − seem to pause from their endless cycles of violence only long enough to argue who struck the first blow when, and thus to determine who is the *real* terrorist and the *real* anti-terrorist. Israel, Syria, Iran and their Lebanese understudies reach back to originating myths (of "Judea and Samara," a "Greater Syria," or the "*dar al-Islam*" of the *jihad*) to justify their own actions − a "surgical" air strike, an indiscriminate shelling, a refugee camp massacre, a car-bombing, or a kidnapping − as an anti-terrorist action taken against terrorist foes.

At a less abstract, much more personal level, the distinction between retaliation and revenge, deterrent and destructive violence, combatant and noncombatant becomes almost meaningless. When asked by a visiting Arab-American delegation to release their hostages because they were innocent, the Hizballah captors of US citizens Joseph Cicippio and Terry Anderson replied that their family members killed by sixteen-inch shells from the US battleship *New Jersey* in 1984 and American bombs dropped from American planes piloted by Israelis had been just as innocent.[57] When terrorism persists, when its acts of violence intensify,

accelerate, and accumulate, the word games behind it become super-
annuated. People *forget* the originary reasons, and blood feuds and
revenge cycles take over. In "civilized" countries, it often becomes the
task of intelligence agencies to carry out the "necessary" retributions
that the public would not or could not sanctify. Cases like the Israeli's
secret assassination campaign against PLO agents (that mistakenly killed
an innocent Palestinian in Norway), former CIA director William Casey's
support for the car-bombing of Sheikh Fadlallah (the bomb missed him
but killed 80 others), a Lebanese leader of Shiism implicated in the
bombing of the Marine barracks and the kidnapping and murder of
CIA station chief William Buckley, or the KGB's retaliatory kidnapping
and mutilation of a relative of Hizballah terrorists (resulting in the
release of three Soviet envoys) are only the exposed skirmishes of what
is probably a much deeper and wider intelligence war.[58] In "*de*-civilized"
countries, like Lebanon, Columbia, and El Salvador, where feudal terror
resurfaced and spread, anti-terrorist forces did not solve the terrorist
"problem": they became just one among many warring militias and
guerrilla groups.

PURE TERRORISM

Very little attention has been paid to the relationship between the
nuclear balance of terror and modern terrorism. A few experts in the
field have envisaged an ultimate bonding of the two, where a handful of
terrorists steal or make their own nuclear device – or chemical weapon,
biological contagion, or computer virus – to hold millions at a time
hostage. But it is another kind of terrorist fusion – not this think-
tank, worst-case scenario of what could be called "hyper-terrorism" –
that warrants serious consideration.

First, we need to consider a possible paradox: has the nuclear stalemate,
by bringing into an already violent family of nations a guarantee of
limited peace – or more precisely, a state of non-war based on massive
retaliation – served as the step-father to conventional terrorism? Historical parallels with another epoch point toward a possible answer. The
classic foundations of colonization – a new mobility of power, technological superiority, and the cultivation of a pervasive fear of retribution –
reappeared as attributes of the superpower system of nuclear terror.
And like earlier apologists of colonization, those who have made a
dogma of nuclear deterrence celebrate the stasis of a nuclear "peace"
while denying any responsibility for the displacement of persistent

rivalries and conflicts into new forms of violence.[59] Social critic Paul Virilio has tenaciously pursued this trend toward, in his words, *pure war*, declaring that "The art of deterrence, prohibiting political war, favors the upsurge, not of conflicts, but of *acts of war without war*."[60] In the global pure war that ensued, terrorism has emerged as its most virulent expression, triggering in turn an antibody reaction, anti-terrorism, that has proven, I believe, to be more devastating than the original "infection."

Socio-terrorists and anarcho-terrorists may of course claim, as did the Red Brigades in Italy and the Tupamaros in Uruguay, that this is the very purpose of terrorism — to reveal the repressive face of the state. However, this moral imperative of terrorism, treated as a truth that can only be proven by deed, is exposed as nothing more than a blood-soaked truism when the state provoked reveals its violent core once again — and nothing changes. To be sure, at world-historical moments like the French, Russian or Chinese revolutions, when governments lose the ability and the will to rule (usually in the aftermath of a major war) and some other group, class, or people is mobilized and ready to take power, then terrorism can indeed take on an important and usually spectacular role in transforming societies. But it should be clear from the weight of the cases outlined above that the heroics of terrorism, acting as a substitute for a mass movement, have only served to fortify the worst aspects of the modern state: its propensity for surveillance and secrecy, vigilantism and surrogate violence.[61] To push the family analogy one step further: fostered by the displacement of superpower violence, and orphaned by the masses in whose name they act, the modern terrorist in some ways resembles the repressed child who grows up into a serial killer, unable to distinguish the guilty parent from the innocent bystander. Conversely — sometimes perversely — we constitute and preserve our own "normalcy" by the terrorist's deviance.

This is not to belittle the moral turpitude of the terrorist — or the oppressive, alienating conditions that can give rise to terrorism. It is, rather, to highlight how pervasive and potentially universal terrorism — in all its guises — really is. As I stated at the outset, the fact that terrorism kills people should not be buried under a pile of words. But, contrary to prevailing moral *and* materialist views, the meaning and power of terrorism will not be found — to put it morbidly — under a pile of its victims. A new form of *pure terrorism*, as immaterial and diffuse as Virilio's pure war, has emerged as an international political crisis in which the violent intimidation and manipulation of a global media audience creates a pervasive state of insecurity and fear. This means that the critical production and distribution of the terrorist threat is not *territorial*, as is the case in conventional war, but *temporal*: its power is increasingly derived from the instantaneous representation and diffusion of violence by a global communication network. But before anyone assigns villainy to the disseminators of terrorist violence – as did former British Prime Minister Margaret Thatcher when she repeatedly called the media the "oxygen of terrorism" – they should recognize the *receptive* and *interpretive* power of a mass audience for whom (and often in whose name) terrorist rituals of violence are committed.[62]

Take again the bracketing terrorist acts of the 1980s: the murders of Aldo Moro and Colonel Higgins. Of the Red Brigade kidnapping of Moro, Claire Sterling wrote that "For speed, mobility, reconnaissance, logistics, staying power, and refinements in psychological warfare, it was a matchless performance."[63] True, but in stating the obvious she misses the more important point. "The real terror network" does not go through Moscow or Libya or Iran, but through a non-place, a cyberspace that reproduces and contextualizes the terrorist act for the global audience. In a manner, Sterling mimics the terrorist, attributing a surplus of power to the "heroic" individual as the author of violence, when it is the interventionist power of governments, the representational practices of the media, and the conformist interpretations of the audience that reconstitute and magnify the force of terrorism. The day after the Red Brigades released the photograph of Moro holding the 20 April issue of *La Repubblica* in his hands, it appeared on the front pages of over 45 major newspapers around the world.[64] I am sure that the video of Colonel Higgins hanging from a noose "captured" an even wider audience. The journey from the original terrorist deed to its propagandized destiny remains, I believe, the most important and under-studied area of terrorism.[65]

THE FUTURE: POST-MODERN OR NEO-MEDIEVAL?

In the Middle Ages, power was fragmented along overlapping lines of religious, class, and national loyalties; a tenuous order was regularly shaken and reconfigured by kidnappings, hostage-takings, and assassinations; and, aside from rare and brief rebellions, a peasant majority was terrorized into a fatalistic subservience. In the 1980s, we read of Latin American drug "lords" and their retinues, equipped with small arms, anti-tank weapons, and air forces, challenging the sovereignty of states;

of Shiite plots, hatched in Iran, to attack Israeli and American targets; and of warring fiefdoms in Lebanon, one side calling on Christian nations to help break a five-month old sea blockade, the other side vowing to fight "the new crusade" and to kill hostages should any Western power intervene.[66] The end of the Cold War merely added to the violence, with the demise of a Soviet endo-colonization producing new forms of endo-terrorism in Armenia, Georgia, Rumania, and, worst of all, in Yugoslavia.

Is modern terrorism now a containable "crisis," or is it a telling sign of a major shift "back to the future," from a world order based on the eminent domain of nation states to a segmented and sectarian system of warring economic, religious, political powers? Is the continuing terrorization of global politics, especially in the Middle East, a harbinger of a re-territorialization, as was the religious and civil terror that presaged the Thirty Years War of the seventeenth century? Or, more likely, a post-modern simulacrum of the Middle Ages, to be played out in C^3I omni-deterrence centers, covered by ABC News simulations with Peter Jennings, and — if necessary — fought out with secret or mercenary armies? In short, not the global village of interdependency die-hards, but something between Disneyland and Beirut as the model for the new global castle of antidiplomacy?

These speculations run against the grain of peace-mongering that marked the end of the 1980s. Perhaps there *are* reasons to be more optimistic, to discern emerging alternatives to national identities built upon violent antipathies. As a sign of the fractured state of the world order, hope for global solutions — sometimes in the guise of a new nostalgia — has gained ground. Full of promise were the globalist adherents of *nove myshlenie* ("new thinking") that advised Gorbachev, the democratic parties in East/Central Europe, and the transnational social movements with various shades of Green in their politics.[67] More peculiar and still popular have been the New Age schemes, that range from the *est*-ian exhortations to think our way beyond war, to the apocalyptic musings of Ronald Reagan, that took on a science fiction character at one of his last question and answer sessions when he spoke longingly for the arrival of a *truly* alien threat to bring the world together in a final fight for good against evil.[68]

Contrary to the globalists, I believe that there are — and there will remain — irreconcilable differences and *many* evils at large in the world. Hence my hopes are on a smaller scale and come with a longer time span. For alternative models to terrorism for national liberation, social change, and other forms of self-determination, I look to the remarkable beginnings (yet incomplete accomplishments) of the Palestinian *intifada*, the journey of the Baltic national movements from underground to parliamentary status, the self-liberation of Central and Eastern Europe, and the fledgling democratization of formerly repressive regimes in Latin America. In these cases terrorism was confronted in all its forms and rejected in favor of a (relatively) non-violent resistance. They have done more to devalue the currency of terrorism than all of the official dealers in the anti/terrorist discourse. They also provide, I might add, an important lesson for everyone who profits by the terrorist discourse, a lesson once taught by history's most famous practitioner of non-violence who upon discovering that his house of prayer had become a den of thieves left the chief priests alone — but threw out all the moneychangers.

But we are left with a much more secular concern: What to do? I have no global solution for the problem — and I would hope that the diverse and complex array of terrorism that I have presented in this chapter serves as a sufficient repudiation of national policy-makers *and* global salvationists who think that there is one. We can no more remedy the problem of terrorism than we can wipe out difference in the world; and were that possible, it would lead not toward a better world but a *final* solution. Alternatively, I offer in this chapter a much more modest yet potentially radical prospect, that through the deconstruction of the terrorist discourse we make possible a new constructive power to mediate antidiplomatic violence.

Notes

1   We have already noted how terrorism was on the top of the agenda at the first National Security Council meeting of the Reagan administration, and a primary target of Bush's. For a breakdown and explanation of terrorist incidents from 1980 to 1988, see *Patterns of Global Terrorism: 1988* (Department of State Publication, March, 1989), pp. 1–11 and 85.

2   Probably the best of a very large lot is *Inside Terrorist Organizations*, edited by David Rapoport (New York: Columbia University Press, 1988). The Rand Corporation churns out an enormous amount of material on the subject, including the very helpful if intimidating (with over 3,500 entries from 1968 to the present) *Chronology of International Terrorism*. In the Rand collection, I found articles by Brian Jenkins on the multiple strategies of terrorism, Jeffrey Simon on the perception of terrorist threats, and Bruce Hoffman on extreme right-wing terrorism the most useful. For those who need a quarterly fix of terrorist discourse, there is *Terrorism: An International Journal*, edited by Yonah Alexander.

3   See Claire Sterling, *The Terror Network: The Secret War of International Terrorism* (New York: Holt, Rinehart, and Winston, 1981); Christopher

Dobson and Ronald Payne, *Terror! The West Fights Back* (London: Macmillan, 1982); Benjamin Netanyahu, *Terrorism: How the West Can Win* (New York: Farrar, Straus, Giroux, 1986); Yossi Melman, *The Master Terrorist: The True Story of Abu-Nidal* (New York: Avon Books, 1986): and *Fighting Back: Winning the War Against Terrorism*, edited by Neil C. Livingstone and Terrel E. Arnold (Lexington, MA: Lexington Books, 1986).

4 Paul Wilkinson's *Terrorism and the Liberal State* (London: Macmillan, 1977), Walter Laqueur's *Terrorism* (Boston: Little, Brown and Company, 1977), and *Terrorism, Legitimacy, and Power: The Consequences of Political Violence*, edited by Martha Crenshaw (Middletown, CT: Wesleyan University Press, 1983), are good examples of this genre. *Terrorism and International Order*, by Lawrence Freedman and other British international relations generalists (London: Royal Institute of International Affairs, 1986), offers a more philosophical and historical analysis. Official US policy in the eighties has vacillated between the conspiracy and liberal camps, but the most astute synthesis is Secretary of State Shultz's "Terrorism and the Modern World," an October 1984 address at the Park Avenue Synagogue in New York (Bureau of Public Affairs, Current Policy No. 629). For a critical examination of the liberal attitudes toward terrorism, see Richard Rubenstein's *Alchemists of Revolution: Terrorism in the Modern World* (New York: Basic Publishers, 1987); and for a refreshingly anarchistic view, see Noam Chomsky's *Pirates and Emperors: International Terrorism in the Real World* (New York: Claremont, 1986). Finally, I believe three works stand out from the crowd, effectively using literary theory and cultural analysis to say something new about terrorism: Robin Wagner-Pacifici's *The Moro Morality Play: Terrorism as Social Drama* (Chicago: University of Chicago Press, 1986); Khachig Tololyan's "Cultural Narrative and the Motivation of the Terrorist," in *Inside Terrorist Organizations*, pp. 217–33; and *Terrorism and Modern Drama*, edited by John Orr and Dragon Klaíc (Edinburgh: Edinburgh University Press, 1990).

5 *Taking the Stand: The Testimony of Lieutenant Colonel Oliver North* (New York: Pocket Books, 1987), pp. 26–7.

6 After Colonel Higgins's captors released the video of his hanging, 58% of those polled were for negotiations, 39% against; 40% supported a commando rescue attempt even if lives might be lost, while 50% were opposed; and 33% advocated the bombing of terrorist hideouts in Lebanon even if innocent people were killed, while 60% were against it. See *Time*, 14 August 1989, p. 15.

7 This is something I attempted to show in chapter 4.

8 Shultz, "Terrorism and the Modern World," pp. 5–6.

9 Hedley Bull, "International Relations as an Academic Pursuit," *Australian Outlook* (26, no. 3, December 1972), pp. 264–5. While I clearly believe current world politics fully warrant Bull's *classical* stance of "political nihilism," I believe it can be positively supplemented by "post-classical" or "post-modern" approaches. Against charges that post-modernist and post-structuralist approaches are nihilist (like classical realism?), I have found the best theoretical defense to be William Connolly's account of a "projectional interpretation" that:

> draws part of its sustenance from an always-already-operative attachment to life as a protean set of possibilities exceeding the terms of any

identity into which it is set ... It then strives to thaw perspectives which tend to stay frozen within a particular way of life, to offer alternative accounts of threats to difference created by the dogmatism of established identities, and to advance different accounts of danger and possibilities crowded out by established regimes of thought.
(From "The Irony of Interpretation," *Politics and Irony*, edited by John Seery and Daniel Conway, St Martin's Press, 1992).

10   William Hazlitt, quoted in *The Complete Works of Shakespeare* (London: Collins, 1981), p. 277.

11   The expansion and acceleration of interdependence was recently highlighted in an event that warranted only a few inches in the *New York Times* (7 January 1990, p. 15), when world financial markets dipped on the news (later proven false) that Gorbachev had cancelled some upcoming meetings with foreign leaders to deal with domestic problems. For theoretical analysis of radical changes in international relations, see Paul Virilio, *Defense populaire et luttes ecologiques* (Paris: Editions Galilée, 1978); R. B. J. Walker, *One World, Many Worlds: Struggles for a Just World Peace* (Boulder, CO, 1988); and chapters 6 and 7 below.

12   "Semiotics" in this context refers to systems of sign usage – including words, visual images, codes, or any signifying practices ("languages") – that convey relations of power and constitute meaning.

13   For those still unfamiliar (or just familiar enough to be contemptuous) with "deconstruction," it can be described as a skeptical (or in some hands, subversive) reading of "texts" – any verbal or nonverbal sign-systems – that elicits the paradoxes, indeterminacy, and contradictions of any language-generated reality.

14   With an additional dash of hyperbole, French social critic Jean Baudrillard levels a similar charge: "Hence the stupidity and the obscenity of all that is reported about the terrorists: everywhere the wish to palm off meaning on them, to exterminate them with meaning which is more effective than the bullets of specialized commandoes ..." See "Our Theater of Cruelty," *In the Shadow of the Silent Majorities and other essays* (New York: Semiotext(e), 1983), p. 117.

15   *New York Times*, 25 June, 1985, p. 1. More recently and in (unusually) clearer prose, former Secretary of State Alexander Haig echoed Weinberger in an editorial article: "We cannot allow a hostage crisis to paralyze the Government to the neglect of everything else ... But it is crucial to realize that we are in a war – a twilight war, to be sure, a war of unusual tactics – but one that requires continuing, strenuous efforts, not just a spasmodic reaction to the headlines." (*New York Times*, 15 August 1989, p. 21).

16   Weinberger's belief that the US should not use military force unless fully supported by the American people and Congress and only as a "last resort" became a matter of public record after his 18 November 1984 speech to the National Press Club. This view would seem to preclude pre-emptive or retaliatory anti-terrorist operations, and, indeed, Weinberger was opposed to the sending of the Marines to Lebanon *and* the hijacking by F-14 Tomcats of the Egyptian plane carrying the *Achille Lauro* terrorists. In his major statement on terrorism Secretary of State Shultz was much less equivocal on the equation of war with terrorism and the need for military retaliation: "We now recognize that terrorism is being used by our adversaries

as a modern tool of warfare. It is no aberration. We can expect more
terrorism directed at our strategic interests around the world in the years
ahead. To combat it, we must be willing to use military force." See Jane
Mayer and Doyle McManus, *Landslide: The Unmaking of the President,
1984–1988* (Boston: Houghton Mifflin, 1988), pp. 52–4, 140–2; and
Shultz, "Terrorism and the Modern World," p. 5.

17 Brian Jenkins, *International Terrorism: The Other World War* (Santa
Monica, CA: Rand, 1985), p. 12.

18 Although it is obvious that I am referring to *international* war and *international* terrorism, I have avoided the word because it is a misnomer: war
and terrorism fought on individual, tribal, class and other terrain can have
multi-level effects. Probably *global* is a better modifier for the phenomena
under discussion, but I do not want arbitrarily to delimit the area to be
investigated.

19 For a persuasive account of the roots of violence in "mimetic desire," and
the historical attempt to control violence in substitutive rituals of sacrifice,
see René Girard, *Violence and the Sacred* (Baltimore, MD: Johns Hopkins
University Press, 1977).

20 For instance, see Georges Sorel's study of how the myth of violent collective
action in the form of a general strike can act as a revolutionary force, in his
Reflections on Violence, trans. T. E. Hulme and J. Roth (New York:
Collier, 1961).

21 See N. Cohn, *The Pursuit of the Millennium* (London: Paladin, 1970);
David Rapoport, "Fear and Trembling: Terrorism in Three Religious
Traditions," *American Political Science Review*, 38, 3 (September, 1984),
pp. 658–77.

22 *New York Times*, 17 June 1906. The setting up of a modern counterpart
was also noted by the *New York Times* (9 December 1988), p. 14:

Anti-Terror Unit To Talk Strategy

... The assembly, commonly known as the "Trevi" group after their
signing of the European Convention for the Prevention of Terrorism,
will primarily deal with problems that have arisen concerning the
extradition of terrorists.

23 Although Richard Rubenstein presumes in the label of "anarcho-
communism" what needs to be historically demonstrated, his opening
chapter to *Alchemists of Revolution*, "The Bogeyman, the Hero, and the
Guy Next Door," is the best study to date of the complex psychological,
political, and historical factors behind terrorism.

24 Sergey Nechaev, "Catechism of the Revolutionist," in *The Terrorism Reader*,
edited by W. Laqueur and Y. Alexander (New York: Penguin, 1987),
pp. 68–72.

25 See Laqueur, *Terrorism Reader*, pp. 47–9 and pp. 395–7, for useful
bibliographical notes.

26 Saint-Just, *Fragments sur les institutions republicaines*, edited by A. Soboul
(Turin: Einaudi, 1952), p. 49, quoted by F. E. and F. P. Manuel, *Utopian
Thought in the Western World* (Oxford: Blackwell, 1974), p. 567.

27 W. Laqueur, *Terrorism* (London: Weidenfeld and Nicolson, 1978), p. 17.

28 Karl Marx, *Political Writings Volume III*, "The Civil War in France"

(New York: Vintage, 1974), pp. 228–31.

29 Ibid., p. 230.

30 Leon Trotsky, "Terrorism and Communism," *The Basic Writings of Trotsky*, edited by Irving Howe (New York: Vintage Books, 1965), pp. 142–53.

31 Ibid., p. 146.

32 Ibid., p. 151.

33 V. I. Lenin, "Where to Begin?", in *Selected Works* (Moscow: Progress Publishers, 1968), pp. 38–9.

34 Ibid., p. 459.

35 See also Lenin's 1920 essay, "Left-Wing Communism – An Infantile Disorder," in which he attacks the "Socialist-Revolutionary Party" since it "considered itself particularly 'revolutionary', or 'Left' because of its recognition of individual terrorism, assassination – something that we Marxists emphatically rejected." *Selected Works*, p. 521.

36 See Leon Trotsky, *Their Morals and Ours* (New York: Pathfinder Press, 1969), where he uses the exigencies of the civil war to defend the Decree of 1919 – which called for taking hostages of relatives of commanders suborned from the Czar's Army – against "the institution of family hostages [by which] Stalin compels those Soviet diplomats to return from abroad" (p. 37–9).

37 See, for example, Eric Wolf, *Peasant Wars of the Twentieth Century* (New York: Harper and Row, 1969).

38 Franz Fanon, *The Wretched of the Earth* (Harmondsworth, UK: Penguin, 1967).

39 Judging from the pre-history of the key players, like Shackley, Clines, and Secord, re-exposed in the Iran–Contra affair, it would seem that fiction rang truer than fact, or at least Eliot Abram's version of it.

40 *Arizona Republic*, 7 April 1989, p. 1. Less humorous and more threatening to civil liberties is the single-mindedness of US Democrats and Republicans on the threat of narco-terrorism. Senators Joseph Biden (Democrat, Delaware), and William Cohen (Republican, Maine) have co-sponsored a bill to establish a "Counter-Narcotics Technology Assessment Center" (CONTAC). It's task would be to "coordinate research into high-technology anti-drug-trafficking techniques, including surveillance, advanced computers, artificial intelligence, and chemical and biological detection systems." See William Uncapher, "Trouble in Cyberspace: Civil Liberties at Peril in the Information Age," the *Humanist* (September/October 1991), pp. 10–11.

41 See *The International Narcotics Control Strategy Report* (Department of State Publication, March 1989). It is interesting to note that the United States is not included in the "Country and Regional Summaries" (pp. 19–24), nor in the list of "Worldwide Production Totals" (p. 15), in spite of the fact that the United States' annual rate of marijuana production rose during the 1980s to rival Columbia and Mexico as a major supplier. Since Section 481(h)(2)(A) of the Anti-Drug Abuse Acts of 1986 and 1988 requires that the President certify whether major drug producing and drug transit countries have "cooperated fully" with the United States "to enforce to the maximum extent possible the elimination of illicit cultivation," the question arises whether the US should cut off aid to itself, or at least the marijuana-producing states within the US.

42 See *International Narcotics Control Strategy Report*; and Michael Massing, "Dealing with the Drug Horror," *New York Review of Books*, 30 March 1989, pp. 22–6. The *New York Times* does, however, report a rise in police officers killed in drug-related incidents to 14, out of a total of 78 for 1988 ("A Record 14 Officers Killed in '88 in Drug Incidents," 3 September 1989, p. 22). See also Michael Massing, "Noriega in Miami," *The Nation* (2 December 1991), pp. 697–704.

43 A sampling of this school would include Alfred McCoy's classic study, *The Politics of Heroin in Southeast Asia* (New York: Harper and Row, 1972); Peter Maas, *Manhunt: The Incredible Pursuit of a CIA Agent Turned Terrorist* (New York: Random House, 1986); Edward S. Herman, *The Real Terror Network: Terrorism in Fact and Propaganda* (Boston: Southend Press, 1982); and Jonathon Kwitney's *Crimes of Patriots* (New York: Norton, 1987).

44 See *Report of the Congressional Committees Investigating the Iran–Contra Affair* (Random House, 1988), pp. 130–1 and pp. 318–21.

45 Both narco-terrorism and the war against it can also be the occasion for insurgency and counter-insurgency on the sly: Juan E. Mendez, executive director of Americas Watch, has recently reported on the collusion between the Columbian military and the drug cartels in attacks on members and sympathizers of the leftist group *Union Patriotica* and guerilla movements (*New York Times*, 31 August 1989). In Peru, it would appear that the Maoist group *Sendero Luminoso* (Shining Path) has set up protection "rackets" with coca growers and tactical alliances with narco-traffickers. See also Eduardo Gamarra, "Militarizing Narcotics War may Threaten Latin Democracies," *Orlando Sentinel* (26 May 1991), p. G-1; Laura Brooks, "US Military Extends Drug War into Central America," *Christian Science Monitor* (25 June 1991), p. 1; and Charles Gepp, "US, Peru Sign New Anti-Drug Pact," (16 May 1991), p. 28.

46 President Bush confirmed this suspicion six months later in a speech, in which he stated that the cocaine cartels "are taking on the pretensions of a geopolitical force" and so "they must be dealt with as such by our military." Address by George Bush at the Commonwealth Club of San Francisco, 7 February 1990 (White House Office text). The most sophisticated argument for a non-military solution to the drug problem comes from Ethan Nadelmann, "US Drug Policy a Bad Export," *Foreign Policy* (Spring 1988), pp. 83–108.

47 See Michael Massing, "Dealing with the Drug Horror."

48 The State Department's Bureau of International Narcotics Matters spends about $100 million a year, of which only $3.6 million goes to crop-substitution and development assistance, while $45 million goes to eradicating crops, and $35 million on law enforcement and interdiction. See Massing, "Dealing with the Drug Horror."

49 One folly could well beget another: on 18 May 1989, the *Washington Times* reported that "House Democrats said yesterday that they will try next week to take money from President Bush's Strategic Defense Initiative research to pay for full funding of the war on illegal drugs." (p. 2). See also "In Drug War DoD Forces Had to Learn to Walk, but Now are Running," Jack Dorsey, *Sea Power* (January 1991), p. 76.

50 *Patterns of Global Terrorism: 1988*, p. v.

51 Shultz, "Terrorism and the Modern World," Current Policy No. 629, p. 2. President Reagan added some hyperbolic flourishes to say much the same thing at an address to the American Bar Association in July, 1985:

So, there we have it: Iran, Libya, North Korea, Cuba, Nicaragua — continents away, tens of thousands of miles apart, but the same goals and objectives. I submit to you that the growth in terrorism in recent years results from the increasing involvement of these states in terrorism in every region of the world ... [A]nd we're especially not going to tolerate these attacks from outlaw states run by the strangest collection of misfits, looney tunes, and squalid criminals since the advent of the Third Reich.

(Quoted from "The New Network of Terrorist States," Bureau of Public Affairs, Current Policy No. 721, pp. 2—3).

52 See, in particular, the section of the CIA's Nicaragua manual, *Psychological Operations in Guerilla Warfare* (republished by Random House in 1985), on "Implicit and Explicit Terror," which instructs the Contras to "Kidnap all officials or agents of the Sandinista government and replace them" (pp. 52—5).

53 Shultz, "Terrorism and the Modern World," p. 3.

54 Although "anti-terrorism" and "counter-terrorism" are often used inter-changeably in both the official and academic terrorist discourses, I prefer to use only the term "anti-terrorism" to describe violent operations against terrorism. *Counter*-terrorism (the preferred term of the US State Department) implies, I believe, a competing structure (in the manner that Gramsci refers to a "counter-hegemony" or Foucault to a "counter-justice") that could, or intends to take the place of terrorism, although the stated policy is to deter and if possible *negate* terrorism rather than replace it with something else. For the official US policy of counter-terrorism — based on no concessions, and retaliation, legal prosecution, and law enforcement assistance — see the introduction to *Patterns of Global Terrorism*, pp. iii—iv. For a theoretical discussion of the anti/counter distinction, see A. Gramsci, *Selections from Prison Notebooks*, trans. and edited by Q. Hoare and G. N. Smith (London: Lawrence and Wishart, 1971), pp. 206—76; and M. Foucault, "On Popular Justice: A Discussion with Maoists," in *Power/Knowledge*, edited by C. Gordon (New York: 1980), pp. 33—5.

55 Although the roles of anti-terrorist and counter-insurgency forces, as well as the rationales of low-intensity conflict and covert action often overlap, I will focus only on anti-terrorism since the other topics are well-covered elsewhere. For a reasonably sober-minded assessment of the various military units involved, see James Adams, *Secret Armies* (New York: Bantam Books, 1989); and for a more analytical account of the doctrine of low-intensity conflict, see Michael Klare and Peter Kornbluh (eds), *Low-Intensity Warfare* (New York: Pantheon, 1988).

56 Nor do you hear much in the anti-terrorist lore of the Egyptian attempt to rescue a hijacked airliner in Malta that resulted in 57 of the 98 passengers and crew dead. Anti-terrorism, like its evil *doppelgänger*, relies heavily on the myth of invincibility; hence, much is made of its vaunted capabilities, and very little of its shortcomings — except through the blatant failures or occasional press leak.

57 "The Captors' Reasons," *New York Times*, 27 August 1989.

58 See Bob Woodward, *Veil: The Secret Wars of the CIA 1981–1987* (New York: Simon and Shuster, 1987), pp. 396–8, 416.
59 This begs the question of whether Western leaders have been too quick to dismiss as opportunist the claims of Southern leaders who have discerned a legitimating affinity between anti-colonial struggles and some modern forms of terrorism. A critical reading of the biennial UN General Assembly debates on international terrorism during the 1970s and 1980s could possibly shed some light on this question.
60 Paul Virilio, *Pure War* (New York: Semiotext(e), 1983), p. 27. See also Virilio's *Defense populaire et luttes ecologiques*, where he describes nuclear deterrence as being at the same time the catastrophic process of "une colonisation totale" (pp. 35–6).
61 "One cannot use violence against what is already violence, one can only reinforce it, take it to extremes – in other worlds, to the State's maximum power." Virilio, *Pure War*, p. 51.
62 We can find a sociological, historical and political equivalent to this diabolical conformity, to this evil demon of conformity, in the modern behaviour of the masses who are also very good at complying with the models offered to them, who are very good at reflecting the objectives imposed on them, thereby absorbing and annihilating them. There is in this conformity a force of seduction in the literal sense of the word, a force of diversion, distortion, capture and ironic fascination. There is a kind of fatal strategy of conformity.
     See Jean Baudrillard, *The Evil Demon of Images* (Sydney: Power Institute, 1987).
63 Sterling, *The Terror Network*, p. 80.
64 Actually Moro's hands are not visible, which at the time raised some doubts of the authenticity of the photograph. The artist Sarah Charlesworth has captured this terrorist cybernet in her presentation of 45 photographic facsimile of newspapers that carried the image of the hostage Moro. Part of a much larger series, *Modern History* (1977–79), the collection was at New York's International Center of Photography in the summer of 1989. In the exhibition she goes beyond the obvious, Sterlingesque point that the Red Brigades made effective use of the media. Charlesworth's blanking out of all written text save the bannerheads of the newspapers reveals the power of context in terrorist discourse. For example, the Roman newspaper that originally received the photograph, *Il Messaggero*, filled two-thirds of the front page with it, with no other news pictures to distract the reader, while *l'Unita*, the newspaper of the Italian Communist Party, ran a much smaller one with two other photos of the forces of law and order, the *carabinieri*, busy at the scene. The London *Times* ran a small, tightly cropped photo of Moro, dwarfed by what *seems* to be a large photo of the Queen holding her new grandson, until one moves down the gallery wall, past the *Irish Times*, the *New York Times*, and the *Baltimore Sun* with multiple news photos as well, to the Toronto *Globe and Mail* which has the smiling monarch blown up three times the size of Moro. Stripped of the verbal signs, the newspapers reveal their ability to impart powerful meanings before the first caption or article is attached, through the image's cropping, placement, size and relation to other photographs. The viewer/reader is drawn into the processs, to see how even the subtlest aspect of media

coverage of terrorism becomes an indispensable part of the re-territorialization of global political conflict.
65 To be sure, there are many works on media coverage of terrorism. For
    example, see Alex Schmid and Janny de Graaf, *Violence as Communication:
    Insurgent Terrorism and the Western News Media* (Beverly Hills, CA:
    Sage, 1982); and *Terrorist Spectaculars: Should TV Coverage be Curbed?*
    (New York: Priority, 1986). But I believe Jean Baudrillard is the first to get
    inside the relationship of the global audience, the media, and terrorism,
    what he sees to be a circle of simulation that is not only ruptured from
    material referents but now engendering a political *hyper*-reality. See *A
    l'ombre des majorités silencieuses* (Paris: Cahiers d'Utopie, 1978), *Simulacre
    et Simulation* (Paris: Galilée, 1981), and *Les Strategies fatales* (Paris: Bernard
    Grasset, 1983); the edited translations in the Foreign Agent series (New
    York: Semiotext(e), 1983), *In the Shadow of the Silent Majorities* and
    Simulations; or *Jean Baudrillard: Selected Writings*, edited by Mark Poster
    (Stanford, CA: Stanford University Press, 1988).
66 See "Columbians Seize Drug Ring Suspect and 134 Aircraft" (p. 1); "Egypt
    Arrest 41; Sees Shiite Plot" (p. 6); and "France Says It Plans No Military
    Role in Lebanon" (p. 7) in *New York Times*, 22 August 1989.
67 It would appear that anti-terrorism is fast becoming (after disarmament) a
    primary site for cooperation with the Soviet Union. Confronting an increase
    in terrorist incidents (for instance, Aeroflot has suffered at least 11 hijackings
    since 1973, compared to the next highest airlines, TWA, Air France, and
    Kuwaiti, which have all been hijacked twice), the Soviet Union has set up a
    new hostage rescue unit and called for more intelligence-sharing on terrorism
    with Interpol and the CIA. There have also been high-level discussions on
    how jointly to combat terrorism: in January 1989 a group of 10 American
    and 10 Soviet experts met in Moscow; in September 1989, Lt General
    Fjodor Sherbak, former deputy head of the KGB, and Maj. General Valentin
    Zvezdenkov, former head of KGB counter-terrorism, met at the Rand
    Corporation for closed-door talks with William Colby, former CIA Director,
    and Ray Cline, former CIA Deputy Director; and in 1990 Secretary of
    State James Baker and Soviet Foreign Minister Eduard Shevardnadze met
    to hold a second round of official talks on terrorism. See Glenn Schoen and
    J. Derleth, "KGB Fields New Hostage Rescue Unit," *Armed Forces Journal
    International* (October 1989), p. 22; and Robin Wright, "US and Soviets
    Seek Joint War on Terrorism," *Los Angeles Times*, p. 1.
68 The speech was to the National Strategy Forum in Chicago in May, 1988,
    and his response was to someone who asked what he thought was the most
    important unsolved problem in international relations. The last part of his
    reply was:
        But I've often wondered what if all of us in the world discovered that
        we were threatened by a power from outer space — from another
        planet. Wouldn't we all of a sudden find that we didn't have any
        differences between us at all — we were all human beings, citizens of
        the world — wouldn't we come together to fight that particular threat?

SPEED

6

THE (S)PACE OF INTERNATIONAL RELATIONS

Speed is the essence of war.
                              Sun Tzu, *The Art of War*

There is more to life than increasing its speed.
                   Gandhi, "Banana Republic" advertisement

SPEED: THE FINAL FRONTIER

In 1909 Filippo Marinetti gave notice in his famous *Futurist Manifesto* of an avant-garde movement for the modern industrial state: "The Futurist writer will make use of *free verse*, an orchestration of images and sounds in motion to express our contemporary life, intensified by the speeds made possible by steam and electricity, on land, on the seas, and in the air."[1]

To break out of the inertia of the prison-state as well as the prison-house of language, the Futurists exalted in paintings the image of the masses in perpetual motion, in race cars, airplanes, and city streets; and in poetry and manifestos the emancipation of words from syntax, punctuation, the requirements of reason itself. Paintings and writings bore titles like *Dynamic Expansion + Speed* and *Technical Manifesto of Futurism*. The technology and "polyphony" of the urban space was their church and litany. The Futurists soon feel victim to their project of marrying an ideology of the avant-garde with art-in-action, which in Italy in the 1920s meant falling in with Mussolini's Fascist movement. But they burned brightly in that period, and they powerfully illuminated a new force in modern industrialized societies: speed.

In this chapter and the next I present and test the proposition that international relations is shifting from a realm defined by sovereign places, impermeable borders and rigid geopolitics, to a site of accelerating flows, contested borders, and fluid chronopolitics. In short, pace displacing space. I turn to one thinker in particular to explain this development: Paul Virilio. He has almost single-handedly brought the issue of speed back into political and social theory. Trained as an architect, Virilio has curated museum exhibitions, studied military strategy, and written several remarkable books on topics that range from the deterritorialization of international politics to the relationship of war to cinematic practices.[2] It is not my intention − and I doubt whether it is possible − to summarize the vast and diverse body of Virilio's work in a single chapter. However, given the obvious and growing importance of speed in international relations − from the velocitization of weapon delivery and concomitant decrease in human response time, the increase in speed and the decline in state control of the global flow of information and capital, the appearance of real-time representation and surveillance of the globe, to the acceleration of history itself − it does seem strange that Virilio's work has gone largely unnoticed in the discipline of international relations.[3]

To be sure, speed has gained some attention as a consequential factor in the disintegration of the Soviet bloc and the end of the Cold War. For example, the French IR specialist Dominique Moisi wrote that "Europe's renaissance is made possible by the historical encounter between the superpower fatigue that has been produced and accelerated by the arms race and European integration itself."[4] The Hungarian writer Mikios Vasarhelyi said of East Germany that "What was most surprising was the speed with which it happened."[5] A few journalists did take note that Mr Gorbachev's first and foremost slogan of economic reform was not glasnost or perestroika, but "Acceleration!" Yet there was little theoretical analysis of speed itself as a significant political factor.[6] North American IR theorists find "regimes" operating just about everywhere that they look: but they seem not to have noticed the "speed regime" seeking to regulate the process of reform that developed between the USSR and the United States. Prompted by the message of concern about the speed of Lithuanian independence that Bush sent to Gorbachev, one journalist did remark that "At a time when American interests have become increasingly entangled with Mr Gorbachev's political fortunes, Administration officials are privately expressing surprise, and apparently some frustration, that Mr Gorbachev has not gained more control over the pace of Lithuania's quest for independence."[7]

Yet another example would be the resistance of war planning to new factors of speed. Most intelligence experts had concluded by the end of 1989 that political changes in the Soviet Union and Eastern Europe, the pull-back of forward-based Soviet troops, and Soviet cuts in conventional arms would assure the US of one to three months' warning of a possible attack on Europe. Yet for well over a year the Pentagon's Defense Planning Guidance stayed with a warning time of 14 days, reducing its military value but probably helping to keep the budget cutters away from the European theater for that much longer.[8]

There are now instances where speed itself has become a paramount value in the formulation of a foreign policy. The rapidity of change since 1989 has made its study an intelligence premium. Commenting on President Bush's selection of Robert Gates to become the CIA's new director, former Deputy Director Bobby Inman interpreted it as a sign that the acceleration and diversity of international events required a commensurate transformation of the intelligence process:

> It tells you of a change in the world we live in. For twenty-five years, how good you were in conducting operations against the Soviets was the fastest ticket to the top. Now it's trying to understand this changing world.[9]

And many shared the speculations of the journalist who wrote before the Persian Gulf War began that "Mr Bush seems to have calculated that if and when the war starts, public support will depend not on the number of casualties but the speed and size of success."[10] Once the war began, all concerns about the principles, goals, and means of fighting the war were reduced to one, de-politicized question: "How soon can we win?"

As an inadequate compensation for this intellectual neglect, and in the hope that it might encourage others to read his work rather than excoriate it, I offer here a brief account of Virilio's ideas which have served more as backdrop than script in this book. They will come to the foreground in the two chapters to follow.

SPEED, WAR, AND PERCEPTION IN VIRILIO

In a word, Virilio's project is to politicize speed. The politics and power of wealth, war and media have been studied but not their political relationship to speed. In the sub-field of international political economy steps have been taken to understand the relation of national wealth to violence, empire, and military power. There has not, however, been serious consideration of political power in relation to the speed of systems of weapons, communications, decision-making. Virilio is concerned about the issue, because he believes a revolution has taken place in the regulation of speed. He outlined this argument in an interview with Sylvere Lotringer:

> Up until the nineteenth century, society was founded on the brake. Means of furthering speed were very scant. You had ships, but sailing ships evolved very little between Antiquity and Napoleon's time. The only machine to use speed with any sophistication was the optical telegraph, then the electric telegraph. In general, up until the nineteenth century there was no production of speed. They could produce brakes by means of ramparts, the law, rules, interdictions, etc. ... Then, suddenly, there's the great revolution that others have called the Industrial Revolution or the Transportation Revolution. I call it a *dromocratic* revolution because what was invented was ... a means of fabricating speed with the steam engine, then the combustion engine. And so they can pass from the age of brakes to the age of the accelerator. In other words, power will be invested in acceleration itself.[11]

In *Speed and Politics* Virilio presents the hypothesis that the great revolution of the industrial age was not national but, as he describes it, "dromocratic" in character, in the sense of a kinetic energy of machines and masses taking hold in the cities. Cities, as disorganized flows of population and capital, or sites of "habitable circulation," begin to challenge the military and political hegemony of the static absolutist state.[12] He sifts through political and strategic theory to provide an intellectual basis for his claims, from the writings of Machiavelli and Montesquieu (who declared somewhat prematurely that "With the invention of gunpowder, the impregnable place ceased to exist") to the military thinkers of the nineteenth century trying to cope with technological innovation, like Colonel Delair ("The art of defense must constantly be in transformation; it is not exempt from the general law of this world: *stasis is death*") and General de Villemoisy ("Out of 300 seiges conducted by the Europeans since the beginning of this century, there have only been about ten in which the fortification fell first").[13]

Virilio is preoccupied with the violence of speed, and running through his various works is the political theme that speed, as Sun Tzu noted many centuries ago, is the essence of war. It is speed that transforms the hand into a fist, or as Napoleon applied the concept to military strategy,

"Force is what separates mass from power."[14] But speed coupled with the other technological changes has even further altered the battlefield:

> Space is no longer in geography — it's in electronics. Unity is in the terminals. It's in the instantaneous time of command posts, multi-national headquarters, control towers, etc. ... There is a movement from geo- to chrono-politics: the distribution of territory becomes the distribution of time. The distribution of territory is outmoded, minimal.[15]

A radical claim, one that Virilio believes to be supported by the equally radical transformation of our visual representation of war. Virilio uses the language and experience of military phenomena to show how the violence of speed, coupled with the other technological innovations, has altered the representation of war — the face of battle itself — as well as the war of representations that goes on in advanced industrial societies. The victim of this "pure war" is reality, or rather any *given* reality. All realities are generated, mediated, simulated by technological means of reproduction; hence, "truth" becomes an instrument and product of perception. His last three books, *Guerre et Cinéma*, *La Machine de vision*, and *L'inertie polaire* make up a trilogy on the logistics of perception, which he interprets as increasingly replacing antiquated phenomenologies of reality.[16]

In his book *War and Cinema* Virilio gives a detailed history of the logistics of military perception and the use of cinematic techniques in warfare. As hand-to-hand combat gave way to long-range conflict, the enemy receded from sight. An urgent need developed to accurately *see* and *verify* the destruction of the enemy at a distance. The necessity of collapsing distance, of closing the geographical space between enemies, led to the joint development of modern techniques for war filming and killing.[17] In modern warfare, as the aim of battle shifts from territorial, economic, and material gains to immaterial, perceptual fields, the war of spectacle begins to replace the spectacle of war.[18] We shall see in the final chapter how true this was of the Persian Gulf War.

Virilio's analysis of the increasing strategical significance of battle-sight over against the more traditional battle-site can be verified in articles from a variety of defense journals.[19] But what lies between the texts in such journals is particularly illuminating. For instance, an advertisement in *Defense Review* for General Electric's computerized simulation "COMPU-SCENE V" extolls the "visionic edge":

In combat, the eyes have it: you watch the environment; you stay in contact with the threat; you aim the weapon; you search for cover. The more you see, the more you win. You see without being seen; you see first; you have tactical vision.[20]

General Electric can provide this military advantage because it "builds the best visionics simulation and training systems in the world." It would seem that as the "real" arms race begins to slow down, a "simulation race" is speeding up:

GE continues to set the pace with COMPU-SCENE V, the most powerful member yet of the COMPU-SCENE family of computer image generators. COMPU-SCENE V delivers true photo realism, it comes with a mission generation capability that translates raw photography into real-world databases and it simulates the full range of visionic devices – a major step toward full mission rehearsal capability.

To read Virilio and then the technostrategic discourse provides an important message for students of war and peace: as image becomes more credible than fact, time displaces space as the more significant strategic "field," and as the use-value of the ultimate power, nuclear weapons, is increasingly called into question, the war of perception and representation deserves more of our attention and resources than the seemingly endless collection and correlation of data on war that goes on in IR. One does not need to look any further than the latest generation of weapons and strategy, Star Wars, the Stealth Fighter Bomber, the Lacrosse satellite, AirLand Battle, and their first real outing in the Persian Gulf War to find ample proof that the empires of simulation, surveillance and speed are growing in significance everyday.

SPEED AND THE DOPPLER CONUNDRUM

Over the last few years we have witnessed a rapidity of change that has left many IR scholars in the dust. Virilio's attentiveness – bordering on obsession – with speed offers an important corrective to the disposition of the field to focus on the institutions and continuities rather than the disorganized flows and disruptions of world politics. Within the mainstream there are some exceptions: in recent works Jim Rosenau and John Ruggie have interpreted the turbulence and discontinuity of international relations as an intellectual imperative to open up the discipline to questions of cultural difference, national identity, and spatio-temporal approaches.[21] But I think they and others who are grappling with the issue of change might be making a possibly fatal error: they seem to be running to catch up to events that are in fact bearing down on them at very high speed.

I shall make an argument of this in the next chapter, but a few out-takes from the recent events in Eastern and Central Europe might make the claim clearer. First, there is the widely (but not very deeply) covered speech by President Havel to the joint session of the US Congress. His opening remarks highlighted the acceleration of history:

> The human face of the world is changing so rapidly that none of the familiar political speedometers are adequate. We playwrights, who have to cram a whole human life or an entire historical era into a two-hour play, can scarcely understand this rapidity ourselves.[22]

Curiously, the *New York Times* excerpted the above remarks in the following day's paper, but expurgated Havel's completion of the thought:

> And if it gives us trouble think of the trouble it must give to political scientists who spend their whole life studying the realm of the probable and have even less experience with the realm of the improbable than the playwrights.[23]

The easy criticism, one that does not break from the rationalist per-spective, is that political scientists are too *slow* to understand *immaterial* change: they/we have lost the alacrity and celerity to keep up with events engendered by a rapidly moving aesthetics of information. This echoes some recent criticisms from the International Political Economy field, that methods of analysis are failing to evolve in synchronicity with structural changes in world politics. But this leaves out of the equation an important new force in IR: the acceleration of mass by information.

A second out-take: the circle of Peter Jennings quoting playwright (not yet President) Vaclav Havel who was quoting the scholar—journalist Timothy Garton Ash:

> In Poland it took ten years, in Hungary ten months, in East Germany ten weeks; perhaps in Czechoslovakia it will take ten days.[24]

Events in the Soviet Union, Eastern Europe, and Central Europe give eloquent testimony to the pace, improvisation, and intertextuality of change. The lessons, however, clearly exceed rationalists' prescriptions for understanding rapid change. With the real-time representation and transmission of global change, it is no longer a matter of running to keep up with these events. In international relations, we are passing, I believe, from what could be called a classical *Heraclitean dilemma* to a postmodern *Doppler conundrum*. In effect, there is a new game of chicken being played out in IR, between the onrushing event and the sometimes recoiling, sometimes advancing observer. We become unsure of the source and direction of change: is it varying according to its relative velocity to the observer? Is our perception of the event being warped by the mediation of transmission? If we increase our speed to keep up, will time itself, as Einstein claimed, slow down? Is the event, in short, objectively knowable, before it is upon or beyond us? Strange speculations perhaps, but ones we need to ponder. For we now witness global change as closely and as similarly as the passing of a train is first experienced: we seem to be simultaneously repelled from and attracted to the waxing and warping of a new power that might just leap the rails.

Speed makes an object of change that eludes our scientific grasp. It is not Virilio but his French cohort in hyperbole, Jean Baudrillard, who from behind the wheel of a Big American Car in the Southwest gives the sharpest impression of the conundrum of speed:

> Speed creates pure objects, it is itself a pure object, since it erases the ground and territorial references, since it runs ahead of time to annul time itself, since it moves more quickly than its own cause and annihilates that cause by out-stripping it. Speed is the triumph of effect over cause, the triumph of instantaneity over time as depth . . . But perhaps its fascination is simply that of the void, for there is no seduction where there is no secret. Speed is simply the rite of initiation into emptiness: a nostalgic desire for forms to revert to immobility, concealed behind the intensification of their mobility.[25]

But where does this leave the IR scholar? Out of breath as walls fall and statues topple; or full of bluster about an "end to history?" Deterritorialized by a now truly global capitalism; or newly patriotic after a hyperreal Gulf War? A third, cinematic out-take for the bewildered: it is always better to bank on an immobile meta-narrative than risk a moving adventure story:

But Mr Norris said when it comes to ideas for screenplays, he's staying away from the fast-moving events in Eastern Europe.[26]

Alternatively, for the less trepidatious, a fourth out-take: from Adam Michnik, Solidarity leader, a powerful rebuttal and lesson to those who might find the events in Eastern Europe peculiar and exceptionalist:

A striking characteristic of the totalitarian system is its peculiar coupling of human demoralization and mass depoliticizing. Consequently, battling this system requires a conscious appeal to morality and an inevitable involvement in politics. This is how the singular anti-political political movement emerged in Central and Eastern Europe ...[27]

Call it a dialectic, a dialogic, or simply the irony of history, but what Michnik refers to is the process by which the very bankruptcy and stasis of politics gives rise to a reaction that ends up as a new political movement: antipolitics. The term, first coined by the Hungarian writer Georges Konrad, was taken up with revolutionary effect by constructive oppositionists and dissidents throughout Eastern and Central Europe. Konrad defines antipolitics as the "ethos of civil society, and civil society is the antithesis of the military society."[28] But of greater interest is his prescription for realizing an antipolitics, which might have seemed laughably utopian to realists when it was written in 1982, but now should command, I think, some intellectual respect. He writes:

What I have in mind is not some kind of anarchic, romantic rising; the time for that is long past. ... The most effective way to influence policy is by changing a society's customary thinking patterns and tacit compacts, by bringing the pace-setters to think differently.[29]

Is it not possible to judge in a similar way the new antidiplomatic forces arrayed in this study, producing simultaneously their own discursive negation of the stasis of geopolitics as they open up a new intellectual appreciation of the possibilities produced by a new chronopolitics? The next two chapters do not deliver a verdict: they show the two faces of an antidiplomatic diplomatic dialogue.

Notes

1   See G. Lista, trans. by C. Clark, *Futurism* (New York: Universe Books, 1986), pp. 12–14.

2   See Paul Virilio: *Bunker Archéologie* (Paris: Centre de George Pompidou, 1975); *L'Insécurité du Territoire* (Paris: Galilée, 1977); *Vitesse et Politique* (Paris: Galilée, 1978), trans. by M. Polizzotti *Speed and Politics: An Essay on Dromology* (New York: Semiotext(e), 1986); *Defense populaire et Luttes écologiques* (Paris: Galilée, 1978), trans. by M. Polizzotti *Popular Defense and Ecological Struggles* (New York: Semiotext(e), ˙1990); *Esthétique de la Disparition* (Paris: Balland, 1980); *Pure War* (New York: Semiotext(e), 1983); *Guerre et Cinéma: Logistique de la Perception* (Paris: Editions de l'Etoile, 1984), trans. P. Camiller *War and Cinema: The Logistics of Perception* (New York: Verson, 1989); *L'espace critique* (Paris: Christian Bourgeois, 1984); *L'horizon négatif* (Paris: Galilée, 1984); and *La machine de vision* (Paris: Editions Galilée, 1988); and, *L'inertie polaire* (Paris: Christian Bourgeois, 1990).

3   The Anglo-American-centricity of IR and the lack of translations might partially explain the neglect, but I would like to pre-empt any criticisms of his difficult style by noting that his two most widely available translations, *Pure War* and *Speed and Politics*, are much more aphoristic and impressionistic than his much larger body of untranslated work. The superfluity of his thought can, at times, be annoying, but the subject often demands the style.

4   D. Moisi, "Germany's Unity, Europe's Rebirth," *New York Times* (12 December 1989).

5   "Three Dissident Voices From Eastern Europe," *New York Times* (18 November 1989), p. 6.

6   See "Four Gorbachev Years: Turning the Soviet Thaw Into a Chill," *New York Times* (3 February 1991), p. 12. On the importance of the acceleration of change, see Philip Taubman," Gorbachev Calls on Party Leaders to Increase the Pace of Change," *New York Times* (30 July 1988), p. 1. Three exceptions stand out: Timothy Luke, "The Discipline of Security Studies and the Codes of Containment: Learning from Kuwait," *Alternatives*, 16 (1991), pp. 315–44; Michael Shapiro, "Sovereignty and Exchange in the Orders of Modernity," *Alternatives* 17 (1992); R. B. J. Walker, *Inside/Outside: International Relations as Political Theory* (Cambridge: Cambridge University Press, 1992).

7   Andrew Rosenthal, "Bush Urges Gorbachev to Avoid A Military Assault in Lithuania," *New York Times* (23 March 1990), p. 1.

8   See Michael Gordon and Stephen Engelberg, "Soviet Changes Mean Earlier Word of Attack," *New York Times* (26 November 1990).

9   "Bush Choice for C.I.A. is Man of Strong Views", *New York Times* (15 May 1991), p. 1.

10 "Meeting Would Put Pressure on Two Sides," *New York Times* (13 January 1991), p. E–3.

11 *Pure War*, pp. 44–5.

12 *Speed and Politics*, pp. 5–7.

13 *Speed and Politics*, pp. 9–18.

14 *Pure War*, p. 31.

15 *Pure War*, p. 115.

16   The warping of reality by the logistics of perception has entered the living room as well. Using time-compression machines, broadcasters are able to shave up to 10 minutes off old films (even *Casablanca* has been squished) without cutting any scenes, leaving 10 more minutes for commercials. See Albert Scardino, "TV's Pace and the Ads Increase as Time Goes By," *New York Times* (11 September 1989), p. D10.

17   See *Guerre et Cinéma*, p. 123:

> Si la première guerre mondiale est donc bien le premier conflit média-tisé de l'Histoire, c'est parce que les armes à tir rapide supplantent la multitude des armes individuelles. C'est la fin du corps à corps systématique, de l'affrontement physique, au profit du carnage à distance où l'adversaire est invisible ou presque, *à l'exception des lueurs de tir* qui signalent sa présence. D'où cette impérieuse necessité de la visée optique, du grossissement telescopique, l'importance du *film de guerre* et de la restitution photographique du champ de bataille, mais aussi et surtout, la découverte du rôle militaire dominant de l'aviation d'observation dans la conduite des opérations.

18   See *Guerre et Cinéma*, p. 10:

> Des premières armes spatiales de la seconde guerre mondiale à l'éclair d'Hiroshima, *l'arme de théâtre* a remplacé le *théâtre d'opération* et, bien que démodé, ce terme d'arme de théâtre employé par les militaires est révélateur d'une situation: *l'histoire des batailles c'est d'abord celle de la métamorphose de leurs champs de perception.* Autrement dit, la guerre consiste moins à remporter des victoires "matérielles" (terri-toriales, économiques ...) qu'a s'approprier "l'immatérialité" des champs de perception et c'est dans la mesure où les modernes belligérants etaient décidés à envahir la totalité de ces champs que s'imposa l'idée que le véritable *film de guerre* ne devait pas forcément montrer la guerre ou une quelconque bataille, puisqu'à partir du moment où le cinéma était apte à créer la surprise (technique, psychologique ...) il entrait de facto dans la catégorie des armes.

19   See, for example, the special simulation issues of *National Defense* (November, 1989), pp. 19–65; *Armed Forces Journal International* (November 1989, pp. 88–92; and *Marine Corps Gazette* (December, 1989), pp. 38–51.

20   *National Defense*, p. 38. General Electric is far from alone in its use of speed and simulation to see weapons systems. Equally aggressive on this front is Loral, which is pushing hard its new laser-based MILES battlefield system: "Via links to the global positioning satellite, it will track every weapon in a simulated battle – simultaneously and in real time – including high angle fire, and helicopter gunships." See *Aviation Week and Space Technology* (8 July 1991), pp. 50–1.

21   See J. Rosenau, *Turbulence in World Politics*, (Princeton: Princeton University Press, 1990); and Rosenau and Ernst-Otto Czempiel (eds), *Global Changes and Theoretical Challenges: Approaches to Word Politics for the 1990s* (Lexington, MA: Lexington Press, 1989). See in particular John Ruggie, "International Structure and International Transformation: Space, Time, and Method," pp. 21–35.

22   *New York Times*, 22 February 1990. Havel also remarked on 28 November 1989, the day that the Czechoslovakian Communist Government gave up

power, that "History has begun to develop very quickly in this country. In a country that has had 20 years to timelessness, now we have this fantastic speed." See Mervyn Rothstein, "A Master of the Parable," *New York Times* (30 December 1989).

23 *Congressional Record*, 22 February 1990. Perhaps this helps us to better understand why Havel met first with Frank Zappa in Prague before he met with political scientists at Georgetown University.

24 Timothy Garton Ash, "The Revolution of the Magic Lantern" (18 January 1990), p. 42.

25 J. Baudrillard, *Amerique* (Paris: Editions Grasset, 1986), p. 12.

26 *New York Times*, 30 March 1990.

27 Adam Michnik, "Notes on the Revolution," *New York Times Magazine*, p. 44.

28 George Konrad, *Antipolitics*, trans. R. Allen (New York: Quartet Books, 1984), p. 92.

29 *Antipolitics*, p. 224.

7

S/N: INTERNATIONAL THEORY, BALKANIZATION, AND THE NEW WORLD ORDER

—

Why do we tell stories? For amusement or distraction? For "instruction," as they said in the seventeenth century? Does a story reflect or express an ideology, in the Marxist sense of the word? Today all these justifications seem out of date to me. Every narrative thinks of itself as a kind of merchandise.
Roland Barthes, *L'Express* interview, 31 May 1970

This chapter is drawn from a travelogue that begins in July 1985 aboard the Baltic Peace and Freedom Cruise and ends in June 1990 at a Billy Bragg concert in Prague. It is both a travelogue in the conventional sense of a record of events that I kept as an observer and minor participant, and a study — in the root sense of *travel* + *logue* — of how words and images travel and take on a discursive power in international relations.[1]

The three sections of this chapter correspond to three political goals. In the first section a genealogy of one concept in particular — "balkanization" — is undertaken to show how discursive practices delimit the conditions of possibility for a new Central and Eastern European order.[2] The second section is an experimental argument for the political and intellectual benefits of a subversive antidiplomacy in international relations. The third is a speculative inquiry: it looks down the road from a moribund nowhere to somewhere new, from the degenerative utopia of the communist order to the possibility of a regenerative heterotopia emerging from the Eastern and Central European experience.[3] In short, this travelogue inscribes the political transformation of a region, the intellectual practices of a discipline, and the prospects for a new world order.

There are many reasons not to take this journey. A foreigner — that is, a generalist without the right papers and worse, carrying French luggage — is not very welcome in the specialist's domain of Soviet and European politics. Yet I believe there are pressing reasons for the incursion. The foremost reason is the manner and method by which the remarkable and rapid transformations since 1989 have been politically charged and intellectually neutralized by a one-sided, parochial triumphalism, in which vocal conservatives declare an end to history, confused liberals choke on its dust, and the rest, the "happy peoples" as Hegel called them in *The Phenomenology of Spirit*, are left with no history.[4] I have argued earlier that the primacy of space over time in international theory — of geopolitics over chronopolitics — has hampered our ability to keep up with let alone presage the impact of real-time representations of rapid political change.[5] In this chapter I move from a critique of stasis in International Relations, to a critical commitment to the opening up of new political possibilities and identities through a dissident antipolitics and antidiplomacy.

A second reason for a travelogue to assess the value of political order is the anthropological advantage afforded by an extra-territorial, alien status. This is not to pretend, by way of a sovereign method, that this will take one out of the power—knowledge loop and onto some detached position of objectivity. Rather, it can help to de-familiarize the orthodox, disciplined process of understanding the world *as it is* (the realist imperative) in opposition to *what it is not* (the utopian fallacy), a binary method of reasoning that invariably works to reinforce and reconstitute the order of things.[6] Hence, this chapter intends to devalue high structural analyses built upon non-contested concepts and parsimonious models by flooding the market-place of international theory with imported, poststructural narrations. In international political economy one might call this "dumping."

A third reason can be found in the nature of language itself. This chapter is a self-reflexive study of "S/N" in international politics. What does this mean? In telecommunications parlance, this refers simply to the signal-to-noise ratio that is produced by the technical reproduction of a sound or image. By now we all have some sense of how noise and nonsense disseminate and accumulate in technologically advanced societies — especially when they approach or engage in warfare.[7] Given the heavily mediated yet heterogeneous nature of world politics, it is not surprising that IR enjoys no diplomatic immunity against the high noise level of late modernity. The only real surprise is the non-recognition of the fact in international theory. A warning, then: this hybrid travelogue contains some videographic out-takes on Eastern and Central Europe that might be considered by some in the field to be too "loud" for scholarly discourse.[8]

But there is (at least) one other important meaning for "S/N." This chapter, in both its content and unconventional style, endorses the possibility of positive change through a *critical pluralism*. In the practice of a critical pluralism, language is not the tool of some external thought or purpose (say, a research program, a professional career, or a revolution), but the very space in which the will to power and truth confronts the empire of circumstance, imagined dialogues take on powerful monologues of the past, and the play of difference challenges the permanent war of essential identities. Hence, the sign "S/N" has a stereographic as well as videographic sense in this chapter. The oblique bar acts as a linguistic sign of the most significant conditions of otherness — and challenge to order — in international relations today: not simply the *State* versus the *Nation* or *Sovereignty* versus *Nationalism*, but all of the differences between — historical, cultural, ideological — that make and unmake both identities. It is this *alternation* — the "other" nation that constitutes sovereign identities — that this chapter re-imagines.

THE MATTER OF THE ORDER OF THINGS

First there is the matter of order, or more precisely, the method by which we make the idea of order matter in international relations. An obvious preliminary point: order matters most when it is lost or in the process of being lost, especially during the break-up of empire. Traditionally, the speculative range at such moments in international theory reconstructs a broad-band spectrum: at the one extreme lies tyranny, at the other anarchy, and *via media*, the optimal order of things. Hedley Bull, following this "trialectic," opens his inquiry into order in world politics, *The Anarchical Society*, with Saint Augustine's view of the best possible order.[9] With one eye on the City of God and the other on Rome under barbarian attack, Augustine defined order broadly as "a good disposition of discrepant parts each in its fittest place." Not a definition that would pass muster with most political scientists, but one nonetheless that evokes the important dualism of a pattern of politics that is necessitated by dangerous exogenous alternatives and made possible by endogenous goals and values.[10]

At historical ruptures comparable to the fall of Rome — like the disintegration of Christendom and the arrival and eventual defeat of

Napoleon — the issue of order arises time and again, causing thinkers to anxiously (or nostalgically) look backward for a reconstruction of the old order while others bravely (or recklessly) look forward to the building of a new order. For instance, one could plot the move from a medieval to a modern view of order with the divergent visions of Dante's *De Monarchia* and Machiavelli's *Prince*, the first calling for a return to a Christian, universalist monarchy, the second for states roughly concurrent with national, particularist interests.[11]

The modern debate in international theory has ranged somewhat further (if not deeper), on the merits and perils of multipolarity over against the stability afforded by hegemonic powers or alliances in a bipolar system.[12] And to be sure, there have been numerous predictions of the imminent end of a world order based on state sovereignty, whether because of technological innovations like the telegraph, radio, or airplane, the coming resolution or revolution of class conflict, the global threat of exterminism, or even the New Age promise of harmonic convergence. But now in the field of international theory, at a time when radical transformation of superpower politics has taken place, the owl of Minerva seems to be grounded.

Not, then, simply a case of being shot down by the ideologues, or left in the jet-stream of events, but grounded by confusion over the question of what might constitute a better, if not the best and fittest, order. The disintegration and reformation of the Soviet bloc — and with it the power to define an order through an alien threat — has led President Bush to declare at National Press Club banquets as well as Veteran of Foreign Wars outings that the new enemies are "uncertainty," "unpredictability," and "instability."[13] Similarly in the Soviet Union, events signaling an impending state of chaos reached such a level that they went unreported in the news — not because of censorship, but because they were no longer thought to be newsworthy.[14]

Of course, some warning noises about the impact of imperial decline on international order have been heard, most notably from thinkers in the historical camp of political economy, like Robert Gilpin and Paul Kennedy, who have read the numbers and seen the symptoms from a bottom-up, materialist perspective.[15] But there is another form of order deserving scrutiny that operates at the level of the *cultural economy*, which I defined earlier as flow and exchange of signs, symbols, and other representations producing value and meaning through discourse. Michel Foucault charts this terrain with remarkable finesse in the Preface to *The Order of Things*, in which he offers his own trialectic of order.[16] He first identifies an order's "system of elements" as the classification of resemblances and differences which define and establish its most basic form. These act as the "fundamental codes of a culture" which govern, and through governance, constitute an order and make us feel at home in it:

> Order is, at one and the same time, that which is given in things as their inner law, the hidden network that determines the way they confront one another, and also that which has no existence except in the grid created by a glance, an examination, a language; and it is only in the blank spaces of this grid that order manifests itself in depth as though already there, waiting in silence for the moment of its expression.[17]

Foucault then locates the other constitutive boundary of an order, the reflexive pale where "there are the scientific theories or the philosophical interpretations which explain why order exists in general, what universal laws it obeys, what principle can account for it, and why this particular order has been established and not some other."[18] Between these two regions lies an extraterritorial expression of order, no less powerful in its ordering effects, that is more resistant to analysis:

> It is here that a culture, imperceptibly deviating from the empirical orders prescribed for it by its primary codes, instituting an initial separation from them, causes them to lose their original transparency, relinquishes its immediate and invisible powers, frees itself sufficiently to discover that these orders are perhaps not the only possible ones or the best ones; this culture then finds itself faced with the stark fact that there exists, below the level of its spontaneous orders, things that are in themselves capable of being ordered, that belong to a certain unspoken order; the fact, in short, that order *exists*.[19]

It is to this space between the codes of a culture and the dominant scientific and philosophical interpretations of the day that this chapter travels, to retrace the path of a concept that moved from a natural position upholding a superpower order, to critical attitudes toward the order of things, and once historically transvalued, to a multiplicity of contested meanings that no single power or doctrine could possibly fix.[20]

THE DISCOURSE OF "BALKANIZATION"

Balkanization is generally understood to be the break-up of larger political units into smaller, mutually hostile states which are exploited or manipulated by more powerful neighbors. It takes only a cursory knowledge of the history of international relations to find some fault with this definition. Indeed, such a definition could be used to describe the entire history of the states-system – from the disintegration of the Holy Roman Empire through the rise of nationalism to the process of decolonization – as one of "balkanization," in which existing structures broke up into smaller pieces.[21] Nor does it take an acute sensibility to sniff out the presence of a great power *telos* operating in the definition: that is, there exists a finite process of state formation leading to the most stable order.[22] Yet this usage of "balkanization" seems to have enjoyed the standing of common wisdom – and thus avoided critical scrutiny. A genealogy of the term is called for, to understand how one meaning gained paramountcy over contending definitions; what kind of order was produced and what served by balkanization; and what its legacy for post-Cold-War politics might be.

The term itself has explicit geopolitical origins. The root of the word, "balkan," means mountain in Turkish, and the history of the politics of the region reflects this geographical fact. Recurrent invasions passed through the valleys of the Danube and its tributaries while the surrounding mountains isolated the settler groups. What developed was a condition described by John McManners in *The Near Eastern Question and the Balkans* as "inner fragmentation and outer accessibility." Rather than forging unity, conquest multiplied the diversity of peoples in the region. A pattern emerged: after the various conquerors left, nationalist and tribal strife would erupt along the fault lines created by years of colonization.

An exemplary case was the Russo-Turkish war of 1876. Abetted by a pan-Slavist movement and a militant Orthodox Church, Russia exploited internal ethnic and religious differences, and then legitimized its intervention in Bulgaria with the Treaty of San Stefano. Great Britain, which had previously fought in the Crimean War not in favor of Turkey but to thwart Russian expansion, grew alarmed by the regional shift in the balance of power towards Russia. Another great power congress was convened, and the Treaty of Berlin of 1878 attempted to redress balance alignments by redrafting the borders of the region. The result? Balkanization in everything but name: Russia and Bulgaria disputed the Dobrya; Serbia and Bulgaria quarreled over the Pirot; Bulgaria and Greece sparred over Thrace; Greece and Albania fought over Epirus; Austria–Hungary annexed Bosnia–Herzegovina – and if there were more synonyms for fighting we could go on about the multiple conflicts that erupted between Bulgarian-speaking Greeks, Greek-speaking Slavs, Albanized Serbs, Turks and Albanians in Macedonia.[23] At the time, these persistent local rivalries with systemic reverberations went under the orientalist rubric of the "Eastern Question." After two Balkan wars, the question – who would fill the power vacuum left by the decline of two empires, the Ottoman and the Austrian–Hungarian – had two eager respondents: Germany, in pursuit of *Lebensraum*, pushed eastward (a carrying forward of the nineteenth century of *Drang nach Osten*); while Russia, full of Slavic fraternalism and seeking warm water ports, pushed westward. Never resolved, the question was to be gorily debated in the first World War.

Although the phenomenon of balkanization was very much in evidence in the late nineteenth century, it was only after the First World War that it gained official linguistic recognition. According to the *Oxford English Dictionary*, it first appeared in two magazines in the 1920s: the *19th Century Magazine* ("Great Britain has been accused by French observers of pursuing a policy aimed at the Balkanization of the Baltic provinces."); and *Public Opinion* ("In this unhappy Balkanized world . . . every state is at issue with its neighbors."). From its original use, balkanization clearly had a negative connotation of hostility toward neighbors and a threat to the existing international order. And the early usage carries with it the sense of the failure of the post-war order, for what was the purpose of the peace following the First World War but to bring an end to the danger of balkanization through national self-determination?

This issue is raised by Arnold Toynbee in *The Western Question in Greece and Turkey*, the only book that I have found to mention alternative origins of the term, although it does so only in passing. Toynbee attributes its origins to German social democrats who used it to describe the deleterious effects that the Treaty of Brest-Litovsk of 1918 between Germany and the Soviets would have on the Baltic provinces, soon to be independent states. With this clue I searched the writings of pre-war German, Russian, and Polish social democrats, Kautsky, Lenin, Trotsky, Luxemburg and Liebknecht among them. I was surprised to discover a meaning of balkanization that never made it into the general discourse of international relations, nor, for that matter, into the *OED*.

In a report from January 1909 in the *Kievan Thought*, a correspondent wrote that the Balkans were "Europe's Pandora's Box and that only a single state of all balkan nationalities, built on a democratic, federative basis – on the pattern of Switzerland and the North American republic

− can bring international peace to the Balkans and create conditions for a development of productive forces." After two Balkan wars and on the eve of the First World War, the same correspondent provided the key elements of balkanization in a 1914 article called "The Balkan Question":

> The balance of power in the Balkans created by the Congress of Berlin in 1879 was full of contradictions. Cut up by artificial ethnographical boundaries, placed under the control of imported dynasties from German nurseries, bound hand and foot by the intrigues of the Great Powers, the people of the Balkans could not cease their efforts for further national freedom and unity.

This essay along with others from the war years would be published in the United States in 1918 under the title *The War and the International*. In bold print the author set out the conditions for peace:

> NO REPARATIONS, THE RIGHT OF EVERY NATION TO SELF-DETERMINATION. THE UNITED STATE OF EUROPE − WITHOUT MONARCHIES, WITHOUT STANDING ARMIES, WITHOUT RULING FEUDAL CASTES, WITHOUT SECRET DIPLOMACY.[24]

Four years later the same correspondent, Leon Trotsky, became the first foreign minister of the Soviet state and led a delegation to those very "balkanizing" negotiations at Brest-Litovsk. Ten years later he applied the concept of balkanization to the Ruhr crisis:

> Victorious France is now maintaining her mastery only by Balkanizing Europe. Great Britain is inciting and backing the French policy of dismembering and exhausting Europe, all the time concealing her work behind Britain's traditional mask of hypocrisy ... Just as federation was long ago recognized as essential for the Balkan peninsula, so now the time has arrived for stating definitely and clearly that federation is essential for Balkanized Europe.[25]

From these quotes and their historical context we can find the intertextual origins of balkanization and the reason for its first political transvaluation. Balkanization was forged as an important conceptual weapon in the Marxist lexicon, to describe what was seen to be a form of endo-colonization in Europe. The persistence of national rivalries was interpreted as a remnant of a feudal past now exacerbated by the uneven development of capital. During the war and for a short period afterwards, Trotsky and others in the Comintern leadership advocated a solution − which never amounted to much more than a slogan − for balkanization: a united state of Europe which would be economically united, politically socialist, and ethnically federated. In this same period Lenin also was taking a liberal view on the nationalist question, likening the right of self-determination to the right of divorce — that is, as rights that should be interpreted as necessary freedoms to maintain a family, not as a moral imperative to break it up. But Trotsky did not find permanent revolution at Brest-Litovsk. With ample assistance from the allied powers, he found a permanent state of "neither war nor peace" that persisted, in one form or another of the Cold War, until 1989. Nor did he find a united state of Europe, unless one is willing to take a long — and highly revisionist — view toward the coming union of Europe in 1992. And Lenin's enlightened view of nationalism was quickly tested by the Poles' bid for self-determination in 1919 — and found wanting when he advocated an invasion of Poland by the Red Army.

At this point balkanization began to travel: to describe the precarious position of the newly independent Baltic Republics, the resurgence of old grievances in the Danube, the state of the world in general. It still carried a negative description of chauvinism gone hostile and of meddlesome intervention by outside parties. But it traveled politically as well, gradually losing the remedial prescription of the social democrats. In other words, balkanization lost its pink petticoats and donned the starched collar of the Wilsonian liberals.[26]

I do not intend to rehearse the history of the failure of these ideals to materialize in either the Communist International or the League of Nations. I wish, rather, to challenge the conventional wisdom that the Marxists and the Wilsonians were at epistemological loggerheads, divided by the formers' materialism and the latters' idealism. A study of their use of balkanization (as well as its use of them) reveals a telling modernist affinity. Both believed geo-economic factors — in particular the size of a state and the internationalization of a single mode of production — to be the critical determinants of a state's viability and an international order's stability. Both shared a progressivist view of history — that a growing economic interdependence would diminish nationalist rivalries and bring about a better, more just order. Both shared epistemologies based on a closed structure of binary oppositions: for the Marxists, balkanization or federation, barbarism or socialism, nationalism or internationalism; for the Wilsonians, balkanization or confederation, despotism or liberal constitutionalism, nationalism or cosmopolitanism. And, most importantly, both world-views proved unable to resolve the fundamental contradiction between the moral principle of self-determination and the political requirements of international order.

To be sure, other cultural, geographical, historical and economic factors evade this simple dichotomization of order versus justice. And sentiments as politically powerful as they are intellectually elusive — like France's desire for revenge over the loss of Alsace and Lorraine and war reparations from Germany, or Germany's resentment over the loss of territory to the Poles — need to be taken into consideration. But from the reconstruction of a post-war order, the conditions for a future balkanization were assured. A third of Poland's population spoke German; Poles, Russians, Germans and Magyars made up a third of Czechoslovakia's population; and over a million Magyars became part of Rumania. And in the two successful cases of nation-state formation, Czechoslovakia and the Baltic Republics, conditions of balkanization were established that led to the two great injustices that assured the outbreak of a second world war: the seizure of the Sudetenland, and the carving up of the Baltic region by Germany and the Soviet Union in the secret protocol of the Ribbentrop—Molotov Pact of 1939. It is then ironic that shortly after the attempted Nazi *putsch* in Austria a learned observer of the Balkans, R. W. Seton-Watson, would write that balkanization was "a cheap phrase about central Europe current after the War."[27] In fact, balkanization clearly had legs.

FLOATING SIGNIFIERS: ABOARD THE BALTIC STAR

15 January [1985]. Received invitation to participate in the Baltic Peace and Freedom Cruise. Sounds like a ship of fools.

22 January. Sounded out friends about cruise and Stockholm conference on the Baltic future. Most of them confused: why a cruise through the "Balkans"? K. and B. [two Soviet specialists] thought it sounded like an émigré provocation, advised against it. Fear of balkanization.

1 February

Dear Mari:

I accept your invitation. To say the least it sounds intriguing, and I think it might just have the potential to break through the intellectual logjam created by academics who don't like to change maps and texts too often and by superpower politicians who like to keep their spheres of influence intact. So, although I am somewhat skeptical of the outcome, I am eager to participate in an area of discussion which has been (not so benignly) neglected. What happens when Baltic peoples assert their right to self-determination; when and under what circumstance might it happen; what will be its effect on the international system; how does the Baltic Question fit into the debate of order versus justice in superpower politics: these are a few of the questions I would like to bring up in my presentations.

25 March. Received program of cruise panel and Stockholm university conference. I think I made a mistake. Boat panel is with Vladimir Bukovsky (ex-*gulag*), Alex Stromas (Lithuanian émigré academic), a Polish Solidarity official, and "Swedish parliamentarian"(?). In Stockholm, with Imants Lesinskis, KGB defector from Latvia. Suspect a set-up: I've been billed as "peace activist, former member of Oxford Mothers Against Nuclear War."

MOSCOW, JULY 15 (TASS) TASS NEWS ANALYST VIKTOR PONOMARYOV

IT HAS BEEN LEARNT FROM THE REPORTS OF FOREIGN NEWS AGENCIES REACHING HERE THAT CERTAIN CIRCLES OF THE NATO COUNTRIES HAVE STARTED A SERIES OF DANGEROUS PROVOCATIONS IN THE BALTIC SEA ZONE ... ONE CAN CLEARLY SEE THE STYLE OF +LANGLEY EXPERTS+ IN THE SCENARIO OF PROVOCATIONS. THE +JUDGES+, +WITNESSES+ AND THE +VICTIMS+ WILL RUBBERSTAMP THE +VERDICT+ WHICH HAS LONG BEEN ENDORSED IN THE QUIET OF THE CIA'S OFFICES, WILL THEN GO TO STOCKHOLM ACCOMPANIED BY A BUNCH OF OVERHEATED +FREE EMIGRE YOUTH+ WHERE A SPECIALLY CHARTERED PIRATIC SHIP IS ALREADY WAITING FOR THEM ... THE SHIP WILL CRUISE IN CLOSE PROXIMITY TO THE SOVIET UNION'S TERRITORIAL WATERS. IN PASSING ALONG THE SEA BORDER IT IS PLANNED TO SEND LARGE QUANTITIES OF ANTI-SOVIET PAPERS ONTO THE COAST OF THE SOVIET BALTIC REPUBLICS USING FOR THIS PURPOSE SPECIAL UNSINKABLE CONTAINERS AND AIR BALLOONS. HEAPS OF SUBVERSIVE LEAFLETS ARE ALREADY BEING DELIVERED FROM THE CIA'S DEPOTS ... THE STAND THAT WILL BE TAKEN WITH REGARD TO THESE PROVOCATIONS BY RESPONSIBLE POLITICIANS FROM THE EUROPEAN GOVERNMENTS, PRIMARILY THOSE OF DENMARK AND SWEDEN WHOSE TERRITORIES AND VESSELS MAY BE USED IN THE PLANNED EXTREMIST ACTIONS, WILL CLEARLY SHOW HOW SINCERE THEY ARE IN THEIR ASSURANCES TO THE EFFECT THAT THEY ARE EAGER TO ACTIVELY PROMOTE THE NORMALIZATION OF THE INTERNATIONAL SITUATION, THE CONSOLIDATION OF GOODNEIGHBOURLY RELATIONS IN EUROPE AND IN THE BALTIC SEA ZONE.

25 July. Arrived in Stockholm and went to the headquarters of the cruise in the Old Town. A bomb scare clears the building. I accuse Mari of staging it for publicity; he seems to have missed the joke. As we walk out and reach the police line there is a very loud bang. Some of the reporters fell to the ground (former war correspondents?). The Swedish police had decided to blow up a suspicious-looking briefcase that had been left in a doorway. Nobody claims it.

26 July. Boarding the boat delayed while dogs sniff every suitcase. Lots of singing, broken up by accusations — anyone with cheap shoes and a camera is suspected of being a KGB agent. One of the accused turns out to be a cameraman for the BBC. TASS hysterical news releases have done the trick: over 40 reps from the Western media are coming along. However, seems to be no one from the US press, except guy from Radio Free Europe (the CIA provocateur?). The news people get the cabins with portholes.

27 July. Gave presentation today. Aside from invective and continuous spray of spittle from S. it went OK. Writer from *Toronto Life* liked the line "better mass whimsy than mass destruction" and bought me a drink in the stern bar. While there overheard the captain of the ship (always in the bar) say to a reporter that "the Soviet Navy, on their way back from their biggest maneuvers in history, will grab my ship and take it to Riga. They will interrogate you for three days and me for two and then let us go." The organizers couldn't get any other ship but this one: on his last voyage the captain miscalculated a turn and hit an island.

Superpower Estrangement and the Baltic National Identity

When I first received your invitation to participate in the Baltic Peace and Freedom Cruise I must admit to some reluctance ... My concern was that this cruise and the Baltic Futures Seminar would be marked by an emotional intensity, at the default of a rational analysis of how the Baltic Question has been a monologue of the superpowers. In the end, I decided to participate in the hope that my empathy for your cause might temper — and render more acceptable — some critical comments I have to make about Baltic nationalism.

I must also say that my doubts were not assuaged by the name of this conference. In the first Cold War and in the new one in which we find ourselves, both words have been appropriated for political and often disinformational purposes: the West has claimed freedom for their own, while the Soviets have staked out peace. My doubts, then, are about the pairing of these concepts: is it a marriage of convenience, to legitimize one more one-sided attack on a superpower? If so, your call for human rights will ring as hollow as Reagan's and Gorbachev's, who see human rights abuses everywhere in the other's sphere of influence, but are blind to them in their own. Or does this represent a genuine attempt at a dialogue, to reunite two concepts, two movements which super-power politics and parochial interests had torn apart in the first place? In the end I decided that the strategy of the peace movement itself dictates participation, for there must be at the very least an initial trust of independent groups' *intentions* if we are to break the political deadlock caused by Cold War obsessions with *capabilities*.

The intention of this floating conference, as I understand it, is to investigate the possibility of opening between the two blocs a space in which Baltic cultures might freely develop in peace. When compared with the military might of NATO and the Warsaw Pact, the capabilities of this cruise do indeed seem paltry. Yet through your imaginative staging of this event, the spontaneous support gained at demonstrations, and a forthright relationship with the media, you have managed to magnify many-fold the raw power of committed Balts. Nonetheless, we should all be aware that the most immediate and tempting capability of this cruise is potentially a negative one: it is much easier – and much more dangerous – to provoke superpowers than to mediate between them. That said, we should not allow the superpowers a monopoly on defining what constitutes a provocation: otherwise, they will surely pre-empt the terrain and rights of independent groups such as your own without a struggle.

[I] think it is a positive act for the Baltic future – and the first sign of a political or cultural organization coming of age – to open the Baltic Question to outsiders, in particular to those from the peace movement who are sympathetic to the problem of human rights but are critical of strategies which entail purely national solutions. For very good reasons, peace activism in the US has involved participation in the debates and struggles against human rights abuses in Central America, South Africa, and other areas in and at the borders of the US sphere of interests. For a variety of reasons, the most obvious one being the political expediency – let's call it what it is – the hypocrisy of President Reagan's human

rights policy – the peace movement has been less inclined to forge
links with human and national rights movements emanating from
the Soviet bloc. This has been less true in Europe, and, as peace
movements also come of age, and come to grips with the complexity
of global politics, I think it will be increasingly less true in the
United States as well. Two examples would be the European
Nuclear Disarmament group in England and the Campaign for
Peace and Democracy/East and West, based in New York but
beginning to find wide support across the US. These groups are
not shouting into the wind: they have formed links and given
support to groups on the other side of the two-bloc divide, independent groups equally committed to human rights and peace
rights, like the Charter 77 in Czechoslovakia, one of the oldest;
Swords into Ploughshares in East Germany; the Dialogue group in
Hungary; the Moscow Trust Group; and most recently, the formation of the Freedom and Peace Movement in Poland. There
have been stirrings in the Baltic as well, with a petition for the
establishment and extension of a Nordic Nuclear Free Zone to the
Baltic region. At least eight of the organizers have ended up in
prison camps or psychiatric hospitals; in fact one of them shared a
cell with the recently released Anatoly Shcharansky. What all
these groups have in common is a history of challenging the Yalta
state of affairs – and state of mind – that puts bloc stability
before civil liberties, and national security before national self-
determination.

I believe it would be a positive action on the part of Baltic
groups in the West to build bridges with these independent, non-
aligned, movements. But some might rightly say, let's be practical:
what does the peace movement have to offer to the Balts besides a
moral position superior to the superpowers? We must acknowledge
that not a single missile has been removed from the European
theatre because of the peace movements. But we should also
measure the success of peace movements and human rights groups
by their ability to demystify the demonology of the Cold War, and
to open between the two superpowers a discursive space in which
alternative strategies for defense and human rights might freely
develop. They have been active in continuous campaigns to publicize
and fight for human and peace rights activists in the Eastern bloc.
They surely can take some credit for the pressure European governments have put on our own government to begin arms talks with
the Soviets. And more importantly for the Baltic cause, they are
working to create the conditions for a detente from below, a

relaxation of tensions which is necessary if there is to be any possibility of better conditions in the Baltic region.

[I] have left for last the question of nationalism because it is the most contentious and potentially divisive issue for peace and human rights activists. Obviously, nationalism has been and can continue to be a positive, powerful force for liberating peoples from conditions of exo- and endo-colonization. Just as apparent, I hope, is the ease with which nationalism can deteriorate into an exclusivist chauvinism. The obvious, however, can sometimes make us oblivious to unpleasant considerations: given the geopolitical position of the Baltic states, a violent expression of self-determination could well be the last refrain before self-extermination. For those who view the Baltic future with a backward-looking nationalism, who remember a post-war state of flux which gave rise to free Baltic states, who envisage similar opportunities from crisis, I say look again, and then multiply the dangers by the megatonnage of destruction in the superpowers' arsenals.

I wish to make it clear that I am not questioning the Baltic right to self-determination; rather, I am challenging the blind advocacy or pursuit of national rights which precludes a discussion of less dangerous paths to that end. The question, then, is not whether but how to rejuvenate and preserve a free Baltic national identity. By now, one historical lesson should have been learned by all Balts: balance of power politics will not do it. You have in the past and perhaps you might again win independence by playing one great power off against another. But you did not and will not keep that independence because smaller powers, in particular those with any geo-strategic significance, are not players but expendable pawns in the great powers' games. Once you seek redress in power politics, you leave the court of international law and human rights behind and enter the international free market of threat-exchange. There is little, if any, autonomy for small powers in this arena: your destiny is determined by secret protocols (like the Molotov–Ribbentrop pact of 1939) or in tacit and not so tacit revisions to the Yalta agreements (like the Sonnenfeldt doctrine).

How then are the Baltic republics to make the transition from occupied, threatening (to both superpowers) non-entities, to liberated, non-threatening entities? It would be supremely arrogant for an outsider such as myself, and indeed presumptuous for Balts living outside of the Soviet Union, to give advice to those who would undoubtedly suffer for it. It is up to them to decide what strategy for peace and freedom is appropriate. But it will help their cause, I believe, to know that they have supporters in the West who are opting for a third way, for a de-aligned, de-militarized, and most urgently, de-brutalized Baltic region, who believe that finlandization is a better prospect for Balts and the world than balkanization, and who are trying to forge links of human, not national interests, in international relations.

I should leave it at that, but "that" is not really adequate. I have attempted an analysis of the Baltic Question in the hope that the moment and movements of change might be advanced. But what can we do now? There is a weapon, one that I have witnessed at close quarters aboard the Baltic Star. I have seen it deflate puffed-up bureaucrats, challenge the arrogance of state security services, and at the same time, boost the morale of Balts. For lack of a better, more impressive academic sounding term, I will borrow from the Czech writer Kundera and simply call it the Baltic Joke, which I have over the last few days enjoyably observed (and often been the butt of) as satire, buffoonery, caricature, wit, and self-deprecation. Against the deadly serious yet absurd superpower strategy of mass destruction, what better way to fight despair and the Yalta powers than a dissident strategy of mass whimsy.

28 July. Toronto Star: "Soviet patrol boat threatens shipload of Baltic protesters"
ABOARD THE *BALTIC STAR* — A Soviet patrol boat last night sped on a collision course off the coast of Estonia for this small ship carrying 400 Baltic exiles — including 20 Canadians — veering away only at the last minute. At the same time, a Soviet fishing trawler cut across the *Baltic Star*'s bow and stopped in its path — forcing the ship's captain to change course.

29 July. Left the bow where a Swedish Liberal Party member was droning on, for the stern bar which was full of other exiles, older Balts; most of them seem to have become disaffected with the youthful, liberal views (and enthusiasms) of the cruise — their anti-communist views not receiving much of a hearing. They were all watching a black and white video, something with Nazis in it and lots of martial music. Suddenly realized it was a German propaganda film of Operation Barbarossa — the German invasion (liberation?) of Russia in 1941. They seemed to be enjoying it.

30 July. Lunch at Stockholm University, before the panel, with Lesinskis, KGB defector. His two Swedish secret service handlers sat on either side of me, looking very athletic and sharp in tailored suits, but with gym bags that clank on the seats. L. very talkative until I ask him about his fellow defector, Shevchenko. Later some confusion about the seating arrangement on stage. In the middle of the introductions one of the handlers comes from behind the side curtain to move a large vase from in front of me to in front of L. I suddenly felt very exposed.

9 *August*. *New Statesman*: "Balts manage to embarrass the Soviets"

> A cruise and conference organised by Baltic refugees from Estonia, Latvia and Lithuania has been trying to get the "Baltic Question" back on the political agenda.
> [The] trip was dogged by practical and political difficulties. Both the ship — the *Baltic Star* — and the organising committee received bomb threats; the ship was shadowed all the way by Soviet, Finnish, and Swedish secret services, and diverted from its agreed course by a Soviet military pincer movement; and 400 Finnish Communist MPs unsuccessfully tried to prevent the ship from docking in Helsinki.
> Following *Baltic Star*'s arrival, the streets of Helsinki witnessed the largest political demonstration for decades — in support of the cruise. After the demonstration, cruise members went to the Soviet embassy but were forced away by police, who made one arrest and two detentions.
> Toward the end of the voyage, participants unanimously agreed to a series of demands for the establishment of peace, human rights and freedom in the Baltic region. Those who took part describe the debates as "non-dogmatic" and "filled with real spontaneity."
> According to one recent visitor to the Baltic states, Balts themselves view the cruise as a positive action. In the words of a representative from the Swedish peace campaign, it seems that "detente from below" might be taking its first but uneasy steps in the area.

STATIC WOR(L)DS

Admittedly this chapter itself, like many pirate videos, has a poor "S/N." With any span of time in the re-telling and editing of stories, distortion and dropouts are inevitable — and, in this case, intentional:

only the totally sovereign power can pretend to transmit a message that gives no sign of its constitutive and often distortive medium. Yet the fictionally sovereign superpowers keep on trying, whether in the form of the socialist realistic projection of Soviet power, or the televisual simulation of America's greatness. Similarly so in international theory, where sovereign methods pursue total transparency in their representational practices, and rationalist models chase after complete congruency with reality. The result: the intractable issues and irrational events of world politics never quite fit into a "research program." Hence this hybrid travelogue.

I have not adapted the form of the travelogue as a prismatic corrective that will yield a more truthful vision of Central European politics. Rather, I have deployed it as a textual experiment in perspectivism (in all of its historical, political, cultural, technical forms) which might convey the extraordinary level of media (in all of its representational forms) interference and influence in world politics that has, for the most part, resisted theoretical scrutiny in international theory. Nor should this travelogue be confused with its nineteenth-century apotheosis: it does not move at the leisurely speed of trains and ships, speak imperially for the mute other, or establish documentary authority through a photographic mirroring of reality. That moment of sovereign certitude has vanished. Or so it would seem, until one crosses genres into the discipline of International Relations which is dominated by a seeming diversity of approaches — neorealism, rational and public choice theory, correlates of war analysis, game theory, neoliberal institutionalism — but nearly all of which continue to share the rationalist perspective of the nineteenth century that all that is reasonable is true.[28]

But has this travelogue taken "balkanization" someplace new? It has shown how the concept traveled almost invisibly from converging Marxist and idealist usages to define its binary opposite, the optimal order of things. Contrasting the historical materiality and ideological baggage of the concept to the abstract, philosophical, or in Foucault's words, "unspoken" nature of order, one can better understand how balkanization came to play such a discursively powerful role in our understanding of what constitutes the "best and fittest" order.

Where might its next port of call be? Surely the demise of a bipolar order and the resurgence of endo-colonization and ethno-terrorism as disordering forces will once again see the revalorization of "balkanization." However, with the institutionalization and formalization of a European union, the concept should begin to shed its eurocentric skin. Perhaps, then, "balkanization" is ready for a return to its Ottoman origins. Take for example President Bush's condemnation of the Iraqi invasion of Kuwait as a "ruthless assault on the very essence of inter-national order and civilized ideals."[29] We know what he means by "the very essence of international order" by its violation — that is, the dictatorial interference in the affairs of another state. But a critical history of how "balkanization" has traveled could yield a very different, much less essentialist definition of "order" in the Middle East. Saddam Hussein was following a great power tradition of solidifying his sphere of interest by the annexation of a much smaller state that only exists because of an earlier colonial balkanization. Yet his actions were met by a level of global solidarity and a hailstorm of rhetoric unmatched since Hitler blitzkrieged into Europe. To be sure, the swallowing up of an oil-producing state is bound to be less digestible than, say, the invasion of Lebanon by Syria or the occupation of the West Bank by Israel.[30]

I will leave the matter of the Persian Gulf War for the final chapter. I believe, however, the early reaction to the Iraqi invasion confirms a conclusion that I have reached from my study of balkanization: the international order is once again being defined by the idealist practices resembling those of the 1920s and 1930s. Or rather, *neo*-idealist.[31] This ground has been theoretically prepared by developments in the field of international relations since the 1970s. The promulgation of Western values, the spread of liberal-democratic capitalism, the decline of the state and the role of force, a belief in progress towards a more unified global order, an emphasis on economic links, a concern for human rights, and a sense of intellectual commitment toward these ends mark much of the interdependency and world order model project theory that came out of the 1970s. Oddly enough, now it and many of its second-generational "institutionalist" adherents go under the rubric of "neo-realism." But I contend that their teleological vision of world order contains cultural, historical, and epistemological blindspots that I hope this travelogue has called into question. Balkanization *can* lead to dis-order, anarchy, a "bad infinity" of political powers. But that threat must be continually weighed against the history of its discursive power to maintain and promote unjust orders.

THE NECESSARY APPENDIX AND THE NATURAL ORDER OF THINGS

Two signs of the acceleration of history have begun to proliferate in the field of International Relations. The first is the conditional footnote leading off many journal articles ("this is the definitive statement as of date X"). The second is the appendix intending to bridge all the unforeseen events taking place between the submission and publication dates. This chapter does not pretend to be an exception to the current rule of circumstance in world politics: it is just slightly less transparent about the fact. As I first began to write this chapter Iraq invaded Kuwait; as I revise it Serbian troops have "invaded" the "independent" republic of Croatia. We have learned that nationalism in the Baltic and the Balkans can still raise the spectre of balkanization, that intervention can take many forms:

> The Bush administration expressed strong concern today about violent clashes involving independence movements in both the Soviet Union and Yugoslavia. But Administration spokesmen made sharp distinctions between the situation in the Soviet republic of Lithuania on the one hand, where it criticized the Soviet Government, and Yugoslavia on the other hand, where it criticized the declarations of secession by the republics of Croatia and Slovenia.[32]

The Persian Gulf War, renewed violence in the Baltic republics, and the secession movements in the Balkans elevated the question of international order to the top of the discursive agenda. And, as I have argued, the words matter more now than in the Cold War period of discursive stasis. Beginning with Gorbachev's reforms, something happened in international political discourse: as the sovereign bipolar powers and truths that determined the exchange-value of key words began to slip, wild fluctuations in the market-place of ideas began to surface. Dangerous, perhaps, but also liberating. Vaclav Havel, in his earlier role as wordsmith rather than powerbroker, wrote of this development:

> No word ... comprises only the meaning assigned to it by an etymological dictionary. The meaning of every word also reflects the person who utters it, the situation in which it is uttered, and the reason for its utterance. The selfsame word can, at one moment, radiate great hopes; at another, it can emit lethal rays. The selfsame word can be true at one moment and false the next, at one moment illuminating, at another, deceptive. On one occasion it can open up glorious horizons; on another, it can lay down the tracks to an entire archipelago of concentration camps. The selfsame word can at one time be the cornerstone of peace, while at another, machine-gun fire resounds in its every syllable.[33]

"To live in truth," as Havel put it, is to establish a credible existence in the face of incredible regimes. We have already seen how keywords of the Cold War were used to maintain rule by deceit: "peace," "freedom," "justice," "human rights" are but a few of the words that were appropriated by both sides for polemical and often disinformational purposes. The US claimed freedom for its own, while the Soviets staked out peace; justice came in two incommensurable forms, economic (Soviet) and political (US); and human rights were understood only as something lacking in the other superpower's sphere of influence. But then, as the superpowers were beset by both internal and external challenges, and their hegemonic hold over words continued to erode, one term became the primary battlefield of the antidiplomatic discourse. And since, as Havel claims, "all important events in the real world — whether admirable or monstrous — are always spearheaded in the realm of words," we must pay heed to this new term.[34]

We (just who is left out by this inclusionary "we" is the subject of the next chapter) are entering, constructing, or perhaps just wishfully invoking a *new world order*. President Bush is often given credit for coining the term; and certainly his liturgical use of it has cleansed the term of its embarrassing roots in Hitler's *Die neue Ordnung*, an altogether different kind of architecture for the world. First given a trial run by the President at a news conference in August 1990, "the new world order" was inaugurated in a television speech to the American public in September, and then formally inducted into the diplomatic lexicon at a February address to the Economic Club of New York. In both cases it was used to describe an American-led, UN-backed system of collective security. But it was the Gulf War that gave the "new world order" its discursive punch. President Bush took it on as his *ur*-text for world politics — and as a cure for the "vision thing":

> When all this is over we want to be healers. We want to do what we can to facilitate what I might optimistically call a "new world order," but that new world order should have a conciliatory component to it. It should say to those countries that are on the other side at this juncture, and there aren't many of them, "Look, you're part of this new world order. You can play an important part in seeing that the world can live at peace in the Middle East and elsewhere."[35]

But surely Soviet diplomacy deserves, at the very least, equal credit. In a September 1987 *Pravda* article (its less than felicitous title of "The Reality and Guarantees of a Secure World" perhaps explaining the lack

of media coverage in the West), Mr Gorbachev presented all the ingredients for the new world order that President Bush would later
popularize: a wider role for international law, a stronger United Nations
Security Council, and new global institutions to deal with environmental,
military, and economic challenges. Moreover, Mr Gorbachev used the
term itself (or at least as *Tass* translated it) well before President Bush
did, informing a gathering of the World Media Association in Moscow
in April 1990 that "We are only at the beginning of the process of
shaping a new world order." And Deputy Foreign Minister Vladimir
Petrovsky, opening the General Assembly debate at the United Nations
in September 1990, declared that it was time to "get down to creative
work on shaping a new world order."

However, before we can begin to assess the import of the "new"
world order, we must have some understanding of what happened to
the "old" one. We have seen how order matters most − more so than
freedom, justice, or even peace − when it is lost or in the process of
being lost, especially during the break-up of empires. Reform in the
Soviet Union, the Soviet withdrawal from Afghanistan, Chernobyl, freedom and democracy movements in East and Central Europe, removal of
intermediate nuclear forces from Europe, the reunification of Germany,
the relative decline of the American economic hegemony − even the
growing hole in the ozone layer − were just a few of the important
transformative events of the late 1980s that challenged the Cold War
norms and ideological practices of superpower diplomacy.

But like all things new and revolutionary in the international system,
it was to be a war that gave birth to a new world order. We have also
seen how neo-Hegelians like Francis Fukuyama, late of the State Department, would like us to believe that it was the *end* of the Cold War,
marked by the demise of communism and the triumph of liberalism,
that ushered in what was to be a peaceful if boring new world order.
But in August 1990 Saddam Hussein rudely reminded the world that
there remain many unhappy people who were willing to exploit and
struggle against the colonial legacy of the states-system. What we were
to witness in the events leading up to the Gulf War was not a Hegelian
"end of history" but an "irony of history." The French social critic Jean
Baudrillard anticipated the deadly irony that might result when the
superpowers chose − or, given the politico-economic costs, had no
choice but − to end the dialectic of superpower deterrence:

> Like the real, warfare will no longer have any place − except
> precisely if the nuclear powers are successful in de-escalation and
> manage to define new spaces for warfare. If military power, at the

cost of de-escalating this marvelously practical madness to the
second power, reestablishes a setting for warfare, a confined space
that is in fact human, then weapons will regain their use value and
their exchange value: it will again be possible to *exchange warfare*.[36]

When the Soviet Union decided first to back the United Nations
sanctions rather than Iraq, its erstwhile regional ally, and then to back
down when President Bush rejected Mr Gorbachev's peace proposal, an
"exchange of warfare" was guaranteed. This is *not* to affix blame on
either one party or another, to endorse a balance of power politics, or
to wax nostalgic over the loss of the nuclear balance of terror. It is
simply to identify a watershed moment for antidiplomacy. Bipolar power
and truths gave way to a new universalism. Note: *uni*-versalism, not
multi-versalism, for much as the "invisible hand" of laissez-faire economics performed in nineteenth-century British foreign policy, the universalist ideals of collective security, liberal economics and politics, and
international law promote — the more critical might say "cloak" — the
unipolar power of the United States. This is evidenced by the suzerainty
that the US exercised over the coalition in military planning and war-
fighting in the Gulf, but also in its broader strategic aims, unchanged
since 1945, of maintaining its position as *the* global military power.

In the next chapter we shall see how words in the Gulf War lost out
not just to war but to images. We were treated to videos of videos of
smart bombs unerringly hitting their targets, cruise missiles seemingly
reading street signs as they made their way down the boulevards of
Baghdad, and a victorious ground war of one hundred hours that ended
in fewer coalition casualties (no one was keeping track of the Iraqi
dead) than in the exercises leading up to it. Of course, images can cut
both ways: the video images of the lone Chinese student staring down a
column of tanks in Tiananmen Square, the foot of an unknown Lithuanian
sticking out from under the tread of a Soviet tank in Vilnius, or a group
of Los Angeles policemen beating a black motorist work against the
power of those prone to use violence before dialogue. But in the Gulf
War the tightly controlled, abstractly clean images presented an appealing portrait of military technology solving intractable diplomatic
problems — what we might call the "aesthetics of antidiplomacy."

As the universalist "new world order" inevitably fails to live up to its
lofty ideals, nostalgia for old order, or worse, calls for a rebirth of an
authoritarian "new order" could result. As ethnic chauvinism, religious
fundamentalism, and economic turmoil grow — or less abstractly, as
Azeris and Armenians, Kurds and Iraqis, Serbs and Croats, Israelis and
Palestinians, European "natives" and "refugees" reach for each others'

throats — I am sure that in both Washington and Moscow there are diplomats who nod at the Islamic saying, "Better 100 years of tyranny than one day of anarchy." We will, I predict, be seeing much more of our friend, "balkanization."

In the harsh terms of *Realpolitik* the end of the Cold War simply means the end of the Soviet Union as a counterbalance to American hegemony. To believe that this is a guarantee of peace and stability requires a leap of faith or a dose of patriotism that is unsuited for the critical thinker. Moreover, the one lesson that should have been learnt from the events of 1989 is that international relations cannot be reduced to the will to power. Events might have been triggered by a relative decline in the superpowers, but in the end it was the will to *truth* that changed the map of Europe.

Therein lies the greatest challenge of balkanization for post-Cold-War diplomacy. Perhaps at one time "one God, one Pope, one Emperor" was necessary and sufficient for the world. But the fragmentation of the diplomatic culture, the diffusion of power along new political and national fault lines, and the continued level of uneven economic development means that the self-sure monologues of the past are no longer feasible — even if they are dressed up in the universalist rhetoric of the new world order. Hope, if it is to be found, lies in our ability to coexist with the cultural difference subsumed and often denied by the discourse of balkanization and the new world order. Indeed, our very existence depends upon it: not (necessarily) in some apocalyptic sense, but in our deep ontological need for otherness in the formation of sovereignty and construction of order.

The insights of two artists might help us better understand this. The first is Billy Bragg, a British singer who is difficult to categorize: saying that he performs solo with an electric guitar and sings militant rock and roll does not really say enough. His performance in Prague, during the week of the first democratic elections in Czechoslovakia since 1948, captured a moment and some disturbing truths about the consolidation of identity through the constitution of difference.[37] Unlike the widely covered Joan Baez concert the night before at the immense People's Sports Palace (piously dull), or the Paul Simon concert two nights later in the packed Old Town Square (drearily sentimental), Havel was not there. Bragg performed in the Zimin stadium, a grand name for an old hockey ring, in front of anarchists, punks, young army recruits still in uniform, and even genuine hippies. The performance was as brilliant as were the asides, and the crowd showed its appreciation by maintaining a kind of Mazurka–St-Vitus–Rokenrol frenzy throughout. But it was the first of three encores that shifted the mood. He brought a Czech up on stage for a word-by-word translation of the first song – The Internationale. After about ten minutes of this, half the audience began whistling (booing) and shouting things like "Communism is Nazism." A few bottles got thrown. Unfazed, he launched into the next song, "dedicated to the ironic soul of the Czechs": "Waiting for the Great Leap Forward". And for the finale, Bragg was joined by Michael Stipe from R.E.M. and Natalie Merchant from 10,000 Maniacs, to sing "The One I Love." In the space of three songs Bragg forced his audience to confront the political difference that had constituted their identities, the ironic difference that allowed them to escape those fixed identities, and the free identity cultivated from a care for difference. And most of the audience had a good time at the same time.

The second insight comes from the great Soviet linguist and literary theorist, Mikhail Bakhtin. Although writing about the work of Dostoevsky, he best plots the link between word and world orders, showing us how diplomacy – like language itself – must negotiate the meaning and values that constitute identity out of difference. He provides what I believe should be the first and last entry for a travelogue of the new world order:

> To be means to be for the other, and through him, for oneself. Man has no internal sovereign territory; he is all and always on the boundary; looking within himself, he looks *in the eyes of the other* or *through the eyes of the other* ... I cannot do without the other; I cannot become myself without the other; I must find myself in the other, finding the other in me.[38]

Notes

1 This chapter attempts at a conceptual and historical level what Edward Said skillfully achieves at a theoretical and literary level in his essay "Traveling Theory," *Raritan* (1, no. 3, Fall, 1984, pp. 41–67), sharing with it some of the way stations that Said sets out in an introductory paragraph:

> There is, however, a discernible and recurrent pattern to the movement itself, three or four stages common to the way any theory or idea travels. First, there is a point of origin, or what seems like one, a set of initial circumstances in which the idea came to birth or entered discourse; second, there is a distance traversed, a passage through the pressure of various contexts as the idea moves from an earlier point to another time and place where it will come into a new prominence; third, there is a set of conditions – call them conditions of acceptance, or as an inevitable part of acceptance, resistance – which then confronts the

transplanted theory or idea, making possible its introduction or toleration, however alien it might appear to be; fourth, the now fully (or partly) accommodated (or incorporated) idea is to some extent transformed by its new uses, its new position in a new time and place.

2 It will take another "story" to explain the related issue of the rise in discursive power of historical concepts like "finlandization," "ottomanization," and "medievalization," and the decline of political concepts like communism, imperialism, capitalism, etc. For instance, consider Jeane Kirkpatrick's statement that "If we hadn't stepped in, Hussein would have gone and finlandized the region," *MacNeil/Lehrer* (3 September 1990).

3 *Utopias* afford consolation: although they have no real locality there is nevertheless a fantastic, untroubled region in which they are able to unfold; they open up cities with vast avenues, superbly planted gardens, countries where life is easy, even though the road to them is chimerical. *Heterotopias* are disturbing, probably because they secretly undermine language, because they make it impossible to name this *and* that, because they shatter or tangle common names, because they destroy "syntax" in advance, and not only the syntax with which we construct sentences but also that less apparent syntax which causes words and things (next to and also opposite one another) to "hold together."

See M. Foucault, *The Order of Things: An Archaeology of the Human Sciences* (New York: Vintage Books, 1973), p. xviii. For an anthropological appreciation of the power of a regenerative disorder, see J. Clifford, *The Predicament of Culture* (Cambridge, MA: Harvard University Press, 1988), pp. 141–2.

4 There is another possibility, that the origins of the new "endism" lie less in ideology or a philosophy of history than in a new sedentariness. In our perpetual desire to avoid the evidence that there is no first principle of truth, final meaning, redemptive end – only eternal recurrence – we mistake our own inertia amidst rapid change for arrival. In his essay "The Last Vehicle" Paul Virilio argues that the speed of travel and information gives an additional priority of arrival over departure, of distance/speed over distance/time, and likens the phenomenon to the Tokyo swimming "pools" in which the swimmer in a greatly reduced space swims vigorously against a current – and stays stationary. A more familiar example would be the step machines, now so popular that people wait for elevators in health clubs to wait in line to use the machines. See "The Last Vehicle," in *Looking Back on the End of the World*, edited by D. Kamper and C. Wulf (New York: Semiotext(e), 1989), pp. 106–19. And for an elaboration on the appeal of "endism," see my "Reply to Rosenau: Fathers (and sons), Mother Courage (and her children), and the End of the World (as we know it)," Roundtable on Superpower Scholars, 1990 ISA Meeting (forthcoming in *International Relations Voices: Dialogues of a Discipline in Flux*, edited by J. Rosenau, Westview Press).

5 See chapter 6 above.

6 See E. Said, *Orientalism* (London: Routledge & Kegan Paul, 1978), p. 259, who quotes Hugo of St Victor: "The man who finds his homeland sweet is still a tender beginner; he to whom every soil is as his native one is already strong; but he is perfect to whom the entire world is as a foreign land."

Richard Ashley and Rob Walker endorse a similar intellectual position of exile in the introduction to the *International Studies Quarterly* Special Issue, "Speaking the Language of Exile: Dissidence in International Studies" (September 1990), pp. 259–68.

7   The reply of the poet Robert Graves to an interviewer's question, why had he not been able to make people understand the nature of the First World War when home on leave, makes the point simply and eloquently: "You couldn't: you can't communicate noise. Noise never stopped for one moment – ever." *Listener*, 15 July 1971, p. 74, quoted by P. Fussell, *The Great War and Modern Memory* (New York: OUP, 1975), p. 170.

8   This does not mean there is a video-tape to accompany the chapter. "Videographic" is used to convey the technical characteristics – time-shifting, channel-switching, erasability of the archive, etc. – as well as the philosophical implications – the intuitive and simulacral power of movement (as external physical reality) and image (as internal psychic consciousness) – of the latest and most pervasive form of representation. The term draws on Henri Bergson's notions of "movement-image" and "cinematographic" illusion, first presented in *Matter and Memory* (1896) and *Creative Evolution* (1907), and reinterpreted by Gilles Deleuze in *Cinema 1: The Movement-Image* (Minneapolis: University of Minnesota Press, 1986) and *Bergsonism* (New York: Zone Books, 1988). For an assortment of views on the philosophical impact of videography, see the special issue of *Block* (Autumn, 1988) on "The Work of Art in the Electronic Age"; Jean Baudrillard, *The Evil Demon of Images* (Sydney: Power Institute of Fine Arts, 1987); Timothy W. Luke, *Screens of Power: Ideology, Domination, and Resistance in Informational Society* (Chicago: University of Illinois Press, 1989); and Michael Shapiro, "Strategic Discourse/Discursive Strategy: The Representation of 'Security Policy' in the Video Age," *International Studies Quarterly* (September 1990), pp. 327–40.

9   See H. Bull, *The Anarchical Society: A Study of Order in World Politics* (New York: Columbia University Press, 1977), pp. 4–5. I believe Benedict Kingsbury first applied the idea of a "trialectic" working in Bull's analysis in a 1986 BISA paper that I have been unable to locate.

10   For a very persuasive account of the influence of Augustine on classical international theory, see Roger Ivan Epp, "Power Politics and the *Civitas Terrena*: The Augustinian Sources of Anglo-American Thought in International Relations" (Ph.D. Dissertation, Queen's University, Kingston, Canada, June 1990).

11   Another example is the first account of the modern world order, A. H. L. Heeren's *Manual of the History of the Political System of Europe and its Colonies*, written in response to what he perceived as the demise of that very old order. In the Preface to the 1809 first edition Heeren stated that "while the author was thus employed in elaborating the history of the European states system, he himself saw it overthrown in most essential parts ... Its history was in fact written upon its ruins." See A. H. L. Heeren, *A Manual of the History of the Political System of Europe and its Colonies* (London: Bohn, 1873), p. x.

12   See K. Deutsch and J. Singer, "Multipolar Power Systems and International Stability," *World Politics* (xvi, no. 3, 1964), pp. 390–406; K. Waltz, "International Structure: National Force and the Balance of World Power,"

Journal of International Affairs (21, no. 2, 1967), pp. 215–31; M. Wight, *Systems of States*, edited by H. Bull (Leicester: Leicester University Press, 1977); R. Keohane, "The Theory of Hegemonic Stability and Changes in International Economic Regimes, 1967–1977," in O. Holsti et al., *Changes in the International System* (Boulder: Westview, 1980); and A. Watson, "Systems of States," *Review of International Studies* (no. 16, 1990), pp. 99–109.

13 Saddam Hussein temporarily gave US foreign policy a purpose and identity again, but the personalities and issues (despite the hyperbolic and historically specious identification of Hussein with Hitler and Kuwait with Czechoslovakia) lack the necessary material threat and grandeur of evil to become a sustainable global threat.

14 See C. Bohlen, "A Glasnost Nightmare: The News is all Bad," *New York Times* (18 August 1990).

15 See P. Kennedy, *The Rise and Fall of the Great Powers* (New York: Random House, 1987); and R. Gilpin, *War and Change in World Politics* (Cambridge: Cambridge University Press, 1981), and *The Political Economy of International Relations* (Princeton: Princeton University Press, 1987).

16 M. Foucault, *The Order of Things*, pp. xv–xxiv.

17 *Order of Things*, p. xx.

18 Ibid.

19 Ibid.

20 This does smell of relativism, even nihilism. For those who consider relativism or nihilism a graver danger to the international society than totalitarian truths, I would recommend large doses of Kundera. Outside of Nietzsche, the two best short statements on the subject come from the previously quoted French literary critic, Maurice Blanchot (see p. 2), and William E. Connolly (see *Identity\Difference*, p. 59):

> The political task, in a time of closure and danger, is to try to open up what is enclosed, to try to think thoughts that stretch and extend fixed patterns of insistence. That is why Nietzsche, Foucault, and Heidegger do not worry too much about the ethicopolitical problematic of "relativism" – partly because we are already located on a field of discourse that is so difficult to stretch and revise in any event and partly because we live in an age in which so many areas of the world are being drawn into the orbit of late modern life. The relativist worry is untimely.

21 I realize the historical specificity of this claim as well, but if we measure the success of Italian (in the nineteenth century) and German unification (1848–1871 as well as the current process of reunification) against the failure of pan-Slavism, pan-Arabism, pan-Africanism, pan-Shiism, etc., then I believe the claim is a valid one.

22 In an Oxford University lecture Hedley Bull stated that the leading theorist of nationalism in the nineteenth century, Giuseppe Mazzini, also believed that there was a finite number of nations seeking liberation.

23 For an exhaustive account of the pre- and inter-war ethnic conflicts of Europe, see Elie Kedourie, *Nationalism* (London: Hutchinson, 1961), pp. 118–31.

24 L. Trotsky, *The War and the International* (Wellawatee: Wesley Press, 1971), p. 34.

25 L. Trotsky, *The First Five Years of the Communist International*, vol. 1 (New York: Monad Press, 1972), pp. 341–3.

26 There is some evidence to suggest that the appropriation was direct and nearly coterminous: one source claims that Woodrow Wilson had asked the publisher for the proofs of Trotsky's 1914 pamphlet in which he advocated self-determination, democratic principles, and an end to secret diplomacy. See the preface to *The War and the International*, p. xi.

27 R. W. Seton-Watson, "The Danubian Problem," *International Affairs*, (September–October, 1934).

28 "The nineteenth century began by believing that what was reasonable was true, and it would end up by believing that what it was a photograph of was true." See William M. Ivins, Jr, *Prints and Visual Communications* (1953), quoted by Andy Grundberg, "Ask It No Questions: The Camera Can Lie," *New York Times* (12 August 1990).

29 "We must not delude ourselves. Iraq's invasion was more than a military attack on tiny Kuwait; it was a ruthless assault on the very essence of international order and civilized ideals." George Bush, Address to the Veterans of Foreign Wars, *New York Times*, 20 August 1990.

30 A comparison of the reaction to the 1923 crisis between France and Germany over the Ruhr, a vital coal-producing region, might be edifying.

31 The use of this term and much of my analysis of it comes from an Oxford University lecture that Hedley Bull gave on the subject – much of it a dissection of the work of Joseph Nye and Robert Keohane, which he categorized as "neo-idealist."

32 See "US on Secession: It Depends," *New York Times* (28 June 1991), p. A8.

33 V. Havel, "Words on Words," *New York Review of Books* (18 January 1990).

34 Ibid.

35 "What the US Has Taken On in the Gulf, Besides a War," *New York Times* (20 January 1991), p. E3.

36 "Fatal Strategies," in *Jean Baudrillard: Selected Writings*, edited by M. Poster (Stanford, CA: Stanford University Press, 1988), p. 191.

37 I borrow the phrasing on identity\difference from William Connolly.

38 M. Bakhtin, *The Problems of Dostoevsky's Poetics*, trans. C. Emerson (Minneapolis: University of Minnesota Press, 1984), pp. 311–2.

WAR

8
CYBERWAR, VIDEOGAMES, AND THE GULF WAR SYNDROME
—

Let us take a limited example, and compare the war machine and
the State apparatus in the context of the theory of games.
Gilles Deleuze and Felix Guattari, *Nomadology:
The War Machine*

This is not a final chapter; it does not conclude. It happens to come at
the end of a book and at the beginning of a "new world order," which
is sufficient reason to apply the theoretical claim of this book — that
new technostrategic, antidiplomatic forces in international relations
require a poststructuralist approach — to the first, and surely not the
last, late modern war.

Let me stress — in case the "excess of writing" is not emphatic
enough — the word "approach": not "analysis," "system," "method-
ology," or "model," but an "approach," which recognizes the impossi-
bility of pure congruence of thought and object, and yet draws the self
into the event. Social scientific theory can act as a proxy in war, as did
organization and systems theory in Vietnam, to distance the observer
from the secondary reality of war, the killing of another human, in the
name of studying the primary purpose, to vanquish the enemy. A
poststructuralist approach closes the distance to death, asking first
before any other question, how is my own identity implicated in a study
of the killing of others? This is not to take up an a priori pacifist
or belligerent position, but to understand fully the forces in a de-
territorialized, hyper-mediated, late modern war already at work to *fix*
that position before one has even begun to consider it. During the war,
as the level of killing became inversely proportional to the level of
knowing the Other, I tried to disturb that position. This chapter is the
unfinished result.

MIND GAMES

Do we not feel the breath of empty space?
                                    F. Nietzsche, *The Gay Science*

BC — Before Cyberspace — our leaders read books during world crises.

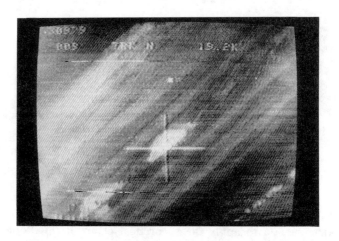

Much has been made of the fact that during the Cuban Missile Crisis John Kennedy was heavily influenced by Barbara Tuchman's *Guns of August*. In his memoirs of the event, Kennedy's brother Robert claims that the President's decision-making was tempered at critical moments by Tuchman's account of how Europe stumbled into the First World War.[1] In the midst of the Persian Gulf War I wondered what George Bush was reading: after watching George Bush, Saddam Hussein, and even a note-taking journalist watch CNN, I stopped wondering and watching, and started reading (mainly Oswald Spengler's *The Decline of the West*) and writing again.[2]

With this war, cyberspace came out of the research labs and into our living rooms. The written word lost out to the video of a video of a bomb that did not need books to be smart; to cruise missiles that read the signs of Baghdad's streets better than most of us read the signs of the war; to a hyperreal Gulfspeak that "attrited" all critics who clung to the archaic notion that words meant what they said and said what they meant. The result is that the majority of Americans — not just the President — had neither the time nor the ability to read, write, or even reflect effectively about the war. For six weeks and one hundred hours we were drawn into the most powerful cyberspace yet created, a technically reproduced world-text that seemed to have no author or reader, just enthusiastic participants and passive viewers. This is not to reify or deify some new technological force in our society. But it is to recognize the possibility that we have become so estranged from the empty space left by the decline of American hegemony and the end of

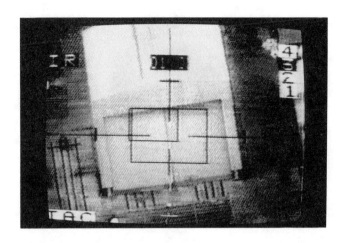

the Soviet threat that we eagerly found in cyberspace what we could no longer find in the new global disorder – comfort and security in a superior technostrategy.[3]

But do not misread me: this chapter is not a literacy campaign, a neo-Luddite attack on new technologies, or an exercise in cyber-bashing. I am merely offering a cautionary tale, of how the technical preparation, execution, and reproduction of the Gulf War created a new virtual – and consensual – reality: the first *cyberwar*, in the sense of a technologically generated, televisually linked, and strategically gamed form of violence that dominated the formulation as well as the representation of US policy in the Gulf. In name only, cyberspace had its origins in science fiction: its historical beginnings and technological innovations are clearly military (from NASA's primitive flight simulators of the 1940s to the ultra-modern SIMNET-D facilities in Fort Knox, Kentucky), and now its widest civilian application has been by the media, continuing the Gulf War by the most technical and immediate means. Yet clearly it is science fiction that alerted us to the dangers of cyberspace, and now popular culture that drives the message home.[4]

Indeed, popular journalism seems much more attuned to the

phenomenon than academic critics. Consider, for instance, these two assessments of the Gulf War:

> The trouble is that order is a 19th century term that suggests Metternichian arrangements of large, heavy, somewhat static entities. History in the late 20th century seems to belong more to

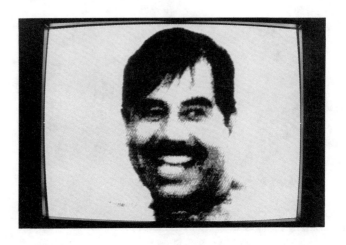

> chaos theory and particle physics and fractals — it moves by bizarre accelerations and illogics, by deconstructions and bursts of light.[5]

and:

> It will not suffice to do extended textual readings of Pentagon briefings or Hussein's speeches. One must also know something about American culture, Iraqi history, etc. The whole deconstructive line of solipsism is obviously worthless or worse in this case. Are we talking about a discourse or are we talking about a war?[6]

When *Time* magazine (the first quote) begins to read like a critical theorist, and a critical theorist (the second quote) begins to read like *Time*, one begins to suspect that not only the Iraqi Republican Guard was out-flanked in the Six Weeks and One Hundred Hours War. Like old generals the anti-war movement fought the last war, while popular journalism and popular culture represented a new war of speed, surveillance, and spectacle — a "pop" war ready-made for the video arcade. As the critics of the war hunkered down for a long war and high US body counts, the rest of America climbed aboard the accelerating, solipsistic, deconstructive war machine. In effect, the "New" Left fought a disastrous war of position, constructing ideologically sound bunkers of facts and history while the "New" World Order fought a highly success-

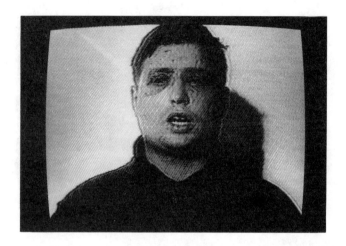

ful war of maneuver, enfilading the horrors and ugly truths of war with high-speed visuals and a high-tech aesthetics of destruction.[7]

The modernist school of criticism ignored the new phenomenon of cyberwar and carried on with the important task of building an edifice of facts unobfuscated by false consciousness and disinformation, à la Chomsky ("Just take a look at the logic of the situation as it is evolving in the Gulf").[8] But efforts to construct a critical *and* universal counter-memory were handily isolated as anti-American and dismissed as utopian. Just as a foreign implant is set upon by antibodies, the "radical" lessons of the Vietnam war and the Cold War not only suffered pathological rejection but became the perverse justification for a hot, curative war ("By God, we've kicked the Vietnam Syndrome once and for all," said George Bush the morning after).

An alternative, late-modern tactic against total war was to war on totality itself, to delegitimize *all* sovereign truths based on class, nationalist, or internationalist metanarratives, à la Lyotard ("we have paid a high enough price for the nostalgia of the whole and the one").[9] Let me once again put my cards on the table: this is the strategy of this chapter, as it was for the presentations that I made at teach-ins and

conferences on the war. Contrary to the claims of some of the New
Left, I found neither quietism nor conservatism but activism and
imaginative criticism coming from deconstructionist, feminist, literary
and cultural critics with a bad (po-mo) attitude who organized and
participated in anti-war events. To be sure, the attitude comes with a
highly advertised side-effect: there is no absolute guarantee that a new

pragmatic basis for justice and truth − rather than an infinite regress
of language-games and textual free-play − will result from political
encounters. But better strategically to play with apt critiques of the
powerful new forces unleashed by cyberwar than to hold positions with
antiquated tactics and nostalgic unities. As was proven by the accelerated
pace of this war, to overcome someday is already a day too late.

All critics of the war, however, were caught (with apologies to the
Rolling Stones) between Iraq and a hard place, between the history of a
civilization and its sanctioned destruction, between the new Hitler in
the bunker and Bush at the helm of the New World Order. From the
start patriotic reflexes, journalistic practices, and presidential politics
worked to sublate this difference into synthetic moral ends: naked
aggression must be stopped, a nation-state's sovereignty restored, and a
new regional peace constructed. Translated: We must war for peace.
Vindication came in the aftermath: roughly 100,000 Iraqi military dead
minus precisely 266 US dead equals victory. What was left for the
critic? Only the less decidable *after-image*, the still unfinished product
of the war between matter and perception that would determine the
dominant memory of this conflict.[10]

Here we might learn a lesson from the military: let the target determine the strategy. The most powerful objective of a post-war, anti-war movement must be the instant after-image, the war that was technically reproduced on the screen between the events and us. This site of perceptions was immediately targeted by the state and the war machine to provide what the economy no longer can: the foundation for a

resurgent American hegemony. What was it that made the image so irresistible, and the after-image so resistant to criticism? Conversely — and inevitably — what new foundations will be produced by resistance to it?

I believe that these questions of position and maneuver, of theoretical bunkers and critical de-bunking, require a mix of modern and late-modern armaments. This chapter is a cross-border operation, violating the territorial principle of non-intervention that delimits both the theory and the system of international relations. Hence my use of still photographs of moving images, the crude black and white alienation from a living color war, and the play of agonistic video-games, to reveal what scientific procedures of causality cannot: how an immaterial conflict was given such serious substance through a war of simulations. In my targeting of the after-images of war I aim to transgress disciplinary boundaries and at the risk of regressing with multiple representations. But this is, I believe, the only means by which the critical theorist might approximate and expropriate the language, video, and war games of the strategists of a late-modern war.

Where better to begin and end than with the first and last *shot* of the

Six Weeks and One Hundred Hours War: the night bombing of Baghdad and the night liberation of Kuwait City, reproduced by television cameras equipped with night-vision technology and transmitted in real-time by portable satellite link-ups. The grainy, ghostly green images of the beginning and the end of the war stick. They seem more real, more authentic than all the packaged images that were sandwiched in between.

Call it the new *video vert*: a powerful combination of the latest technology, the lowest quality image, the highest representation of reality. It reproduced a twisted Manichean truth: light — a tracer bullet, a secondary explosion, a flaring match — is danger; darkness — by camouflage, stealth, the night — is safety. Correspondents quickly learned that in wartime it was better to dwell and deal in the latter. The motto "We own the night" (originating in the 7th Infantry Division) became the slogan of the war and the reality of its coverage. When obfuscating military briefers and mandatory "security reviews" extended the ownership beyond the battlefield, the press and the public, already blind-sided in Grenada and neutered by the pool system in Panama, eagerly seized on the hi-tech prosthetics offered by the military. Words became filler between images produced by gun-cameras using night-vision or infrared that cut through the darkness to find and destroy targets lit-up by lasers or radiating heat. Perhaps if a few journalists had known what all night-fighters know, that night-vision degrades depth perception, then the appeal of the videographic reproduction of the war might have been diminished. But from the beginning moving images took out fixed words, and photocentrism triumphed over logocentrism. The combination of surgical video strikes and information carpet bombing worked. To be sure, for every public viewing of the war there was also a private perspective. I for one missed the collective moment of first images. Circling over Chicago's O'Hare airport when the bombs started to fall on Baghdad, I first heard of the war on the radio of a taxi. The first mediation came from the driver, who had not said a word during

the trip until he turned around to give me change. In the thickest of Russian accents he said: "They told me it would be over in three weeks – I was in Afghanistan for three years."

The discordance of the first word with first images lasted right up to the last day of the war. Fast forward to the end of the Ground War, to the televised victory briefing by "the chief architect of the ground war," better known as the commander of allied forces in the Persian Gulf, General Norman Schwarzkopf. Working his charts full of red and blue markers, he presented the keystone to the building that Norm built.

I think this is probably one of the most important parts of the entire briefing I could talk about. As you know, very early on, we took out the Iraqi Air force. We knew that he had very limited reconnaissance means. And therefore, when we took out his air force, for all intents and purposes, we took out his ability to see what we were doing down here in Saudi Arabia. Once we had taken out his eyes, we did what could best be described as the Hail Mary play in football.[11]

Stretching from the first days of the Six Weeks War to the last minutes of the One Hundred Hours War, these two simple statements by two disparate "mud soldiers" frame the architecture of cyberwar. The construction and destruction of the enemy other would be:

- measured in time not territory

- prosecuted in the field of perception not politics
- authenticated by technical reproduction not material referents
- played out in the method and metaphor of gaming, not the history and horror of warring.

In short, a cyberwar of chrono-strategic simulations for pax Americana II.

VIDEO GAMES

> It is precisely when it appears most truthful, most faithful and most in conformity to reality that the image is most diabolical ...
> Jean Baudrillard, *The Evil Demon of Images*

The simulated nature of the war was apparent at the outset, but took on a critical consciousness when ABC correspondent Cokie Roberts asked General Schwarzkopf, via satellite link-up, to comment on it:

Roberts: You see a building in a sight — it looks more like a video game than anything else. Is there any sort of danger that we don't have any sense of the horrors of war — that it's all a game?

Schwarzkopf: You didn't see me treating it like a game. And you

didn't see me laughing and joking while it was going on. There are human lives being lost, and at this stage of the game [*sic*] this is not a time for frivolity on the part of anybody.

In the space of a single sound-bite Schwarzkopf reveals the inability of the military and the public to maintain the distinction between warring and gaming in the age of video. We were enchanted by the magic of applied technologies, seduced and then numbed by the arcane language of the military briefers, satisfied by the image of every bomb finding its predestined target. The wizards in desert khaki came out from behind the curtain only long enough to prove their claims on TV screens, to have us follow their fingers and the arcs of the bombs to the truth. At some moments — the most powerful moments — the link between sign and signifier went into Möbius-strip contortions, as when we saw what the nose-cone of a smart bomb saw as it rode a laser beam to its target, making its fundamental truth-claim not in a flash of illumination but in the emptiness of a dark screen. William Tecumseh Sherman meets Jean-Paul Sartre in a sick syllogism: since war is hell and hell is others, bomb the others into nothingness.

Schwarzkopf's difficulty in separating war from its gaming is under-
standable. Back in October 1990 Schwarzkopf revealed in a *USA Today*
interview that the US military was ready for war in the Gulf over a year
before, because two years earlier they had learned that Iraq "had run
computer simulations and war games for the invasion of Kuwait."[12] He
did not mention – it is doubtful that he did not know – that the

software for the invasion simulations was supplied by an American
company. In the same interview Schwarzkopf stated that he programs
"possible conflicts with Iraq on computers almost daily." Having been
previously stationed in Florida as head of the US Central Command –
at the time a "paper" army without troops, tanks, or aircraft of its
own – he had already earned a reputation as an adept simulation
jockey.

In fact, Schwarzkopf sponsored a highly significant computer-simulated
command post exercise which was played in July 1990 under the code-
name of Exercise Internal Look '90.[13] According to a Central Command
news release issued at the time, "command and control elements from
all branches of the military will be responding to real-world scenarios
similar to those they might be expected to confront within the Central
Command AOR consisting of the Horn of Africa, the Middle East and
Southwest Asia." When Kuwait was invaded by Iraq, the war game
specialist who put Exercise Internal Look together, Lt General Yeosock,
was moved from fighting "real-world scenarios" in Florida to taking
command of all ground troops – except for the special forces under
Schwarzkopf – in Saudi Arabia. The war gamers went to cyberwar.

WAR GAMES

How much better is this amiable miniature than the Real Thing! Here is a homeopathic remedy for the imaginative strategist. Here is the premeditation, the thrill, the strain of accumulating victory or disaster – and no smashed or sanguinary bodies, no shattered fine buildings, nor devastated

US ARMY COMPUTER SIMULATION

countrysides, no petty cruelties, none of that awful universal boredom and embitterment, that tiresome delay or stoppage or embarrassment of every gracious, bold, sweet, and charming thing, that we who are old enough to remember a real modern war know to be the reality of belligerence.

H. G. Wells, Little Wars

What Cokie Roberts and her journalist cohort had only begun to suspect, that the line between war and game was becoming irrevocably blurred, was common knowledge in the realm of popular culture – and down at the mall video arcade. Two films stand out as genre setters. The first is the late seventies, post-Watergate, pre-*Challenger* film *Capricorn One* based on the premise that the military and NASA would – and had the technological capability to – simulate a successful Mars landing after the "real" mission aborts. The second is the Reagan-era film *War Games*, a story of a young hacker who taps into an Air Force computer simulation and nearly triggers a nuclear war between the superpowers.

There are as well the ubiquitous video-games. "Tank," one of the earliest and most popular, was a stripped-down version of an Army training simulation. Its graphics and sound effects now seem neolithic when compared to the simulations available for home computers. To name a few: from Navy simulations there is *Harpoon, Das Boot Submarine, Wolf Pack,* and *Silent Service II*; from the Air Force, *Secret Weapons of the Luftwaffe, Nighthawk,* F-117A *Stealth Fighter,* A-10

Tank Killer, and F—15 *Strike Eagle.* Judging from a sampling of "non-military" (narrowly defined) games, the future appears to be neo-medieval, inter-galactic, and eco-sensitive in nature. A keyboard jockey can choose among: *Warlord, Crusades of the Dark Savant, Dusk of the Gods, The Two Towers, Hyperspeed, Rules of Engagement, Armada 2525,* and *Xenocide*; and for those seeking eco-simulations, *Populous, Civilization, SimCity, SimEarth,* and *Global Dilemma.*

Of course, simulations — *the continuation of war by means of verisimilitude* — have a much longer and much wider history.[14] Prussia used *Kriegsspiel* ("war play") before their victories over the Austrians at Sadowa in 1866 and the French in 1870; Major William Livermore of the Army Corp of Engineers joined William McCarty Little and Rear Admiral Alfred Thayer Mahan at the Naval War College to set up the United States' first modern system of war gaming in 1889; and Japan made effective use of war games to achieve an unexpected victory over the Russians in 1904. Moreover, there is something of a law of uneven development at work in the field of war gaming. For instance, the Afghanistan resistance combined highly flexible sand box and toy soldier war games with hi-tech weaponry like the Stinger to defeat their far superior enemy, the Soviets — who, one could argue, were fighting the wrong war game. In this same period the US military research labs began to develop simulations for smart ground and air weapons-systems that operated without pilots or drivers, taking us further along the slide into sci-fi war gaming and robotic war-fighting.

LOGOS WARS

What entered Megavac 6-v as a mere *logos* would emerge for the TV lenses and mikes to capture in the guise of a pronouncement, one which nobody in his right mind — especially if encapsulated subsurface for fifteen years — would doubt.

P. K. Dick, *The Penultimate Truth*

The most powerful dialogue of the TV cyberwar —·if measured by the allocation of image resources — was the war of logos. It speaks for itself, but a genealogy helps us to understand how the media construct their own simulation cyberspace. Just around the time that Schwarzkopf wrapped up Operation Internal Look, the networks began to prepare their own war simulations. Most of them booked time at National Video on 42nd Street in New York City, a cutting edge video graphics lab known for its production of MTV logos.

NBC, cash-poor, went for the see-cubed-eye look, no fancy graphics, of the image of the news set as command and control HQ of *America at*

War. CBS and ABC revealed the limits of simulated imagination when they replayed *Time-Newsweek*'s simultaneous cover story of Bruce Springsteen: both came up with *Showdown in the Gulf*. ABC had the distinguishing underlay of a radar screen, but soon jettisoned the High Noon theme for a simpler logo, *The Gulf War*.

But it was ABC's *Primetime Live* and CNN's *Headline News* that

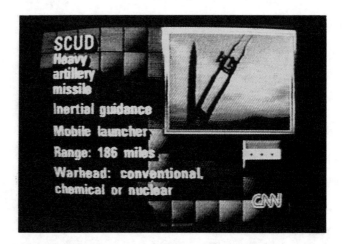

would be the front runners if there were an Emmy award in the special category of War Graphics. *Primetime* went for the Cruise Missile simulation. In successive frames the missile goes through some remarkable ground-hugging, terrain-following maneuvers, and just as it looms large − as the viewer realizes who the target is − *The Gulf War* logo and Diane Sawyer fade in. CNN, riding a high ratings wave, took the most innovative approach. It used as an underlay the military video of the week, and as the smart-bomb or missile homed in on the logo, *War in the Gulf*, block-lettered in fascistoid orange and black, rotated in over the destroyed target. Scary enough to hope that hologram TV never arrives.

To be sure, a more significant logomachy was in evidence at the less graphic, more subtextual level of semantics. Before the first shot was fired, language was enlisted in the war effort. Until we had sufficient troops in place "to deter and defend," the hostages in Iraq were cautiously referred to as "detainees." In late fall, after 250,000 more troops had arrived, George Bush shifted linguistic gears and called for the "unconditional surrender" of Saddam Hussein. When reminded shortly afterwards that this demand exceeded the requirements of the UN resolutions, he replied "that's just semantics." By February, with the air war going well and ground exercises for invasion taking place daily, General Colin Powell stripped US strategy toward Iraq of any nuance or ambiguity: "First we're going to cut it off, and then we're going to kill it."

But enough has been said about the systematic corruption of language by military practices. It quickly became a commonplace that truth was

the first casualty of war.[15] But this was a slogan in need of a theory, of how truth is *produced* in the continuation of war by other, simulated means.

THEORY GAMES

> In short, by opposition to the philosophico-juridical discourse which addresses the problem of sovereignty and law, this discourse which deciphers the permanence of war in our society is essentially a discourse where the truth functions as a weapon for a partisan victory, a discourse sombrely critical and at the same time intensely mythical.
> Michel Foucault, *Résumé de Cours* (Collège de France, 1975–76)

Writing for the *Frankfurter Zeitung* in 1926, marveling at the immense popularity of the newly constructed picture palaces in Berlin, Siegfried Kracauer chronicled the emergence of a "cult of distraction." It is in these new "optical fairylands," he wrote, that "distraction – which is meaningful only as improvisation, as reflection of the uncontrolled

anarchy of the world − is festooned with drapes and forced back into a
unity that no longer exists."[16] In Kracauer's view the picture palaces
served as a kind of Hegelian asylum from Weimar disorder, ornate
spaces where the alienated Berliner could seek reunification through a
new, totally imaginary, cinematic (yet organic) *Zeitgeist.*

Taking his first measure of film production, Walter Benjamin wrote
in his 1936 essay, "The Work of Art in the Age of Mechanical Reproduction," of the corresponding loss of authenticity, aura, and uniqueness
in art. Benjamin believed mechanically reproduced art, especially film,
to be especially useful to if not generative of Fascism, for the rendering
of politics into aesthetics had the advantage of mobilizing the masses
for war without endangering traditional property relations. He quotes
the Futurist Marinetti to chilling effect:

> War is beautiful because it establishes man's dominion over the
> subjugated machinery by means of gas masks, terrifying mega-
> phones, flame throwers, and small tanks. War is beautiful because
> it initiates the dreamt-of metalization of the human body ... War
> is beautiful because it creates new architecture, like that of the big
> tanks, the geometrical formation flights, the smoke spirals from
> burning villages, and many others ... Poets and artists of Futur-
> ism! ... remember these principles of an aesthetics of war so that
> your struggle for a new literature and a new graphic art ... may
> be illumined by them![17]

Surveying the rise of a consumer society, anticipating the failure of
conventional, radical, *spatial* politics in 1968, Guy Debord, editor of
the journal *Internationale Situationniste*, opened his book *Society of the
Spectacle* with a provocative claim: "In societies where modern conditions
of production prevail, all of life presents itself as an immense accumulation of *spectacles*. Everything that was directly lived has moved away
into a representation." At the root of this new form of representation
was the specialization of power, with spectacle coming to speak for all
other forms of power, becoming in effect "the diplomatic representation
of hierarchic society to itself, where all other expression is banned."[18]

After analyzing the political economy of the sign and visiting Disneyland, Jean Baudrillard, the French master of edifying hyperbole, notified
the inhabitants of advanced mediacracies that they were no longer
distracted by the technical reproduction of reality, or alienated and
repressed by their overconsumption of its spectacular representation.
Unable to recover the "original" and seduced by the simulation, they
had lost the ability to distinguish between the model and the real:

"Abstraction today is no longer that of the map, the double, the mirror or the concept. Simulation is no longer that of a territory, a referential being or a substance. It is the generation by models of a real without origin or reality: a hyperreal."[19]

Paul Virilio's project to politicize the violence of speed, reviewed in chapter 6, illuminates the events of the Gulf War. Indeed, his account of the linking of the logistics of military perception and surveillance to the use of video in warfare anticipates many of the representational practices of the first "real" cyberwar. The last years of the Vietnam War foreshadowed the hi-tech display that bedazzled the public and befuddled the critics. Recounting a Vietnam pilot's story of how he was sent back repeatedly to bomb the same target, just to please the photo interpreters, Virilio remarks: "People used to die for a coat of arms, an image on a pennant or flag; now they died to improve the sharpness of a film. War has finally become the third dimension of cinema."[20] In the Gulf War, the necessity of speed and capabilities of new technologies made video "the third dimension of war." This was confirmed by Colonel Tom Diamond, commander of Combat Photography in the Gulf:

> In the field, any time and anywhere in the world, we could take a photo, point a portable satellite cellular phone system, and send images as fast as we could take them, so that the time between when the event occurred and when we could get it to the national command authority was reduced to forty seconds transmission time. Now we were helping decision-making. We can make a difference in a battle.[21]

The consequence, foreseen by Virilio, is that in modern warfare, as the aim of battle shifts from territorial, economic, and material gains to immaterial, perceptual fields, the spectacle of war is displaced by the war of spectacle.

This is not to claim that in the Gulf War the truth was collaterally damaged as some incidental victim of a necessary violence. The truth — in the Nietzschean sense of "illusions whose illusionary nature has been forgotten"[22] — was constructed out of and authorized by spectacular, videographic, cyberspatial simulations of war.

GAME WARS

I hate to say it, but once we got rolling it was like a training exercise with live people running around. Our training exercises are a lot harder.
Captain Kelvin Davis (after American troops captured Kuwait City)[23]

We were primed for this war. Simulations had infiltrated into every area of our lives, in the form of news (re)creations, video games, flight simulators, police interrogations, crime reenactments, and, of course, media war games. Six days into the invasion of Kuwait Tom Brokaw on *NBC News* staged a war game with former US officials standing in for Hussein and Bush. It ended with "Hussein" threatening to "send home body bags every day" and Brokaw warning us that "before too long we may have the real thing." In October 1990 Ted Koppel on *ABC Nightline* weighed in with his "Ides of November" war game. This war game differed from previous ones presented by Koppel (two on terrorism and one on nuclear war): there was not a pasha from Kissinger Associates in sight, and the talking-heads barely had equal time with the video simulations. Constructed and narrated by the authors of the book *A Quick and Dirty Guide to War* and the wargame *Arabian Nightmare*, the program featured stock clips of war exercises, computer simulations of bombing runs, many maps, and a day-by-day pull-down menu of escalating events. The post-game commentary (known in the ranks as a "hot wash-up") was conducted by two military analysts armed with pointers, James Blackwell and Harry Summers, Jr. They ended with a split decision — and a final cautionary note that "no plan survives contact with the enemy."

By the first ultimatum in January, the representational boundary between the simulation and the "real thing" was as attenuated as a fuse wire. War continued by means of simulation in its media representation as well as through its military preparation. Before the ground war the

US conducted a series of highly publicized war exercises, the largest being an amphibious Marine landing called "Imminent Thunder." In fact, no landing crafts were used because the seas were running too high. Nonetheless, the simulation "worked." When the allied troops reached Kuwait City they found in a school house used by the Iraqi military as a headquarters a room-sized model of the city. On a sand tableau there were, to scale, wooden ships, buildings, roads, barbed wire — and all the Iraqi guns pointing toward the sea attack that never came.

For those still retaining some control over their television sets during the war, there were illuminating intertexts to be seen on non-news channels. My local movie channel ran a Eastwood—Norris—Bronson—Stallone series to coincide with the real thing. But it was in switching over to the *Fox* station that I discovered the hoariness of the simulation theme when an episode on war games appeared on *Star Trek* — not on *The Next Generation* with its virtual reality holodeck, but on the toggle-switch and blinking-lights original. Called the "Ultimate Computer," the episode pits Kirk against the "M5 Multitronic Unit" in a wargame. After the crew is removed from the ship, Kirk is told by the

creator of the computer "to sit back and let the machine do the work."
As machine proves more adept then man, Kirk goes through several
existential crises; that is, until the machine mistakes the game for war
and destroys another ship by unfriendly fire. Angered and impassioned,
Kirk stops soliloquizing and regains control of the ship by convincing
the computer that by killing humans it has violated its primary purpose

of protecting them.

It took Captain Kirk to pull the plug on the national security double-
speak of the Gulf War: we kill to live. Ironically, it was Peter Arnett
reporting not from Baghdad but from Ben Tre, Vietnam, who had
recorded an earlier instance of that naked mechanical truth: "it became
necessary to destroy the town to save it."

Science fiction offers other insights that journalism and lagging social
science cannot provide. In the movie *Aliens*, when the Colonial Marines
are being buffeted as they enter the atmosphere of the planet where the
unknown awaits them, Ripley (Sigourney Weaver) asks the obviously
anxious Lieutenant how many combat drops this is for him. He replies
"Thirty-eight," pauses, and then adds "– Simulated." He quickly proves
incapable of responding to situations that do not follow his simulation
training. Both Kirk and Ripley should have been on the bridge of the
USS *Vincennes* on 3 July 1988 when its radar operator and the tactical
information coordinator mistook – after nine months' simulation
training with computer tapes – an Iranian Airbus for an attacking
Iranian F-14 and shot it down.

Even more useful is the intertext of strategic power and popular culture provided by Tom Clancy. Clancy's first bestseller, the *Red October*, has a hyperbolic blurb from former President Reagan. His second novel, *Red Storm Rising*, a thinly fictionalized mosaic of NATO war games, was authoritatively cited by Vice President Quayle in a foreign policy speech to prove that the US needs an anti-satellite capability. In his third, *Patriot Games*, Clancy magnifies the threat of terrorism

to the prove that state counter-terrorism works; a view endorsed by Secretary of Defense Weinberger in a laudatory review of the book for the *Wall Street Journal* — which was then reprinted in the Pentagon's *Current News* for the edification of the 7,000-odd Defense and State Department officials who make up its readership. His fourth novel, *The Cardinal of the Kremlin*, in which Clancy plots the plight of a mole in the Kremlin, affirms the need to reconstruct the impermeable borders of the sovereign state with Star Wars. His fifth novel, *Clear and Present Danger*, opens with a quote from Pascal, "Law, without force, is impotent," and closes with the unrepressed message that the US will be impotent if it does not use — prudently of course — its technological edge in night-vision, GBU-15 laser-guided bombs, and satellite surveillance against drug cartels.

Taken together, Clancy's novels anticipate the strategic simulations that filled our screens during the Gulf War. Jammed with technical detail and seductive ordinance, devoid of recognizably human characters, and obliquely linked to historical events, they act, from the Cold War to the Drug War, as free-floating intertexts for saving the reality principle of the national security state: namely, that the sovereign state's boundaries, like those between fiction and fact, simulation and reality, can once again be made impermeable to any threat posed by this year's model of evil.

There is of course a fundamental and ultimate difference between war and its game: people die in wars. But this distinction also suffered erosion in the Gulf War. If we subtract the number of Coalition soldiers

(the Iraqi dead never "figured") killed or injured by "friendly fire" and accidents, there were more casualties in the war exercises leading up to "G-Day" (the beginning of the ground war) than during the war itself.

END GAME

> This is a war universe. War all the time. That is its nature. There may be other universes based on all sorts of other principles, but ours seems to be based on war and games. All games are basically hostile. Winners and losers. We see them all around us: the winners and the losers. The losers can oftentimes become winners, and the winners can very easily become losers.
>
> William S. Burroughs, *The War Universe*

Was this a just war, or just a game? For the winners, both: for the losers, neither. To suggest as I have done in this video-essay that it could be both or neither simultaneously is to challenge the US effort to construct out of this war a new world order based on one truth, one winner, one loser. To offer as I do nothing in its place but a Nietzschean "breath of empty space" is to risk those familiar charges of relativism, or worse, nihilism. But this cyberwar is the *result* of the US effort to fill and to delimit the new void left by the end of the Cold War, the end of the old order, the "end of history." While the architecture of the new world order may be built of simulations, its hegemonic effect will be all

too real for those nation-states that have little to gain from it.

Of course, the post-war historical possibilities are not so clear-cut, a nihilistic case of either all or nothing being permitted. But "the end of the Cold War" — that is, the end of the Soviet Union as a counter-balance to American hegemony — *has* re-opened a space — as illustrated above by Baudrillard's quote — for *both* war and peace."[24]

But Baudrillard does not get it quite right. If anything has been proven by this war, it is that simulations now rule not only in the war without warring of nuclear deterrence, but also in the post-war warring of the present.[25] It was never in question that the US would win the military conflict. But it did not win a "war," in the conventional sense of destroying a reciprocating enemy. What "war," then, did the US win? A cyberwar of simulations. First the pre-war simulation, Operation Internal Look 90, which defeated the Made in America Iraqi simulation for the invasion of Kuwait. Second, the war game of AirLand Battle which defeated an Iraqi army that resembled the game's intended enemy, the Warsaw Pact, in hyperreality only. Third, the war of spectacle, which defeated the spectacle of war on the battlefield of videographic reproduction. And fourth, the post-war after-simulation of Vietnam, which defeated an earlier defeat by assimilating Vietnam's history and lessons into the victory of the Gulf War.

Have we, "by God," kicked the Vietnam Syndrome in Iraq? I am sure that as long as there is a great global gap in power and wealth there will be tenacious under-dogs with a taste for grey flannel — and more swift kicks to follow. But the score is being kept. Almost 25 years ago at the Bertrand Russell War Crimes Tribunal in Stockholm, Jean-Paul Sartre rendered a verdict that bears remembering:

> It [the US] is guilty, by plotting, misrepresenting, lying and self-deceiving, of becoming more deeply committed every instant, despite the lessons of this unique and intolerable experience, to a course which is leading it to the point of no return. It is guilty, self-confessedly, of knowingly carrying on this *cautionary* war to make genocide a challenge and a threat to peoples everywhere. We have seen that one of the features of total war was a constant growth in the number and speed of means of transport; since 1914, war can no longer remain localized, it must spread through the world. Today the process is becoming intensified; the links of the *One World*, this universe upon which the United States wishes to impose its hegemony, are ever closer.[26]

Perhaps it is time to diagnose a "Gulf War Syndrome," the pathological need to construct and destroy a lesser enemy to restore and revive US hegemony in the "new world order." Iraq served its purpose well as the enemy other which redefined our own essential identities: but it was the other enemy, the new threat posed by the de-territorialization of the state and a disintegrating bipolar order that required the violent reconstitution of new monological truths.

The new disorder requires a commensurate de-territorialization of theory. We can no longer reconstitute a single site of meaning or reconstruct some neo-Kantian cosmopolitian community; that would require a moment of enlightened universal certainty that has long past. Nor can we depend on or believe in some spiritual, dialectical or scientific process to overcome or transcend the domestic and international divisions, ambiguities, and uncertainties that mark the antidiplomatic age of spies, terror, speed, and war. Rather, we must find a way to live with and recognize the very necessity of difference, the need to assert heterogeneity before we can even begin to understand our role in the lives of others. This is not yet another utopian scheme to take us out of the "real" world, but a practical strategy to live with less anxiety, insecurity, and fear in what Mikhail Bakhtin described as "exotopy," and Michel Foucault as "heterotopia." These environments make poss-ible broader realms of freedom where the heteroglossia of language bespeaks a heterodoxy in world politics, where radical otherness in international relations is assumed and asserted in dialogue, not repressed and expressed in violence.

The strategy from the first to this last chapter, to construct a counter-simulation to war and antidiplomacy, is in the end only one of many beginnings towards one of many heterotopias. Not an endgame, then, but a game with no end, no winners, no losers, no rules but one: play in peace.

Notes

1   See Robert F. Kennedy, *Thirteen Days: A Memoir of the Cuban Missile Crisis* (New York: W. W. Norton, 1971), pp. 40, 105.

2   The inspiration for the chapter comes mainly from the powerful (and admittedly, orientalist) opening to Spengler's chapter on "Problems of the Arabian Culture." See Oswald Spengler, *The Decline of the West* (New York: Viking, 1927), vol. II, chapter 7, pp. 186–9:

> In a rock-stratum are embedded crystals of a mineral. Clefts and cracks occur, water filters in, and the crystals are gradually washed out so that in due course only their hollow mould remains. Then come volcanic outbursts which explode the mountain; molten masses pour in, stiffen, and crystallize out in their turn. But these are not free to do so in their own special forms. They must fill up the spaces that they find available. Thus there arise distorted forms, crystals whose inner structure contradicts their external shape, stones of one kind presenting the appearance of stones of another kind. The mineralogists call this phenomenon Pseudomorphosis.
>
> By the term "historical pseudomorphosis" I propose to designate those cases in which an older alien Culture lies so massively over the land that a young Culture, born in this land, cannot get its breath and fails not only to achieve pure and specific expression-forms, but even to develop fully its own self-consciousness. All that wells up from the depths of the young soul is cast in the old moulds, young feelings stiffen in senile works, and instead of rearing itself up in its own creative power, it can only hate the distant power with a hate that grows to be monstrous.

3   This begs the onto-theological question that I raised in the Introduction (see p. 4)

4   The most comprehensive definition of cyberspace that I have heard comes from Michael Benedikt (professor of architecture at University of Texas at Austin), taken from the *Collected Abstracts from the First Conference on Cyberspace*:

> Cyberspace is a globally net-worked, computer-sustained, computer-accessed, and computer-generated, multi-dimensional, artificial, or

"virtual" reality. In this world, onto which every computer screen is a window, actual geographical distance is irrelevant. Objects seen or heard are neither physical nor, necessarily, presentations of physical objects, but are rather − in form, character, and action − made up of data, of pure information. This information is derived in part from the operation of the natural, physical world, but is derived primarily from the immense traffic of symbolic information, images, sounds, and people, that constitute human enterprise in science, art, business, and culture.

See also Philip K. Dick, *The Simulacra* (New York: Ace Books, 1964) and *The Penultimate Truth* (London: Triad, 1984); and the book in which William Gibson coined the term "cyberspace," *The Neuromancer* (New York, Ace Books, 1984).

5   Lance Morrow, *Time*, 18 March 1991, p. 21.

6   Todd Gitlin, "Theory in Wartime: An Interview with Todd Gitlin," *Linguafranca*, February 1991, p. 26. Another position of radical critics that I witnessed at various teach-ins and in journals like *Z* and *Lies in Our Times* was to attribute the war to a plan by the US and Israel to lure Saddam Hussein into Kuwait and then spring the trap. This was such a perfect conspiracy that these same people were predicting as late as January US casualties in the several thousands, a protracted war, and mass resistance. When this scenario failed to develop they fell back on a conspiracy theory to explain why the war was so popular, so swift, and so total − and why their theoretical analysis was so far off.

7   See P. Virilio, *Bunker Archéologie* (Paris: Centre Georges Pompidou, 1975), p. 42, on the dangers of "bunker architecture": "Le bunker est devenu un mythe, à la fois présent et absent, présent comme objet de répulsion pour une architecture civile transparente et ouverte, absent dans la mesure où l'essential de la nouvelle forteress est ailleurs, sous nos pied, désormais invisible."

8   See N. Chomsky, *On Gulf Policy* (Westfield, New Jersey: Open Magazine Series, 1991), p. 1.

9   See J. -F. Lyotard, *The Postmodern Condition: A Report on Knowledge* (Minneapolis, MN: University of Minnesota Press, 1984), pp. 81−2.

10   See Henri Bergson, *Matter and Memory* (New York: Zone Books, 1988), and Walter Benjamin, "On Some Motifs in Baudelaire," in *Illuminations* (New York: Schocken, 1969).

11   *New York Times*, 28 February 1991, p. A8. I doubt whether we will ever see a "Norm knows football" advertisement (Bo can rest easy), for the only "Hail Mary" play of the war was Iraq's desperate long bomb SCUD attacks. Charles Hables Gray (from the University of California at Santa Cruz) later pointed out to me that the appropriate football analogy for the Allies' strategy was using the air game to set up the ground game, followed by a fake up the middle and power sweep around the left side. And most of the military officers that I interviewed referred to it as the "end-run" play.

12   *USA Today*, 8 October 1990, p. 8.

13   See J. Der Derian, "War Games May Prove Deadly," *Newsday*, 9 December 1990.

14   See T. Allen, *War Games: The Secret World of the Creators, Players, and*

Policy Makers Rehearsing World War III Today (New York: McGraw Hill, 1987); and P. Perla, *The Art of WarGaming* (Annapolis, MD: Naval Institute Press, 1990)

15   Since journalists were as reluctant to credit the quote as they were keen to repeat it, it should be noted that Senator Hiram Johnson said in 1917 that "[T]he first casualty when war comes is truth." Of course, the corruption of language is not always intentional. For instance, General Colin Powell's reference to the US forces as "Desert Storm Troopers" during a victory speech before a convention of Veterans of Foreign Wars went unreported, probably because it was considered to be an innocent slip.

16   See F. Kracauer, "Cult of Distraction: On Berlin's Picture Palaces," trans. by T. Y. Levin, in *New German Critique*, 40 (Winter, 1987), p. 95; and Kracauer's *Das Ornament der Masse* (Frankfurt a.M.: Suhrkamp Verlag, 1963), forthcoming as *The Mass Ornament*, translated and edited by T. Y. Levin (Cambridge, MA: Harvard University Press).

17   See W. Benjamin, "The Work of Art in the Age of Mechanical Reproduction," *Illuminations*, edited by H. Arendt (New York: Schocken, 1969), pp. 241–2.

18   See G. Debord, *Society of the Spectacle* (Detroit: Black and Red, 1983), no. 1, pp. 1 and 23. In a more recent work, Debord persuasively – and somewhat despairingly – argues that the society of the spectacle retains its representational power in current times: see *Commentaires sur la Société du Spectacle* (Paris: Editions Gerard Lebovici, 1988).

19   See J. Baudrillard, *Simulations* (New York: Semiotext(e), 1983), p. 2. The original French version, *Simulacres et Simulation* (Paris: Editions Galilée, 1981), has more on the simulacral nature of violence in cinema. See in particular his readings of *China Syndrome, Barry Lyndon, Chinatown*, and *Apocalypse Now*, pp. 69–91.

20   See *War and Cinema*, p. 85.

21   Tom Diamond, "Combat Camera," *Arts and Entertainment* documentary, 22 November 1991.

22   Paul de Man, *The Resistance to Theory* (Minneapolis, MN: University of Minnesota Press), p. 67.

23   *Newsweek*, 11 March 1991, p. 17.

24   See "Fatal Strategies," in *Jean Baudrillard: Selected Writings*, edited by M. Poster (Standford, CA: Standford University Press, 1988), p. 191, quoted in chapter 7:

Like the real, warfare will no longer have any place – except precisely if the nuclear powers are successful in de-escalation and manage to define new spaces for warfare. If military power, at the cost of de-escalating this marvelously practical madness to the second power, reestablishes a setting for warfare, a confined space that is in fact human, then weapons will regain their use value and their exchange value: it will again be possible *to exchange warfare.*

Backing up Baudrillard's claim is a recent report that the Pentagon has produced, in secret, seven "illustrative" post-Cold-War "war scenarios," all of them potential regional conflicts except for the last, which envisions the rise of an "REGT" (Resurgent/Emergent Global Threat) by the year 2001. See Patrick Tyler, *New York Times*, 17 February 1992, p. A8.

25 "The art of deterrence, prohibiting political war, favors the upsurge, not of conflicts, but of *acts of war without war*." See Paul Virilio, *Pure War*, p. 27. See also Timothy Luke, "On Post-War: The Significance of Symbolic Action in War and Deterrence," *Alternatives*, 14 (July 1989), pp. 393–62.
26 See Jean-Paul Sartre, "Vietnam: Imperialism and Genocide," in *Between Existentialism and Marxism* (New York: Pantheon, 1974), pp. 82–3.

INDEX

—